# Preacher Spurs

# 2<sup>nd</sup> Edition

By Lamont H. Fuchs, EdD

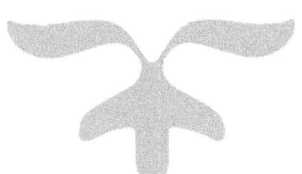

**MARCH 1, 2025**

# Table of Contents

# Endorsements for Preacher Spurs 2<sup>ND</sup> Edition

There are Ten Commandments that God gave Moses on Mount Sinai. I suppose we could produce Ten Commandments for preachers. Some might be:

- Thou shalt not think by the inch and speak by the yard, lest thou get the foot to boot you out the door.
- Thou shalt not demand from those in the pew what the man in the pulpit will not do.
- When thou hast said all that is needful, stop.
- Thou shalt put the cookies on the shelf where thy people can reach them.

Doubtless, you could think of others. One that I would include is: "Thou shalt not be boring!"

Yet, that is a challenge when you are speaking most every week, multiple times each week, and even several times a day. Imagine preaching for decades at the same church. I spent 25 years with one congregation. While the well of God's Word never goes dry, we may have trouble finding the bucket! This book gives you a bucket to lower into the well.

I was blessed to serve as a pastor to the author, Monty Fuchs, and his wife. They are dear Christian people, and his desire is to help pastors. This is another tool for your sermon preparation toolbox. Some of these thoughts may not find their way into your sermon, yet as you read them may strengthen you personally, and that is crucial for your preaching. I read this:

"The better the man, the better the preacher," (Clarence Macartney, Preaching Without Notes).

In addition to stirring your devotional life, this book can stimulate your homiletical juices. That is a good thing. If the message does not stir you, it is unlikely to awaken the sleepy saints! I hope it "spurs" you onward to better preaching. Our churches need it!

Dennis Thurman, Mission Strategist for Haywood Baptist Association

The task of preaching and teaching God's people is a great privilege. For many, however, that task can be a burden. Life brings a busyness that often serves as an interruption to the preparation time of even the most gifted preachers and teachers. Dr. Fuchs has provided a gift to the church with *Preacher Spurs.* This practical work will serve as an invaluable tool to the busiest proclaimers of God's Word. It is a book that should be in the library of pastors, Sunday school teachers, and lay preachers. It will serve as a useful resource for preparation and study. I am excited to endorse *Preacher Spurs.*

Dr. Nick Smith, Senior Pastor, Junaluska First Baptist, Clyde, NC

# Preacher Spurs

Teaching or preaching with inspiration from God is a great blessing but can also be a burden. It is a blessing to have the motivation to create devotions, teach lessons, or preach sermons with your unique approach. However, it can be burdensome because they are expected to deliver a sermon or lesson every Sunday. The inspiration to provide a message to expound on God's Word must be carefully gathered, researched, and logically presented. Many pastors start preparing weeks or even months in advance. Sometimes, the final preparation time is just before you preach, and unfortunately, the inspiration may not always be there.

I am not a judge, and I ask God to prevent me from speculating about why He withholds His divine inspiration from us or whether we are not right with Him at times to receive it. We know, however, the speaking event is coming, and sometimes the stimulus or impetus is not. I empathize. Ministry is service to God. If that describes you, this book was written for you.

The following verse is the impetus for the title.

Hebrews 10:24–25 (NIV)

> *And let us consider how we may spur one another on toward love and good deeds, not giving up meeting together, as some are in the habit of doing, but encouraging one another—and all the more as you see the Day approaching.*

I was looking for a word similar to the word *stem*. A stem is what some writers use as a short statement that provides an idea or the beginning of a paragraph. This verse and the word *spur* captured

3

my meaning. The difference is that I wanted to offer more than a stem-type statement. I thought I would provide enough information to encourage someone to finish what is provided with confidence to teach or preach without the work involved in starting from scratch.

As a faithful layman, Sunday school teacher, and occasional preacher, I have witnessed and can relate to those who bring forth a solid lesson or sermon week in and week out. God inspires them; they are gifted with talent by God and inspired by the subject matter or applicable Scripture to teach or preach. Many laypeople, teachers, and pastors lean on notes taken, books read, or Scripture studied as resources and stems to make a spiritual discourse.

This resource is a compilation of Spurs to help you create your presentations. Preachers, teachers, and laypeople who use devotional material each week for any number of Christian gatherings can find material in this book to teach or inspire others.

# Foreword

There are times in the career of every pastor and teacher when they struggle with the lack of inspiration to create sermons or lessons. The ideas fade after months and years of multiple weekly presentations, especially during periods of life when events and tribulations require time and dedication to other pressing matters.

Bi-vocational pastors get caught in this dilemma purely because there are only so many hours in a day. This book is for them too. Books, websites, and prepackaged discourses can be purchased to assist those in need. Hopefully, you will find this book full of content that will spur you on to lessons and sermons packed with your creative flavor and uniqueness. If a Spur you read here inspires you to only make a point within your original, then this book's purpose is being served.

An old pastor friend told me that occasionally, when he was in a tight spot to speak and did not have a sermon to warm up like an old biscuit, he searched for content in books available to him to read or hear someone else's discourse from someone he admired. Then, he took that sermon and made it his, much like my wife takes a brand-name jar or can of spaghetti sauce off the shelf and proceeds to make it her own. She adds some meat, mushrooms, onions, and other seasonings to make it better, but it is really … not from scratch. He then gave a soft, gentle warning. Somehow, people know when it is not one of your originals. "It is hard to plant another man's field" is how he referenced it. You are always better and more comfortable when you hear the voice of God as He inspires you to make your sermon or devotion from scratch. These Spurs are only to get those creative juices flowing. Each Spur outlined in this book has been preached on, prayed over, and designed with the concept of preaching or teaching the gospel. We must firmly believe in Isaiah 55:11:

*So shall my word be that goeth forth out of my mouth: it shall not return unto me void, but it shall accomplish that which I please, and it shall prosper in the thing whereto I sent it.*

When purely imparting God's Word, how can you go wrong?

God made us. He molded us. He is the potter, and we are the clay. Paul said in 1 Corinthians 15:10, better known as the "Popeye Speech":

*But by the grace of God I am what I am: and his grace which was bestowed upon me was not found vain; but I labored more abundantly than they all: yet not I, but the grace of God which was with me.*

That is an excellent stand-alone Spur right there. However, what we should get from that is this: We had no choice in the most significant things that made us who we are. God chose those things. He designated the most important things for us before time began. He ordained when we were born, where we were born, who our parents were, what color we are, where we grew up, our sex, our looks, and you can list a dozen more.

After that, I was out of control of many other things that made marks on my life through the experiences He controlled. Let us start with the church I grew up in, the influence of my teachers, bosses, relatives, and friends, and my daily life experience. All these were appointed to me by God for my life flavoring, learning, and experience. If psychologists and psychiatrists can espouse that we are a product of our environment, believe them, but none of it was fate. God is in control—past, present, and future. I take no power away from God. He has it all and always has. If you doubt this, read Romans 9, the whole chapter.

Furthermore, the surroundings that molded me and created my pillars of belief, social behavior, personality, and experiential foundations result from God's will—handmade and mastered for me. God's plan was etched in stone for my life and yours before the creation of this earth. You and I are the results of the environment He created. God is the artist, and we are the clay (present tense) because you are assured—He is not done with us yet. However, after saying all that, this book is not about me. It is to glorify God through His calling to you. You have the class or congregation; you are His prophet.

His purpose, to me, is a no-brainer—are you a disciple of the Lord? Were you called to minister, preach, or teach? As I was recently reminded, if we call ourselves Christians, then we are all ministers. Then, speak about what you know, who you are, and where you come from. God gave you that life experience for a reason—before He called you to serve Him. Why? So you could share it. This statement is true if you are eighteen or eighty-eight. Look forward to each day's experiences and what God reveals to you through them. Whether blessing or a tribulation, there is a reason you are there.

You are probably thinking, *Who is this guy to tell me this common-sense stuff? I know this.* I intend not to insult your intelligence or judge whether you know it; make your lessons by using these Spurs, trusting God, and recalling the experiences He has given you. You will have more than just forty minutes of content to expound upon. Someone asked Billy Graham how long it took to prepare a sermon. He answered, "A lifetime" (Phelps).

My prayers for you and the goals of this book are to provide Spurs for you to study and think about while bringing together your presentation. You are invited to use each Spur to evoke your experiences and unique bent on the subjects provided. Ask God to speak through you and the life He gave you and make it His discourse. Another of my prayers over these Spurs and for you is to reach those who are lost, the ones He invites to hear the gospel and draw closer to Him through you. After all, if that is not our ultimate goal, then we are wasting time.

Many preachers and speakers concern themselves with iterating others. No one wishes to be a plagiarist, and to do so is a theft of another's intellectual talent. Intellectual rights are protected and should be. The Christian community is usually much freer to borrow another's concepts when promoting the Word of God. It is not always true, but if one gives the respect of annotating the credit of the origin or even mentioning where their inspiration came from, most Christian authors permit others to use their work in another.

There is a difference when authoring a book or article for remuneration; authors might be more protective. However, public speaking, especially within a sermon or classroom within the confines of the church sanctuary, is different. Most pastors give credit when quoting a famous author or using someone else's illustration. Some will tell their congregation they are expanding on a sermon they heard or read from another pastor. Nevertheless, sometimes you cannot say it better than the person who received their inspiration from God in the first place.

I am okay with others using my illustrations and even flattered that someone would use these ideas and stories in their preaching or teaching. I credit those within these Spurs, as I received inspiration to write them. No credit to me or this writing is required. Humbly, I seek no glory but for God alone. I intend you to read these Spurs and weave them into *your* sermons and teaching. They are hardly standalone as complete sermons or lessons, only snippets of ideas for you to expound upon. I have nothing to brag about but my Lord and Savior, Jesus, and someday, when I qualify to meet my Lord, I pray I will receive my rewards, if any are due. They are all on deposit through the Spirit in heaven. We should all look forward to hearing our Lord say our name, followed by the praise of being a good and faithful servant as He welcomes us to our eternal home.

# Chapter Breakdown

Each chapter is organized in the same manner. This book is not designed to be read from cover to cover but used as a reference for your preaching and teaching. Each chapter stands alone.

After the title, the following sections are *CONCEPTS* and *PURPOSE*. These are placed before the *SCRIPTURE BASE* so readers can decide whether to read or research the Stem further. This format ensures the reader does not get too deep into the trees before they decide they might be in the wrong forest for their purpose. These two sections are written to inform the reader of the *what* and *why* for the Stem. The *SCRIPTURE BASE* section is provided for further research into the Stem. The following section, *BACKGROUND*, provides additional content that provides a perspective from my personal experience or the global experiences of the target audience. These help the reader identify and possibly remember a unique experience they can use in their lesson or sermon. Finally, the *SPUR* is the meat of the chapter to provide content for the message.

*PRAYER* follows each Spur because each Spur needs a fervent request to God to bear fruit when used. Finally, the *CREDITS AND/OR INSPIRATION* section lets the reader know where the Spur likely originated. Solomon states it concisely in Ecclesiastes 1:9: *What has been will be again, what has been done will be done again; there is nothing new under the sun.*

Except in specific cases, the Bible translation used throughout this text is the American Standard Version (ASV). It is considered a Public Domain edition for easy referencing and free use. The ASV version may distract you as a user if you have read or memorized a familiar passage from another translation and find the ones used here different. Please use your preferred translation, as the verses will be referred to by book, chapter, and verse. The meanings and interpretations should not be affected.

2 Timothy 3:16–17

> *Every scripture inspired by God is also profitable for teaching, for reproof, for correction, for instruction which is in righteousness: that the man of God may be complete, furnished completely unto every good work.*

Care to begin? After reading this first explanation, continue to use this book by the Table of Contents. These Spurs are an aid, not a crutch. Do not preconceive or judge the typical subject of the Spur by its title. Some titles are misdirected, and others are spot-on. Some of these Spurs can be combined to steer the direction of God's message for His purpose. Many are single concepts, and others are multifaceted. You also may not agree with my view or interpretation of the Scripture. That's okay. Don't stop reading the rest of the Spurs. If you find only one that brings someone to Christ, all costs are worth the time and effort.

Not everyone will like every chapter of this book. My defense is written in Acts 5:32: *And we are witnesses of these things; and so is the Holy Spirit, whom God hath given to them that obey him.* Obeying God's inspiration, in my opinion, is being led by His Spirit. Humbly, I pray that is what I have done authoring this book—glorify God and Him alone.

Glorifying satan is *not* my agenda. I am very aware that the name *satan* should be capitalized as a proper noun, but I chose not to capitalize his name unless it begins a sentence. To capitalize the name of satan would be to recognize the name as a proper noun for a thing that is not proper in any way.

Again, I pray these Spurs will provide you with many lessons to modify personally and that God's Spirit will invite many souls to know Him through Jesus, our Lord and Savior.

# Sources

Dennis Phelps. "9 Things We Can All Learn from Billy Graham's Preaching." Sermon Central. June 26, 2021. First published by NOBTS.Edu. https://www.sermoncentral.com/pastors-preaching-articles/dennis-phelps-9-things-we-can-all-learn-from-billy-graham-s-preaching-1678?ref=PreachingArticleDetails.

# Dedication

To glorify God for He alone is good

And to my devoted wife, Joyce, who keeps me level.

# Cats vs. Dogs

**CONCEPTS**

Bias is natural and becomes part of our thought process without our consent or realizing it occurs. That is why bias is so difficult to overcome, even when we are made aware that we have a critical bias. Racism is like that, but there are many others we need to consider as well. Controlling our bias-based thoughts requires prayer and practice to overcome the effects on our thought processes. It is a daily battle for some; for others, they don't seem to care or realize the impact on others.

**PURPOSE**

This Spur is designed to consider how our bias can keep us from being like Christ, which impedes our ability to spread His word or do His work. The blessings we miss are beyond our ability to understand.

**SCRIPTURE BASE**

Matthew 28:19, Matthew 15:30–37

Other supporting Scripture for the Spur ...

Matthew 8:2–3, Matthew 25:44–45, Mark 2:16, Luke 10:27–29

**BACKGROUND**

Following the above verse is one of Jesus' most famous parables. The story is of the Good Samaritan, in Matthew 15:30–37. Then, in the days of Jesus, bias was prominent, but no more than today. The story continues to have such an impact coming from to-day's pulpit because it strikes at the very root of our bias. Consider who your neighbor is.

## SPUR

This is a story of classic miscommunication. You see, all our lives, we have seen dogs chasing cats. And we assumed that there was an inbred hatred or a natural predator/prey relationship between the two animals.

Some of us have had both a cat and a dog or more than one of each, and we know they can become friends. They can lie down, lick each other's faces, and even share food.

As told to me by a wise old Saudi man, the chase between a cat and a dog is all about miscommunication. It is the very crux of what bias and miscommunication are all about.

When a cat sees another animal, it begins with fear and de-fense, raising its back and tail to make it look bigger or fiercer. But the truth is it is afraid.

When a dog sees another animal, it also begins in fear and raises the hair on its back, but instead of raising its tail, it tucks its tail in a protective mode. When a dog sees a cat, though, all these natural tendencies of the dog and cat are miscommunicated. After all, they can't discuss it; they work entirely off visual indicators.

If the opposing animal is not aggressive, the dog innately be-comes curious and begins to engage and befriend the cat in play. When a dog wants to play, it raises its tail, and when another animal runs, the dog gives chase; that's fun to a dog. So, when a dog sees a cat raise its tail, the dog thinks the cat wants to play and becomes aggressive. The cat, already in fear, sees a dog become aggressive and takes flight to flee from the aggressor. The game is on.

When the cat is cornered or is caught, flight becomes a fight, and the cat goes into self-defense and counterattack. When the dog gets a paw full of claws in its nose, it is immediately confused by how quickly the play turns into a fight.

When they both learn that strange animals are not their friends, cats become dog-haters, and dogs become cat-haters. Fear, hate, and fighting become part of their modus operandi, and when a dog sees a cat, a fight ensues from the beginning. They were groomed into hatred and bias against each other because of miscommunication from the beginning. Our beginnings may have started with our parents who, from their bias, told us to stay away from people like "that."

That's the way Arabs think about it in their colloquial mindset. Arabs, generally, are biased against dogs and adore cats.

Miscommunication. What does this have to do with us? Our conduct is derived from a similar miscommunication. Critical thinking teaches that bias kills our ability to think accurately about anything. Our bias controls our decision-making and general attitude toward whatever we are thinking about. Satan uses that weakness to steer us in directions that keep us from doing the right thing, often the Christian thing. Examples follow.

How often do you see people who are not like you, and your bias keeps you from helping them or witnessing to them? Maybe they are dirty, they are tattooed, they have pink hair, or they are poor. Perhaps they are a different color or foreigners, old, young, business-like, uneducated, beggars, diseased, physically impaired, convicts, or just plain ugly. Do you hate sinners *and* their sins? Possibly, you ignore physically incapacitated people who became that way from injury or were born with a physical disability. Do you shy away from talking with them, looking at them, witnessing to them? Think of the story in Matthew 8 when a leper asked Jesus to heal him. Jesus reached out and touched him. *Touched him*! In that ancient day, touching an unclean leper was social suicide and possibly a life-threatening action.

Part of critical thinking is considering other perspectives. They (those who are different from you) might have also been mistreated, ignored, looked down upon, and even hated for being "different." Of course, some of them hate back. It sounds similar to the story above about cats and dogs.

Imagine if Jesus had held those biases. He wouldn't have been Jesus. Jesus loved the unlovely. Why can't we? Our example is Christ. His marching order to us is called the *Great Commission*. I don't remember seeing any caveats to that order, like spreading the Good News to everyone except those people you don't like.

Matthew 28:19

*Go ye therefore, and make disciples of all the nations, baptizing them into the name of the Father and of the Son and of the Holy Spirit:*

Hate the sin; love the sinner. Think about it. Repenting to become this kind of unbiased person is hard. Ask God to help; He will. Shed the bias and love like Christ.

## PRAYER

Lord, God, and Father, forgive me when I let my bias get in the way of receiving a blessing from You. Help me repent from my attitudes toward the unlovely and help me to show genuine Christian love to my neighbor. I ask, Lord, that You allow me to show the love You have given me to another. In Jesus' name, I pray. Amen.

## CREDITS AND/OR INSPIRATION

A good person who showed me mercy and grace when I was a stranger to them. The credit goes to my wise Saudi friend, who is full of Arab tales.

I belong to a Wednesday morning Breakfast Club of men who fellowship with prayer, sharing devotions over eggs and bacon or biscuits and gravy. Most men in this group are over sixty, and everyone has been either a preacher, deacon, Sunday school teacher, or minister of one type or another. Special thanks to a fellow Breakfast Club member, Richard S., for his moving story of acceptance in love toward others as Christ does.

# Back to Work

**CONCEPTS**

Many of us have worked in the ministry alongside hundreds of good people who relished the opportunity to do for others by being the hands and feet of our Lord and Savior, Jesus. The fields are ripe in the combat zone, but there are few soldiers (mixing metaphors). This Spur is written to encourage others to take action. We need more faithful workers to prepare the soil, plant the seed, and disciple the harvest the Lord brings.

**PURPOSE**

Work will not get you into heaven, no matter what. But God endorses and expects His own to work for ourselves, our family, and Him.

**SCRIPTURE BASE**

Colossians 3:23–24, Hebrews 12:15

Read Romans 16:1–16. In brief, Paul thanks and recognizes fellow workers in Christ (just as we should, by name).

Familiar Scripture to support faith and work, work and faith.

Ephesians 2:8–10, James 2:26, Ecclesiastes 11:4–6, Psalm 90:17, 1 Corinthians 15:58

**BACKGROUND**

I led groups of maintenance technicians in a public school system for many years. I was fortunate that many on each team were

Christians. Occasionally, people need counseling when they become discouraged. Especially in an environment where working hard was expected, but few were ever appreciated or noticed. That's the nature of the maintenance field. I often used these verses.

Colossians 3:23–24

> *Whatsoever ye do, work heartily, as unto the Lord, and not unto men; knowing that from the Lord ye shall receive the recompense of the inheritance: ye serve the Lord Christ.*

The verses worked on the Christians but did not affect those less spiritually inclined. I referenced this passage, especially in the weeks before I retired from that establishment. Pastors and teachers shy away from discussing work for fear that some might think it is a way they can earn their way into heaven, which is far from the truth. Working in the ministry shows love and faith in the Father, who has done exceedingly more for us. It is one way we can tithe by offering the best of ourselves to Christ. After all, God gives all good gifts, including our talents and inspiration.

## SPUR

Romans 16 (see verses 1–16) is a great reference when you wish to honor those who glorify God working in His service. We all know individuals who expect to be praised while others expect nothing because they are humble and desire to serve their Lord.

I've had the extreme privilege of working alongside many excellent and talented people in ministry. To list them all would make me sound like bragging when the reality is I was honored to be among some great Christians who were sold out in service to God. God gives all good gifts, and many come to people as talents and abilities that others do not possess. You don't need to name names; they know who they are, and everyone else knows who they are. They are the ones who organize and promote events, cook the meals, enlist others, gather resources, generate ideas, clean the floors, buy the little extras that are needed, and pick up the pieces, whatever they are.

Sometimes, we might wonder what motivates others to write letters and notes, clean up the messes, stand in the hot sun or cold weather, do the shopping, set up the tents, hand out the bulletins, play music, pull the cables, visit the sick or dying in hospitals, homes, or hospices. I'm speaking of those who may never ask but do it out of love or compassion. After they are asked, some jump in with both feet and tear into their task like a bulldog. As administrators, we sometimes want to put the brakes on their spirited zeal. It is a blessing to have a group of people dedicated to working. A lot can be done, even if it is only a small group of four or five dedicated people. God blesses whenever two or more like-minded servants are gathered together.

The others, not described above, pull down and quench the Spirit. They are often the ones satan can convict to do nothing or worse; they backbite, compromise, tattle, and espouse contrary gossip to other potential workers, undermining the proposed idea or program. These displays, whatever you might call them, are church killers. Sadly, I confess to being guilty; I've been there.

We can't forget the passive-aggressive types, either. These are the ones who were not asked to help, won't volunteer, and now impede the progress with slow hands and feet or cease to show up when needed. They are hard to spot, and you might even identify with them sometimes in your Christian life. It doesn't feel good to know you can identify with them sometimes.

I love being asked and rarely turn down a request, but I seldom volunteer. We should aspire to be the *sheeple* God wants us to be when supporting our church activities. We might not fully agree with the program and may even be somewhat envious of the leaders, but we should never be the ones to quench the Spirit or slow-walk and impede the progress.

Hebrews 12:15

*Looking carefully lest there be any man that falleth short of the grace of God; lest any root of bitterness springing up trouble you, and thereby the many be defiled.*

In other words, don't be that person. Test yourself. If you ask God to search your heart and reveal any evil or wickedness, ask for forgiveness and repent. Everyone will be lifted because of it.

## PRAYER

Lord, God and Father, forgive me when I fall short of doing all I can do. Your Word in James tells us we sin when we know we should do something and fail. Convict me, Holy Spirit, when I should act but make excuses not to do what You have called me to do. Lord, take me, enlist me to be Your hands and feet to do Your will and glorify Your name. Amen.

## CREDITS AND/OR INSPIRATION

Reading Romans 16, Paul's listing of those he thanks for the work within their church and with him serving God.

# Your Engine Light Is On

## CONCEPTS

Critical decision-making instruction is lacking in our basic educational systems. Many organizations teach about critical thinking, but few teach students how to think critically about anything. Religious organizations consider the topic of critical thinking to be somehow New Age and say it should be discouraged in our educational syllabi. As Christians, we must think critically and make good decisions based on the truth of God's Word, not worldly bias or satan's influence.

## PURPOSE

False indications, faulty intelligence, and worldly bias often play a role in the lives of Christians who lose focus on the truth and lose faith in God. Satan is the great deceiver whose only purpose is to confuse and lead us in the wrong direction by pushing us toward wrong thinking.

## SCRIPTURE BASE

Psalm 1:1, 1 Corinthians 2:6–8, Philippians 4:8, Matthew 4:1–11, Romans 8:5–8, Romans 8:38–39

## BACKGROUND

If you had ever ridden with me in my old 2005 pickup, you might have seen my engine light glowing on my dash. It's been like that for about five years. It makes my wife nervous, and it used to bug me too. I've tried fixing it and taken it to several mechanics; they all have prescribed fixes. I've tried those remedies that only cost a few bucks. A few recommendations would have cost a lot of money, and I've not done those. You see, the pickup starts and runs fine with the light on.

There may be a real fix, but it doesn't matter because I know it's not a big deal. I figured out I could get by. I ignore the lie; I don't get excited about it or change my driving habits.

The intel that the sensor and indicator give me is faulty. False intel in life, if believed, can have costly, if not fatal, results. Maybe you have a similar story to use for this Spur. The idea is that sometimes we make bad decisions based on faulty intel. Many times, that intel comes directly from the lies of satan.

## SPUR

False swatting has become a significant problem across the US. You can Google it and find several incidents at schools, businesses, and private homes. An infamous event happened on Dec 28, 2017, in Wichita, Kansas. A local police officer (sniper) fatally shot Andrew Finch after being mistakenly swatted by an online gamer playing *Call of Duty*. The unidentified gamer argued with another online gamer and decided to play a prank. He submitted a 911 call and mistakenly gave the wrong address, resulting in a SWAT team response. Andrew Finch answered the door and was told to put his hands up. When he unexpectedly dropped one hand to his waist, he was immediately shot by the sniper officer. He was DOA at the hospital.

The original intel was false, and the result was permanent. Andrew Finch, a father who had young children, was murdered.

In many ways, we all live with false information that pervades our daily lives. Some of it is the news we receive from all types of media. Some of it is gossip we hear from friends or family. As Christians, we should be diligent in keeping ourselves from falling for these lies and deceptions. Our walk should be in Spirit and truth, but it is much more complicated than just saying so.

Consider how many people do terrible things based on false information. Suicide, murder, abortion, divorce, fights, division—you can name several negative results of people taking action based on false information.

Critical thinking requires us to fight the indicator light. Those lights on your car's dashboard have been called idiot lights by mechanics for years because they know the truth. Indicator lights don't tell you the whole story. You must dig deeper. You have to see all the angles and not jump to conclusions. You cannot let prejudice or even previous experiences tell you what is right or wrong. You have to weigh the evidence and search for the truth. If you don't know the difference between true and false, you can't make a good decision, and you may as well hope for good luck. Do not put your faith in a warning light, regardless of how long it burns.

The warning light urges you to take action and become active in trying to find out what is wrong. Investigative research will lead you to act if needed; sometimes, you must do something as soon as possible. No decision is a decision, and it is usually the wrong one (Elder and Elder).

Peter A. Facione, an identified leader in the use of critical thinking, said this in 2011:

Critical thinking is skeptical without being cynical. It is open-minded without being wishy-washy. It is analytical without being nitpicky. Critical thinking can be decisive without being stubborn, evaluative without being judgemental, and forceful without being opinionated.

All this advice about indicators transfers directly to everyday living. Christians, especially, need to be critical thinkers too. We must know where our truth comes from and never doubt it. Satan is the liar of all liars, and he will invade every thought process you have to skew the truth and give you the false indicator he wants you to react to. Sometimes, bad advice comes from well-meaning friends. Check the facts (Psalm 1:1).

Some of satan's best work is right inside your brain to doubt yourself and who you are. If you believe his lies, he will have you thinking you are not good, intelligent, strong, rich, or powerful enough. Soon, you will give up without even trying. Do not accept the lies. The truth is that you are a child of God, and when you know that, you can brush off all those lies above, having the wisdom God gives through the Spirit (1 Corinthians 2:6–8).

The cartoon that shows the devil sitting on one shoulder and an angel sitting on the other shoulder whispering in the ears of the decision-maker comes to mind. Satan can't control your mind, but he can influence the way you think.

If you are wary that you might be lied to and you begin to accept the lie because the idiot light continues to blink, then it's time to reintroduce yourself to the only book on how to live on earth by God, the author of life.

Philippians 4:8

> *Finally, brethren, whatsoever things are true, whatso-ever things are honorable, whatsoever things are just, what-soever things are pure, whatsoever things are lovely, what-soever things are of good report; if there be any virtue, and if there be any praise, think on these things.*

That devil sitting on your shoulder screaming in your ear, "Loser, Worthless, Unloved, Hated," is lying to you. These accusations come from the father of lies, the great accuser and master of false indicators. So shed that junk and believe what God says. Ask Him for help. Use His Word to combat the fiery arrows being shot at you. Read Matthew 4:1–11 and do what Jesus did when satan tried to sway Jesus into sin.

Romans 8:5–8

*For they that are after the flesh mind the things of the flesh; but they that are after the Spirit the things of the Spirit. For the mind of the flesh is death; but the mind of the Spirit is life and peace: because the mind of the flesh is enmity against God; for it is not subject to the law of God, neither indeed can it be: and they that are in the flesh cannot please God.*

And never forget that God is on your side. You have become a child of God, and as such, who can be against you if God is for you? The battle has been won; stay on the right side.

Romans 8:38–39

*For I am persuaded, that neither death, nor life, nor angels, nor principalities, nor things present, nor things to come, nor powers, nor height, nor depth, nor any other creature, shall be able to separate us from the love of God, which is in Christ Jesus our Lord.*

## PRAYER

Lord, Father of life and Creator of all things, protect us daily from the one seeking to destroy our minds and lives. Remind us through the Spirit to seek Your Word and truth. Help us maintain a Spirit-filled perspective and walk in step with You and Your will for us. Teach us daily and remind us of Your love; all good gifts come from You. Give us Your peace and spare us from evil. Amen.

## CREDITS AND/OR INSPIRATION

Readings from two books with a Christian perspective and bias:

Richard Paul Elder and Linda Elder. *Critical Thinking: Tools for Taking Charge of Your Learning and Your Life*. Fourth edition. The Foundation for Critical Thinking, 2022.

Peter Facione. *THINK Critically.* Pearson, 2010.

# A Soldier's Perspective

**CONCEPTS**

The author is a Vietnam veteran and has worked as an educator with the US and foreign military services for over twenty years. Many military precepts fit the behavior of what a Christian soldier should be and how they would conduct themselves.

**PURPOSE**

Many people can identify with the service of a soldier and the dedication required for honorable service.

**SCRIPTURE BASE**

2 Timothy 2:1–4 and Mark 8:34–38

The "Whole Armor of God" is a military reference to preparing for battle with evil (Ephesians 6:10–20). Use these verses to draw other parallels to a soldier in combat against the spiritual powers of darkness.

**BACKGROUND**

These references might not lead you to create an entire sermon but might help create devotion or become part of another discourse to make a point intended by the preacher. Many of these comparisons are easily transferable and understandable to a majority of any audience. It is also suitable for a Veterans Day or associated Memorial Day service.

## SPUR

There may be people I'm speaking with today who, at some point in their lives, joined the military and went through what most services call "Boot Camp." I'm a veteran, and I went through boot camp. I can tell you it changed my life. If you haven't been in the military and can't relate to this experience, maybe you know someone close to you or a school buddy or friend who joined and became a soldier, sailor, airman, or marine. Did you see a change in them? I assure you—everyone is changed. The military has a unique way of taking any man or woman from any walk of life, color or nationality, background or part of the country, rich or poor, and changing them with a military bearing within an average of sixteen weeks, more or less. They become a different person. Within the chest of most military members is a heart that beats with patriotism, dedication, and a mission in life. That was the intent of the training, and people who went through it know that they changed. This Spur is about the correlation and comparison between the military and being a soldier for Christ.

When we consider the life of a Christian soldier, one might consider Ephesians 6:10–20. Extending the references to many other parts of our lives as Christians is easy. In thinking about them with a military bent, we broaden our understanding of dedication, honor, and victory in Jesus.

What if we consider our church building as a soldier would consider their fort? I am not talking about shooting from the twenty-foot barricade walls but about gathering the troops in a place for recovery, nourishment, training, drill, practice, and the continuous honing of skills. This fort compound teaches doctrine and plans with strategic goals and tactical mission objectives. Imagine the church building a safe place where the injured are cared for and others are refreshed and empowered to go out and fight another day. Our churches should reflect this kind of education and preparedness. Our present-day problem is that too many churches kill off their wounded instead of bandaging them and helping them to heal from their injuries received on the battlefield.

The garrison is where we live, home. It is always close to the fort and relatively safe from the battlefield. This place is surrounded by peaceful people who share the same friendly ways of life. Your home is your fort or protection where you can feed yourself, care for yourself, and study independently. Your home should be a place of rest, love, family, and peace. This might not always be true for some, but you should stay in the fort if you cannot go home to be safe.

The world is the front line. No doubt, this is the battlefield. The battlefield is where you need to have put on all your armor, as written about in Ephesians 6. The enemy is out there, and the enemy is prepared to attack you and fight you over every good deed that glorifies God. For every soul you might lead to Christ. The enemy will use every trick and lie to penetrate, infiltrate, and annihilate you and your efforts. Sometimes (too often), he will break down the walls and walk in the front door of the fort or your place of safety in the garrison. If satan cannot kill you, he will do everything to make you ineffective in battle.

Being a good soldier requires dedication—a good soldier is dedicated and takes an oath to protect and defend. When good soldiers take an oath, they literally write a blank check to give their lives if needed to honor the duty they have volunteered to do. Have you taken an oath to give your life in service to God?

Commitment—with any sworn dedication is a mental commitment to live a life worthy of a good soldier. Many soldiers never let down their guard and are always faithful to behave and live as the military doctrine requires. Some carry the commitment of that integrity into their civilian lives after they have served. I can attest to the adage of "Once a Marine, always a Marine." Few ever take on a private life that leaves behind the ingrained Marine Corps integrity and dedication taught from the first day of basic training. As

Christians, we, too, can and should carry our commitment to Jesus for our entire lives. Good soldiers obey, take orders, and fight to the death for what they believe.

Surrender—soldiers also know what it means to surrender. When ordered, they will submit to the authority of those who hold their lives in their hands. Surrender is seldom a choice, and it is rarely a negotiation; it is not an agreement or a bargain. Surrender is giving oneself over to the total control of one's life to a greater power. God wants each soldier to have surrendered to only One, the One and Only—God. Surrender is an all-in sum of one's life.

2 Timothy 2:1–4

*Thou therefore, my child, be strengthened in the grace that is in Christ Jesus. And the things which thou hast heard from me among many witnesses, the same commit thou to faithful men, who shall be able to teach others also. Suffer hardship with me, as a good soldier of Christ Jesus. No soldier on service entangleth himself in the affairs of this life; that he may please him who enrolled him as a soldier.*

Emphasis:

*No soldier on service entangleth himself in the affairs of this life; that he may please him who enrolled him as a soldier.*

This part of the verse seems strange, and I often wonder about what Paul is saying, implying, or teaching. I get the part about pleasing the one who enlisted him, referring to each of us as those who have accepted Jesus and aim to please the one who enlisted us, but what do you suppose he means about *No soldier gets entangled in civilian pursuits?* When I served in the military, I knew I was at work and under the control of my superiors 24/7. We could be called into battle or war at any time, and we knew we had better show up or be declared a deserter. Sure, during peace, they gave us time off and endeavored to make our lives as normal as possible, but it was not that way in Paul's time. In Paul's day, a soldier was indeed a soldier 24/7. Soldiers (not commanders or generals) but the soldiers in the field, garrison, and fort were always on call and on duty. They did not go to the store; they did not have weekends with their wife and kids; they did not work a part-time job, enjoy hobbies, or take time off to go sightseeing or to a favorite restaurant. If they did any of that, they did it when they were on duty. Even today, the life of a soldier in some military organizations, as then, is a total commitment. Roman soldiers never partook in civilian affairs because they were not civilians. They were often ordered to enforce Roman law on civilians because most military personnel in Paul's time were occupation forces.

I know you did not come for a history lesson on the life of a Roman soldier, but now think about what Paul was saying when he wrote this. As soldiers for Christ, we must be willing and ready as dedicated and enlisted soldiers for His work 24/7 and not be distracted by our civilian life. We are to live all-in as Christian soldiers in our civilian lives. That is dedication, devotion, and surrender.

Considering everything Paul says, people should commit to that intensive enlistment.

Consider what Jesus said to His disciples. In Mark 8, written in red letters beginning with verse 34:

> *And he called unto him the multitude with his disciples, and said unto them, If any man would come after me, let him deny himself, and take up his cross, and follow me. For whosoever would save his life shall lose it; and whosoever shall lose his life for my sake and the gospel's shall save it. For what doth it profit a man, to gain the whole world, and forfeit his life For what should a man give in exchange for his life? For whosoever shall be ashamed of me and of my words in this adulterous and sinful generation, the Son*

*of man also shall be ashamed of him, when he cometh in the glory of his Father with the holy angels.*

The context and the meaning of what Paul writes about being a soldier gets real. The people Jesus spoke to knew exactly what it meant to follow Him.

Do you have that kind of commitment? Living a Christian life takes courage. It takes considerable fortitude to step up or step out and say, "I will." I understand many cannot or will not make that decision for fear of what that kind of enlistment might do to the lives they love to live right now.

So, take the other road and surrender. That is what I said: surrender to Jesus and let Him stand you up to be His soldier. Give yourself over to the higher power, to Jesus, and let Him take your life. You may not be ready for battle. You may need to get in shape. You need to learn how to use spiritual weapons and know and understand the battle plan. You may need to stop some civilian activities that hinder your relationship with God. He will guide you. Once accepted, the Spirit that dwells within you will train and protect you. The Spirit will work on you over time and help you understand what you need to do to become holier. Have faith in God to clean you up and change what you know is not right in your life.

The military takes civilians just as they are and makes them soldiers. Jesus and the Spirit do precisely the same thing. It is a lifetime commitment and a new way of life, but it is a life that has an eternal reward in heaven. So, save your life; give it to Jesus today.

Turn to your hymnal and sing, "Onward Christian Soldiers." It might bring back a few memories of what this Spur is about.

## PRAYER

God and Father, You alone are worthy to follow. Lead my life and be a lamp unto my feet, a light unto my path. Shod my feet with the faith to follow You wherever You lead me. Give me the tools needed to be Your servant and soldier in battle. Please give me the courage to fight and stand firm for the gospel wherever and whenever I am allowed to witness. Amen.

## CREDITS AND/OR INSPIRATION

The author is a disabled Vietnam veteran. He continued completing a twenty-year career working for and associated with the military as a civilian.

# Wash, Rinse, Repeat

## CONCEPTS

Humility is difficult for modern men to attain. Some have it, but they are generally shy and introverted in reality. This Spur isn't about humility alone but Jesus' example of servanthood. It is also about the daily sins that we all commit.

## PURPOSE

There is a threefold lesson available within this Spur. Pick one, two, or all of them.

## SCRIPTURE BASE

1 John 1:10, John 13:9, John 13:14, James 5:16

## BACKGROUND

Years ago, in what almost now seems to be a lifetime ago, I was honored to be in the presence of one of the most excellent pastors and preachers I've ever met. His name was Steve Taylor, and he spent his entire career preaching in one church he started in his garage, now Northside Baptist Church of Northglenn, Colorado. He never used notes, memorized every verse, and sang during his sermons, and when he felt the Spirit moving, he would not quench it but have an altar call on the spot. When my family and I attended that church, there were two services each Sunday, with Sunday school between their morning services. Some preachers leave a "mark" on your heart with the aid of the Holy Spirit. Many sermons have left a mark on my heart. This Spur is about one of those marks.

## SPUR

Pastor Steve Taylor preached toe-stomping sermons frequently. He never let us forget that even though we might be saved and our sins are forgiven, we still fall short of the target and often offend our Lord or sadden His Spirit. If we thought we didn't sin anymore because we were Christians, he'd pull out that verse that would call us a liar.

1 John 1:10

> *If we say that we have not sinned, we make him a liar, and his word is not in us.*

He reminded us that just because we are human and walk around this world every day, we get our feet dirty. And because we do, we need to ask God to forgive us, cleanse us, and show us our sins so that we will repent and stop offending Him.

John 13:9

> *Simon Peter saith unto him, Lord, not my feet only, but also my hands and my head. Jesus saith to him, He that is bathed needeth not save to wash his feet, but is clean every whit: and ye are clean, but not all.*

You see, that is why Jesus said this to Peter. You don't need to wash all of you. You are saved and have been cleansed once and for all eternity, but your feet are dirty and must be washed.

I've said before that I'm not a theologian, but I liked and exactly understood what that means to us. We get dirty sometimes. Jesus was making a point, and He made Himself the example as their mentor, pastor, and Lord.

John 13:14

*If I then, the Lord and the Teacher, have washed your feet, ye also ought to wash one another's feet.*

What do you suppose that means? Some churches do this regularly. As a deacon in one church I attended, we occasionally did this to remind us of how humble it made us. I wasn't humbled to wash another's feet but was genuinely leveled to the ground when another washed mine. I suggest trying this if you have never done it in your church. People will talk about it for months. Some will remember it for years.

But, you know? You can't just bare your feet, get some towels and a wash bin, and sit down to wash each other's feet in our society today. It is a humbling event at church, and it has a purpose, but think of it in another context. Jesus is washing His disciples' feet, but they are not washing each other's feet. Are servanthood and humility the only lessons here? I don't think so. Jesus knew He wouldn't be around them much longer, so His example is clear.

James 5:16

*Confess therefore your sins one to another, and pray one for another, that ye may be healed. The supplication of a righteous man availeth much in its working.*

If you haven't confessed to your brother the sins you have committed so he might pray for you, you'll find that very humbling. You are washing one another's feet, both literally and figuratively. You don't need to provide the details. God knows. But you can tell your brother in Christ you've been screwing up lately, and your faith has been compromised, or you've stumbled and fallen and need Jesus to lift you up. You can say satan is attacking you, and you need prayer to combat the evil you are fighting. Ask a righteous friend to pray for you. We do that when we are sick, injured, or have an upcoming situation that bothers us. But we need to do that when we are sin-sick too.

Praise God, if you have a friend, you can ask for prayer—maybe your pastor, your deacon, or a close friend. Be a blessing and do the same for them; you will also be blessed. If you don't have a friend like that, make one, be one.

## PRAYER

God and Father, Lord of all, thank You for the brothers and sisters in Christ I have to confide in and ask for prayer. I thank You, Lord, that I can be the person people can call and ask for prayer when they have tribulations. Hear those who seek Your face and call upon Your name, Lord. We ask Your will be done, for we pray in Your name. Amen.

## CREDITS AND/OR INSPIRATION

Reverend Steve Taylor, rest in peace. Hope to see you again soon.

# Dog Bones

## CONCEPTS

Our sins are before us, but our past is behind us. Many of us need to remind ourselves of these truths.

## PURPOSE

If we live in our past and constantly relive our sins, we haven't forgiven ourselves even though God has forgiven us. The Scripture Base tells us that is not what God wants. Satan throws our past in our faces to tear us down and make us feel unworthy. Jesus died and was raised again to free us from those chains.

## SCRIPTURE BASE

John 8:36, Romans 8:1, Titus 3:3, Romans 8:6, Philippians 4:7, John 10:9–11, John 14:27

## BACKGROUND

Each Wednesday morning, an eclectic group of men meets for prayer, devotion, breakfast, and fellowship. Our mix of devotees has been or currently are preachers, teachers, deacons, or church leaders. From that mix, we include those who are also military veterans, Christian motorcyclists, computer programmers, musicians, realtors, chemical engineers, newspaper editors, and combinations of those. This group of men's ages varies from thirty-somethings to eighty-year-olds, but each adds to the collection of stories and experiences rich with the flavor of living full Christian lives. We call ourselves the Christian Breakfast Club. The background of this Spur comes from a Wednesday devotion given by one of these men. Marty is a retired Marine from the Vietnam era who did his share of fighting while flying helicopters in battle. He is currently (at the time of this writing) the president of the Western North Carolina Chapter of the Christian Motorcycle Association (CMA) and a former pastor of a local Baptist church.

## SPUR

While sitting in our local Veteran's Affairs hospital waiting room one day, Marty overheard a conversation between two other veterans sitting behind him. One of the veterans was a younger man who had served in combat in Afghanistan and Iraq. The other was an older man who had served in combat in Vietnam. They began cordially talking about the weather and the hospital service they received, and then the younger man began to relate war stories that were haunting him for the things he had seen and done. The older man tried to interject his experience, but the young man wouldn't let him get a word in edgewise. Finally, the old man said, "Let me tell you about a dog I used to have." The young man's attention was taken, as ours was, trying to relate what this guy's dog had to do with the younger man's experiences. The older soldier told a story about how he had a big dog whom he rewarded with a meaty bone from the butcher shop. The dog chewed on the bone for a time, then buried it. After a few days, he dug up the bone, chewed it, reburied it, and left it for a few more days. The dog dug up the bone again a week later, now very rancid. He chewed on it again, but this time, he seemed happy to bury it again for the last time. Everyone got the message except, apparently, the young man.

Did you get the message from that story? Those of us who have lived any length of time have a bad memory in our past that we dig up and chew on. The older it gets, the more that specific sinful past or offense pricks our consciousness. It is best to bury it and forget about it. But some people can't do that, and it destroys them; for others, it is just a bad memory that returns in nightmares for years afterward.

As Christians, we have a Savior who died for our sins and freed us from the chains of guilt and condemnation. Whenever we (or satan) dig up that nasty bone again, we have a bar of soap that cleans that memory out of our minds and gives us a peace only God can provide. It may take years of therapy for non-Christians to forgive and forget if they live that long. I could share how thousands of war veterans have committed suicide, unable to purge the memory of things they've done, seen, or had done to them. But it is not just war victims who suffer these burdens from evil memories and how they can destroy lives. What everyone needs is Jesus. He is the balm that soothes the pain of guilt, condemnation, and unforgiveness. His sacrifice on the cross paid for all those sins. He is the one whose grace covers the pain, guilt, and shame satan holds over us. Others need to hear that. I pray for the young war victim in this story to find Christ and be healed of his burden.

As we witness to the lost and those we meet, our past is a tool to effectively remind others that we all have a sin sickness that only the Holy Spirit of God can heal. Everyone has sinned, and when reminded of it, many seek salvation. No one is getting to heaven with sin on their ledger. As Christians, we know the One who cleans the slate. Lead others to Christ. Jesus saves.

## PRAYER

Lord, God and Father, we praise Your Holy Name above all. Remind us each day that You are good and Your gifts come in many packages. Thank You for allowing us to love and forgive ourselves because You love and have forgiven us. Lord, we pray that others will find Your love, forgiveness, and peace in You. Please help us to show others where they will find salvation from the evil that troubles their minds. Help us to show others where they can see the renewing of their minds through Christ. Amen.

43

## CREDITS AND/OR INSPIRATION

With his permission to relate this story, Marty O'Dell is a Marine combat veteran, my friend, and a fellow Christian Breakfast Club member.

# Fireworks

## CONCEPTS

Pastors, ministers, teachers, and musicians can get lost in their desire to serve the Lord and begin to serve themselves. Maybe you've met some. Perhaps you have fallen into satan's snare of pride. Beware, this Spur defines how easy it is and what is needed to escape the sin of hubris.

## PURPOSE

We are human, and satan is wily to grab our basic instincts and pull us down into selfish pride instead of glorifying God. Unfortunately, it happens, and in recent days, we have seen it much too often. Satan uses fame, riches, and pride to draw disciples away from God.

## SCRIPTURE BASE

Hebrews 12:1–2, Mark 8:34–37

Exodus, Chapters 36–38: Read all three chapters. The first verse of chapter 36 begins this Spur rightly.

Exodus 36:1

> *And Bezalel and Oholiab shall work, and every wise-hearted man, in whom Jehovah hath put wisdom and under-standing to know how to work all the work for the service of the sanctuary, according to all that Jehovah hath commanded.*

## BACKGROUND

Far too many pastors, preachers, and musicians lose their way after being called to glorify God. Sadly, some fall into the sin of exalting themselves, and their motives become skewed. We all need to test ourselves and our motives for what we do in our belief that we do it for God alone. The *Fireworks* title is a pun, but it isn't funny if your works are heading in the wrong direction.

## SPUR

I was born and raised in Montana in the fifties and sixties. The 4th of July was the biggest holiday of the year for me. It was bigger than Christmas or my birthday or anything else. Our family plans always included doing something special. For many years, there were rodeos in Roundup or Red Lodge, and they always always concluded with fireworks. I can't remember too many years since that time when my family and I failed to try to see fireworks whenever we got a chance. It's not always on the 4th of July that you can see fireworks somewhere.

Have you ever seen them? Think about when you heard and felt the booms, saw the colors, the smoke, and smelled the black powder. How glorious the sights and sounds of a good fireworks display are. I can even give you a bona fide rating of a good, bad, or mediocre show. I've spent hundreds of dollars shooting off our shows of fireworks at home, even though it was illegal in some places we lived. But, if you've never lit a fuse, run, and stood back with your eyes to the sky to see the fireworks, then I'd say you may have missed some living.

Do you know who made the fireworks? Have you ever met anyone who mixed the powders or created the internal packages that produced unique displays of red, green, sparkly blues, and gold? How about those guys who lit the fuses and set up the cannons that controlled the direction or the sequence of all those beautiful bursts of light in the sky? We rarely think about or give credit to the explosives maker or the people who lit the cannons. All we see and remember is the glorious display of lights and sounds.

Where is this Spur going? The people who glorified the skies with their service and talent exemplify humility for us. It is the way we should live our lives, glorifying God. We are His hands and feet, and His glory is the light and action, the flashes and sounds that get all the oooohs and aaaahs from those who witness the fury. We are supposed to be the ones who light the fuses, make the cannons, and coordinate the action to give God the glory.

Do you remember who Bezalel was? Read Exodus 36 through 38 again. He was a talented man. He was likely more talented than anyone in history for his artistry and creativity. We know of many ancient artists who gained great notoriety and fame. Bezalel is hardly remembered or famous by world standards, but he was greatly honored by biblical standards for his accomplishments. God inspired him with artistic talent like none other. He was gifted immensely by God. As a result, his fame and glory are lifted to heavenly places, and his name is in the everlasting Word of God.

No one wrote about his houses or cars or jet planes. They didn't talk about his best-selling books or millions in wealth. Instead, Moses wrote how Bezalel made a tabernacle, a tent temple of God that God ordered to be made to His glory. But, of course, the glory was not Bezalel's, whom we hardly remember, but to God and His glory.

That's humility in a nutshell when it comes to ministry. But, unfortunately, for some ministers, preachers, and artists, the desire for the stage becomes a sin, and the crowd's adoration becomes a drug. None of us should wish to be on the pedestal of the crowd. We shouldn't desire to use the pulpit or sanctuary as a springboard to glorify ourselves. Instead, we are to point to the glory of God. We are to light the fuse of the Spirit and give God the stage of light, sound, and fury.

Hebrews 12:1–2

*Therefore let us also, seeing we are compassed about with so great a cloud of witnesses, lay aside everyweight, and the sin which doth so easily beset us, and let us run with patience the race that is set before us, looking unto Jesus the author and perfecter of our faith, who for the joy that was set before him endured the cross, despising shame, and hath sat down at the right hand of the throne of God.*

Mark 8:34–37

*And he called unto him the multitude with his disciples, and said unto them, If any man would come after me, let him deny himself, and take up his cross, and follow me. For whosoever would save his life shall lose it; and whosoever shall lose his life for my sake and the gospel's shall save it. For what doth it profit a man, to gain the whole world, and forfeit his life? For what should a man give in exchange for his life?*

That's it. That's the Spur. Check yourself. What are your motives? Are you an actor? Comedian? Great orator? Are you good at playing an instrument or singing? Check yourself, and when you conclude honestly that your heart and mind are in the right place to glorify God, His glory will manifest itself, and the fruit of the Spirit it yields will be glorious. If you find yourself on the other side of that inspection, do as you might be calling on others to do. Repent. Ask for forgiveness and get your priorities right. Jesus first, always.

**PRAYER**

Lord, God and Father, protect those You have called into Your service. Keep satan at bay, and don't allow him to pull our best, brightest, and most talented down into pride and self-serving motivations. Lord, protect the servants You have called to draw others unto You. Lord, I ask Your Spirit to pour generous portions of wisdom, humility, grace, and peace over those in Your service. Thank You for each one of them and for all they do for You. Amen.

## CREDITS AND/OR INSPIRATION

You only need to look around at the ones failing in their service and understand why.

# It's Hell Without Jesus

## CONCEPTS

Hell is real, and if you have a heart for the lost, you will do everything possible to lead people to Christ for Him to save them.

## PURPOSE

Use this Spur to preach the gospel. The Good News is that Jesus saves believers from hell, a very real place.

## SCRIPTURE BASE

Mark 9:42–49, Matthew 13:36–43, Luke 16:19–31, Matthew 23:33, Matthew 10:28, Luke 12:5, 2 Peter 2:4

## BACKGROUND

We can see how satan minimizes hell and his influence on believers and nonbelievers alike. Hell isn't so terrible; it is a lie. Satan isn't such a bad guy, and that is a lie. People who take either for granted or consider either as less are making a horrendous mistake. Preach heaven as well as the sacrifice and resurrection of Christ with the same enthusiasm as the depth and ruination of an eternal hell.

## SPUR

Preachers don't preach much about hell these days because, to most folks, it's unpopular. Most churchgoers don't care to sit in a pew on Sunday morning and listen to a sermon about a place they are relatively sure they're not going to.

That didn't stop Jesus from teaching and preaching it. Jesus spoke of hell more often than He spoke of heaven, if we are talking about places of eternity.

Heaven is a place, and so is hell. If you don't believe me and don't wish to hear me talk about it, let's consult with God's Word and those words of Jesus written in red in many of your Bibles. I love God's Word and have read it from the table of contents to the maps many times. I love the prophets and disciples and believe in the Bible's lessons and stories. But, for my reasons, I enjoy hearing quotes from Jesus. I don't need anyone to tell me what they think He said or what they heard; we have direct excerpts. I pay more attention to the words directly from my Lord. My mother gave me my first Bible, not my church. I remember reading it soon after I was baptized, and Christ's words were written in red. His words seem to jump off the page at me. I still like it, and I still have it.

I have three main passages of Scripture I would like to bring to your attention. Most of you have read these before and might even have some memorized. I will take these three in a specific order to make my point. These passages are rich with glorious content to preach from, and thousands of pastors have been inspired to preach these verses. I wish to pull from these verses those words that describe hell and try to imagine a place of eternal torment.

Preachers often dwell on the words describing the assaults on Christ and all He endured during His crucifixion. They also dwell on the descriptions of heaven and the beautiful visions we will see as described in Revelation, where there will be no pain, tears, or sorrow. Take an hour and dwell on hell sometime. That reflection will bring the reality of what hell will be for nonbelievers and might make believers in Christ. People are more inclined to think they deserve heaven and all it holds more than they think they could end up in hell. For some people, describing their heavenly home is easy to

51

accept, but fear of hell is remote. Once they realize that hell could be a reality for them, fear becomes very real.

These verses Jesus spoke provided warnings and curses. His words describe horrendous attributes of a place where the unrighteous will go eternally.

Mark 9:42–49 warns "whosoever" causes little children who believe in Christ to sin. Some theologians consider this might mean not just the younger age children who are gullible enough to be led into sin but also new believers (baby Christians). Both are susceptible to being drawn or enticed back into sinful behavior. So how do you cause someone to sin? I consider those who force or coerce others into sin, i.e., child slavers, sex traffickers, drug pushers, pedophiles, porn blackmailers, etc. The result of one who would commit these atrocities against innocents doesn't sound good, for they will suffer at the hands of a righteous God something worse than a heavy stone tied around their neck and being thrown into the sea to be carried to the bottom and drowned.

The rest of the section illustrates several situations where people may habitually sin with their hands, (stealing?) feet, (running to evil?) eyes, (porn?) which are all habits that, if not broken, will lead to hell. The instruction is to do whatever extreme thing you can to break the habit, even if you must cut off a hand or foot or gouge out an eye to stop. The warning is that you will be cast into hell if you do not control these habits. The description here leads your imagination to consider what it must be like to have worms eating your dead body and enduring a fiery torment that will never stop. Everyone cast in this place will feel that unquenching fire.

Sinful habits such as these are tough for some people to break. We have all known Christians who have struggled with something that holds them back from a fruitful and blessed life in Christ. Jesus says, Do whatever you must to break these habits of willful sin. Jesus is saying in plain terms that it is better to enter heaven (saved?) without the sinful hand, foot, or eye than to allow those sins to drag you into eternal hell. Asking for help from Jesus, confessing the problem, and requesting the Spirit to aid in overcoming your sinful desires have helped Christians break sinful habits. Regardless, do not continue sinning. Ask God to show you your sin and make extreme, if necessary, efforts to overcome those habits.

Matthew 13:36–43 is Jesus' explanation and teaching His disciples the meaning of a parable He spoke to the public. Jesus' audiences were comprised of masses of agricultural men and women who would understand sowing seed and reaping crops at harvest. He relates the story spiritually to His disciples to describe the world's end and how it will be at the Rapture. As believers, we should understand what our salvation means at the end of this world. Without His salvation, His description of hell relates to eternal fire for those who cause stumbling or do evil things. Those whom the devil sowed as weeds among the faithful will be gathered separately and thrown (as a conscious soul) into a furnace to burn forever, and the torment seems to be unbearable. Praise God, the righteous conscious soul will shine forth in the Light of God.

In Luke 16:19–31, Jesus tells another parable describing attributes of hell that allow our imagination to understand the boundaries of a very inescapable place again. Jesus describes how the rich man, looking up and in torment, sees his ancestor Abraham and asks for mercy. The rich man only wants some water to cool his tongue, and even in hell, he expects to call upon a servant to relieve his anguish from the flame—what a picture. Instead, Abraham slams him for his life and says that his misery is deserved. The following description sets the boundaries of hell in that a great chasm separates hell from heaven and earth. The abyss cannot be breached, and no one can cross over. Accepting that answer, the tormented rich man asks for another favor—save his family and send Lazarus back as an eyewitness from the dead so his Father's house would repent and be saved from the torment of hell.

I find Abraham's answer to that request interesting, and it should not be lost in the story. Remember, this is Jesus' story. In essence, Abraham says that if they don't believe what is written by Moses and the prophets, they won't be persuaded if one rises from the dead.

Jesus wasn't talking about Lazarus; He was talking about Himself. If you don't believe or have faith in what the Bible says, you likely won't believe that Christ rose from the grave and defeated death. Without this fact, Christians have no hope, and there is no salvation. It is hell without Jesus.

The other verses, as listed above, provide further descriptions of hell and the suffering hell brings. Mathew and Luke relate Jesus as saying whom we should fear (respect). Respect for the One who has the power to destroy body and soul in hell gives us again the description that our spirit is conscious. Our feelings will be filled with pain. Second Peter adds the description that hell's pits are of darkness, without the Light of God, and that if God has done that to His heavenly hosts of misbehaved angels, what is in store for those souls from this world?

I'm convinced. Hell is worse than we can imagine, just as heaven is better than we can imagine. The presence or absence of God establishes the attributes of both heaven and hell. It is God who is beyond our imagination. It will be all or nothing to be with Him or without Him for all eternity.

## PRAYER

God and Father, thank You for Your Son and His excellent gift of salvation from eternal death, the second death unto an indescribable place without You. Only imagining what we can imagine is a dull image with no depth or detail of what heaven or hell might be like. You are the clear choice to live. Thank You, Lord, for Your Word that has provided the Light to my path for eternity with You. Amen.

## CREDITS AND/OR INSPIRATION

I listened to the testimony of a saved man who had once been very bad. Under the influence of alcohol, he was convicted of killing another and was thrown in prison for several years. In all of his experiences, he related that once he realized he was going to hell for his sins, he became grateful beyond expression for the gift Jesus offered. He related that the closer you live to hell, the easier it is to believe it could be worse, and a promise for heaven was worth his devotion to Christ and to live for Him.

# He Thinks of Us

## CONCEPTS

When we think of God, we often think He is there but unattentive until we call upon Him. However, those who forget how close He is must be reminded that our God is mighty and powerful and always with us.

## PURPOSE

The Spur reminds us that God thinks more about us than we think about Him. People give God human attributes, including our capabilities and weaknesses. In doing that, we deny God His divine power, authority, and omnipresence. When we consider who God is, we can only imagine, and even then, we fall infinitely short of how powerful He truly is.

## SCRIPTURE BASE

Psalm 139

## BACKGROUND

I am inspired and awestruck when I try to imagine the grandeur of our God. When I am down or lonely, depressed or confused, I think about how God is there to lean on anytime, all the time. God is good, and these verses are meant to remind us of that.

## SPUR

Psalm 139 is a great place to put God's love in perspective. Verses 13–16 are often used to prove from God's Word that life begins at conception and that God controls our making in the womb.

*For thou didst form my inward parts: Thou didst cover me in my mother's womb.*

*I will give thanks unto thee; for I am fearfully and wonderfully made: Wonderful are thy works; And that my soul know eth right well. My frame was not hidden from thee, When I was made in secret, And curiously wrought in the lowest parts of the earth. Thine eyes did see mine unformed substance; And in thy book they were all written, Even the days that were ordained for me, When as yet there was none of them.*

It is unconscionable to me that anyone could think an unborn person is not a child of God and should not be treated with the same respect as any other person. Only an unbeliever, in my opinion, could think this.

But Psalm 139 contains much more about His love, concern, and thoughts about us. So, if you have gone this far without reading the entire psalm, stop now and read it all.

My intent is not to repeat everything Psalm 139 says but to highlight those parts that might seem fantastic or deeper than how we normally think about the workings of God. The conclusion is obvious to me. We haven't got a clue about the height and depth of God's mind or abilities. These are things people forget when we consider how great is our God.

The psalm begins with how God knows us (*all* of us) and our every move, regardless of how small or insignificant. He also knows our every thought. He knows where you are going, when you will rest, and all your ways of doing things. The psalmist goes on to relate how there is nowhere you can go where God is not there with you, beside you, in front of you, and behind you. He is within you.

The psalm says He knows you better than you know yourself. He has known you since before you were born. He made you. He put you together. He gave you all the talent you need. He protects and surrounds you. He thinks about you more times than the number of grains of sand in the whole world. He is with you, always everywhere. You can't even hide. He loves you more than you love yourself.

Yes, He made you. He knew you from the beginning of this life and before you were given life. He sees your entire life string, and you haven't even finished it yet. He knows what will happen when you don't even know what you will do next or what you will do when you get there. He knows.

He gave you your soul before He gave you life. He will deal with you as long as you are alive and after you die. God is with us.

What should our response be? Verses 19–22 tell us. In a nutshell, we need to know what side we are on and live like it. Identify our enemies and shed the wickedness in our lives.

> *Surely thou wilt slay the wicked, O God: Depart from me therefore, ye bloodthirsty men. For they speak against thee wickedly, And thine enemies take thy name in vain. Do not I hate them, O Jehovah, that hate thee? And am not I grieved with those that rise up against thee? I hate them with perfect hatred: They are become mine enemies.*

Finally, concede what you can't ignore. Embrace the sovereignty of God and request that His ways will permeate your life so you can live righteously.

> *Search me, O God, and know my heart: Try me, and know my thoughts; And see if there be any wicked way in me, And lead me in the way everlasting.*

If you want to put some icing on this cake, read Psalm 36:5–10.

## PRAYER

Father God in heaven and on earth, my prayer today matches verses 23–24. I need You every hour, Lord. Let me lean on You for everything in my life. My life is Yours. You have given me everything to nurture and mold me; everything I am is what You have made me be. Thank You, Lord, for being my God and making Yourself known to me through Your Word. Amen.

## CREDITS AND/OR INSPIRATION

I was inspired by a sermon from a local pastor I admire. He spoke about what is happening with the state abortion laws and how we must support life at conception as Christians. I like to read surrounding verses and was inspired by Psalm 139. I hope you are as well.

# Just Missed Him

## CONCEPTS

A plethora of verses can be found that reveal how all of Israel, except for the disciples and followers of Jesus, discounted Him as Lord. Today's literate world knows of Jesus but only recognizes that He was a prophet or a historical figure. However, many, including Jews and Muslims of today, consider Him a mere notation in their past as a religious figure that has captured the minds of Christians. They don't believe He is the Messiah or Lord referenced in our Old Testament or their Torah and Qur'an.

## PURPOSE

The Jews, Muslims, Christians, and the rest of the world may know about Jesus, but this Spur is dedicated to showing who He is to you and me. JESUS IS LORD!

## SCRIPTURE BASE

John 3:18, John 5:39–40, John 14:6–7 1 John 5:11–12

The following verses support the Stem:

Matthew 11:2–5, John 9:40–41, John 10:24–25, John 10:31–33

## BACKGROUND

The story is in the four Gospels: Matthew, Mark, Luke, and John. They witnessed Christ in the flesh, on earth, and in ministry using His own words. You only need to reread the Gospels to look for those who didn't recognize Jesus as the Messiah, the Son of God, the Son of Man, God, I Am in the flesh. The fact remains that people were looking for the Messiah yesterday and are looking for the Messiah today and will continue to look for Him tomorrow. He's been here, and He's coming back. There is no other.

## SPUR

Many seek God and miss Jesus. The Pharisees and scribes, the Sadducees, and the Jews all studied and sought after the Word of God to find the Messiah, only to look right over Him while He was in their presence. He was standing right before them, and they missed Him. All the clues of the Old Testament, all the miracles He performed, all the things He said of Himself, and they missed Him. People still miss Him.

Ever look for something all over the house, garage, or workplace? You know what it looks like. You're sure it has to be someplace close to where it belongs, but you don't see it. Then someone else points to exactly where it is, and you have already looked over that spot a dozen times. It's like you were blind. Someone might say, "If it had been a rattlesnake, it would have bitten you." That's a strange comparison right there. You can hear a rattler and not see it; if you don't believe what you hear and know your danger, you might die. That's what it's like to search for and miss the kingdom of God. People can learn all about Jesus but miss the relationship that He is Lord and that He saves. It is those who miss that and condemn themselves in disbelief.

John 3:18

*He that believeth on him is not judged: he that be-lieveth not hath been judged already, because he hath not believed on the name of the only begotten Son of God.*

John 5:39–40

*Ye search the scriptures, because ye think that in them ye have eternal life; and these are they which bear witness of me; and ye will not come to me, that ye may have life.*

How did the ancient ones seeking the Kingdom of God respond to Jesus? In their minds, they knew what He was supposed to look like. They decided who He was supposed to be and what they wanted for themselves. In their minds, filled with pride, they were confident that they knew better than their Scripture what the Messiah should be. He was not who they wanted.

That thinking is hubris, conceit, pride, and ultimately blind ignorance. In their defense, they were spiritually blinded. They were preordained to condemn Him. That was the plan. People of today seeking the Kingdom of God want to skirt Jesus and make their own way to heaven. They create their own religion, their own gods, and their own rules. They think they know better too. However, the difference is that the ancient ones were blinded for a grand purpose; you can call upon Jesus to show you the truth through the Holy Spirit.

Who is blinding you? What's your excuse? Satan is a liar and will keep you from understanding who Jesus is if you let satan get in the way. Jesus is stronger, His Spirit is stronger, and He overcomes the wiles of satan. All you need to do is believe and repent, knowing Jesus is Lord God Almighty, and He saves. He is the way to God and the Kingdom of Heaven. Let His Spirit lead you. Ask Him to come into your heart. If you miss Him today, you will miss eternal life with Him. Don't miss Jesus.

John 14:6–7

*Jesus saith unto him, I am the way, and the truth, and the life: no one cometh unto the Father, but by me. If ye had known me, ye would have known my Father also: from henceforth ye know him, and have seen him.*

## PRAYER

Lord, God and Father, we ask that Your Spirit lead and guide us closer to living a Kingdom life with You as our guide. Light our path, direct our feet, and lead us in a closer walk in truth and in Spirit. Thank You, Lord, for revealing who You are so that our faith becomes the belief to accept You as our Saviour and Lord. Teach us how to live in Your light and walk in Your way. Amen.

## CREDITS AND/OR INSPIRATION

The Gospel of John

# Layaway Plan

## CONCEPTS

People relate to their own experiences. In their way, people use their knowledge to perceive a unique concept. Preachers like Billy Graham use these shifts in thought to take people from a "known" to an "unknown," teaching the hearers of God's Word to think differently to move them toward the truth about Christ. This Spur about layaway plans is to reach those who will draw a parallel and relate this concept to salvation.

## PURPOSE

The Spirit works in mysterious ways. No one can tell how people are drawn to accepting Jesus in faith and truth with a desire to change and accept the grace of God. There isn't a one-size-fits-all approach to leading individuals to Christ. For centuries, preachers and teachers have used logical or impressive approaches that they thought might be unique to a particular audience. This Spur might engage some to think differently, turn understanding into faith and belief in Jesus, and recognize the grace He offers each of us.

## SCRIPTURE BASE

2 Corinthians 1:20–22 (NIV)

## BACKGROUND

Small business stores and department stores still use layaway plans. It is better than going into debt, and no interest is required. Sometimes, you can take advantage of excellent deals when you find what you want on sale, but you don't have the money to pay for it. There are worthy comparisons and contrasts to salvation.

2 Corinthians 1:20–22 (NIV)

*For no matter how many promises God has made, they are "Yes" in Christ. And so through him, the "Amen" is spoken by us to the glory of God. Now it is God who makes both us and you stand firm in Christ. He anointed us, set his seal of ownership on us, and put his Spirit in our hearts as a deposit, guaranteeing what is to come.*

## SPUR

Have you ever put a sale item or an expensive purchase on layaway at a store? Maybe you didn't have the money needed to buy it outright. Perhaps you wanted a place to keep it until it was needed. Sometimes, mistakes happen. The store might lose or break what you purchased, and they give you your money back. Sometimes, they might make the mistake of putting it back on the shelf and re-selling it to someone else. Maybe their accounting gets mixed up, and they don't have your purchase record or matching layaway ticket, and you must find those receipts and the payments made.

What happens when Jesus saves you? A layaway plan is when you make payments for something someone else is keeping for you until you pay in full. They usually keep your purchased item in the back room or storage bin. God's layaway plan is better. If anything, it's the opposite of the typical store plan. Jesus has already made the deposit and paid for your eternal future by dying on the cross many years ago in Jerusalem. His one-time sacrifice was for the sins of the world, your sins, and mine. When you earnestly accept His payment by calling on His name to save you from death and sin, He gives you a deposit of the Holy Spirit. You take away the gift of eternal life instantly. Not when you die, but immediately. It's almost like a reverse kind of mortgage. You not only get to live blessed with an eternal deposit, but you get the whole gift to take with you forever. If it sounds too simple and unbelievable, it almost is.

A layaway plan is when you give money as a down payment to get something reserved that the store keeps as you continue to pay for it. Then, when it is all paid for, you will get it sometime in the future.

God's plan is simple; Jesus has already paid for it. His gift is waiting, sitting on the shelf until you accept it. When you accept His gift of love and forgiveness, the additional benefit is eternal life and blessings from the moment the Spirit enters you. It's not only a future blessing; it's an immediate blessing because He changes your life. The Spirit begins to clean your thoughts and actions; He restores you with love for others. The benefits are now, for each day, forever because He is in you—forever. And He promises you that He will never leave you, never forget you, never lose your ticket, and never let you go. He will always be with you, beside you, as your defender, comforter, healer, and friend. A friend better than a brother, a father who provides for your needs with mercy, grace, and rewards of heaven greater than anything you can imagine. You will never die. You will live forevermore with Him in all His glory in heaven.

He made the full payment with His life on the cross so you can live forever with Him. You get the whole gift; all you need to do is believe in Jesus, believe He can save you from your sin, and have faith that He is the only One who can and will do this for you. Take the gift home right now.

**PRAYER**

Lord, God and Father, I ask today that this simple idea might be used to Your glory. I ask that someone will see and understand how simple accepting Jesus is and how permanent the results are. Lord, You have no limits in that You can make Your Word come alive and, with Your Spirit, capture the hearts of those You call unto Yourself. Use this Spur to gather those unto You for Your glory and honor. Amen.

## CREDITS AND/OR INSPIRATION

The Scripture verses of 2 Corinthians 1:20–22 about deposits and guarantees inspired the writing of this Spur.

# Run Away!

## CONCEPTS

I've written a lot about being courageous. Being bold and standing up is an important life skill as a Christian. I've meant every word and have given plenty of Scripture to back it up.

As men, we've been raised to be courageous and never run away, but today is different. This goes for women too. Flee from satan, run from sin, and run to Christ.

## PURPOSE

Christians sometimes get conceited and think they are above certain types of sin. Maybe they have overcome the same sin in the past and have dismissed it as a defeated foe. But, like alcoholism, sin is addictive, and we must take each day and battle our illness of sin. We can ask for help because Jesus has conquered sin, but we still fight daily with the consequences of falling off the wagon. Satan knows where the gutter is and speeds us up so we'll stumble and fall. When we think we're beyond sinning, we should recognize that as pride, and there we go again: sin. We must always be on guard and know when to run.

## SCRIPTURE BASE

Proverbs 3:7, 1 Corinthians 10:14, 1 Timothy 6:10–11, Genesis 39:12, 2 Timothy 2:22, 1 Corinthians 6:18, Proverbs 4:14

## BACKGROUND

How many famous Christians have you been shocked to learn fell into infamous sin? I'm sure we can remember a name or two of solid Christians who fell into sexual sin, the love of money, types of idolatry, or the pride of fame. It can happen to the best and most blessed of us. So keep your head on a swivel, and never underestimate how much satan wants to see you slip and fall. Pray for holy protection.

## SPUR

The Bible sometimes tells us to run from evil. Other times, it tells us to fight evil through the strength of God so that we can stand against temptation. We are always supposed to stand for God and His righteousness. It can get confusing. It is evident in God's Word that when you find yourself trapped or consumed with sinful living, and the Spirit shows you should be uncomfortable with your surroundings, it's time to run and get out.

Proverbs 3:7

*Be not wise in thine own eyes; Fear Jehovah, and depart from evil:*

The three sins common to man that seem to be ones identified to run from are idolatry, love of money, and sexual sin. When you think about it, those are natural within men and women. Another one that you can't run from is pride; I think that's because you'd have to run from yourself.

What takes up your time? What amuses you more than spending more time with God? Is the game on TV more important than going to church on Sunday night? Is reading those tweets and checking your likes more critical on the X/Twitter App than following God in His Word? How about all those other distractions that draw you away from God? Check yourself to see if they haven't become your idols or self-aggrandizement to your ego and pride.

1 Corinthians 10:14

*Wherefore, my beloved, flee from idolatry.*

Jesus and the apostles relate parables throughout the New Testament about money, riches, and the love of anything above God. Paul had his issues with money and described them to Timothy as a warning of the power money can have in the influence of our lives. It is a form of idolatry with the shine of silver and gold.

1 Timothy 6:10–11

>*For the love of money is a root of all kinds of evil: which some reaching after have been led astray from the faith, and have pierced themselves through with many sorrows. But thou, O man of God, flee these things; and follow after righteousness, godliness, faith, love, patience, meekness.*

Again, the Bible depicts many stories about sexual sin. That specific sin draws in many other sins, making it even more dangerous. Residing alongside sexual immorality are pride, idolatry, lying, murder, and different slippery slopes of all kinds of evil beyond the act of fornication. The love of sex pulls in all the sins in Leviticus of what are despicable uses of the body. It destroys our body as the temple created for the Spirit within us. The following stories and verses tell us specifically to run, as Joseph did when Potiphar's wife wanted him to stay and play. Please read all about it in Genesis 39.

Genesis 39:12

>*And she caught him by his garment, saying, Lie with me: and he left his garment in her hand, and fled, and got him out.*

Paul tells Timothy to flee those youthful urges. Do you think Paul knew that hormones rage in youth, as most middle and high school teachers know? Our youth ministers must address this enormous potential of human desire and guide our youth away from temptation.

2 Timothy 2:22

*But flee youthful lusts, and follow after righteousness, faith, love, peace, with them that call on the Lord out of a pure heart.*

Paul takes the sinful act of sex outside of marriage a step beyond the act itself. He tells us it is a sin against our bodies. Engaging in sexual immorality with another joins our physical temple containing the Holy Spirit with sin. Read 1 Cor 6:12–20. The body is the Lord's, and we are members of Christ.

1 Corinthians 6:18

*Flee fornication. Every sin that a man doeth is without the body; but he that committeth fornication sinneth against his own body.*

Draw closer to God and flee from sinful habits or things that distract you from what God wants to show and bless you. Run away. Put away. Uninstall. In Matthew 8:9, the concept of plucking out your eye before you end up in hell emphasizes the seriousness of this issue. Satan is out there to drag you into whatever keeps you from serving, worshipping, praying, or drawing nearer to God. Run away.

Proverbs 4:14

*Enter not into the path of the wicked, and walk not in the way of evil men.*

## PRAYER

Lord, God and Father, we ask for Your mercy upon us in our weaknesses to sin against You. Do not lead us into temptation, but deliver us from evil. Help us to find our feet and direct them straight and away from all sin that offends You. Show us where to repent and forgive us when we fail You. Amen.

## CREDITS AND/OR INSPIRATION

While searching the concordance for another project, I was drawn to the numerous times I read the word *flee*. I initially thought how strange that was, considering how often I had written about being strong and courageous, standing, fighting, and defending against the wiles of satan. But the more thought was given, the more conviction I had to write about what God inspired others to write. So, flee from sin; run to Christ.

# Cracked Pot

## CONCEPTS

How often do you hear people say, "What can I do?" with a voice that sounds like failure? This Spur and your choice to motivate others in service suggest we change these exact words into a tenor of service—"What can I do for God?"

## PURPOSE

God has given each of us a talent or gift to be used for His glory. It comes with a lifetime warranty to be used for as long as we are valuable to Him. (His Word says we are so valuable to Him that He gave His only Son to die for us.) Some gifts and talents may be for a season, which is for a reason, but there is always another gift or talent that can be used for a lifetime. So whether you are young or old, in development or past your prime, engage yourself in service to God, for He has a purpose for you.

SCRIPTURE BASE

2 Corinthians 4:1–2,7–9, Romans 11:29, 2 Corinthians 12:9

## BACKGROUND

From a personal perspective, many retired people have concluded that being retired means doing nothing and being responsible to no one. Others feel they are not gifted or do not want any extra work beyond whatever might bring a paycheck home. Yet, as Christians, we are *all* ministers; as such, we each have responsibilities to glorify God, continuing in the Great Commission in any way we can. Using the talents God gives is also a matter of tithing, in my opinion. God gave you the talent to use to glorify Him.

If you still have the talent, give back to Him in gratitude that you can still use that talent.

## SPUR

The following story is well-known and often used to encourage those who feel inadequate or broken. Maybe they have an evil past. Perhaps they cannot do what they want to do for Christ. Trust God what says; each of us has been gifted through His Spirit to do a good thing for His glory. This story has many attributes to draw to, and this Spur is one of them. The story was copied from (Poonen).

A water-bearer in India had two large pots, both hung on the ends of a pole, which he carried across his neck. One of the pots had a crack in it, while the other pot was perfect and always delivered a full portion of water. The cracked pot always arrived half full at the end of the long walk from the stream to the house. The poor cracked pot was ashamed of its imperfections and miserable that it could accomplish only half of what it had been made to do. After two years of what it perceived to be a bitter failure, it spoke to the water-bearer one day by the stream:

"I am ashamed of myself and want to apologize to you. I have been able to deliver only half my load because this crack in my side causes water to leak out all the way back to your house. Because of my flaws, you have to do all this work and don't get the full value from your efforts." The bearer said to the pot, "Did you notice that there were flowers only on your side of the path but not on the other pot's side? That's because I have always known about your flaws, and I planted flower seeds on your side of the path, and every day while we walk back, you've watered them. For two years, I have been able to pick these beautiful flowers to decorate the table. Without you being just the way you are, there would not be this beauty to grace the house." (Poonen)

The story is relative to the fact that God uses cracked pots. You do not need to be perfect for God to use you. Draw strength in Paul's words to motivate yourself and others.

2 Corinthians 4:1–2

*Wherefore we faint not; but though our outward man is decaying, yet our inward man is renewed day by day.*

2 Corinthians 4:7–9

*But we have this treasure in earthen vessels, that the exceeding greatness of the power may be of God, and not from ourselves; we are pressed on every side, yet not straitened; perplexed, yet not unto despair; pursued, yet not forsaken; smitten down, yet not destroyed.*

As John Wesley wrote, "Do all the good you can, by all the means you can, in all the ways you can, in all the places you can, at all the times you can, to all the people you can, as long as ever you can" (Goodreads).

A. L. Williams, the founder of the term life insurance company Primerica of the '80s, used this quote to inspire his sales force to work harder. As John Wesley wrote above, the motto is good for ministers to live a Christian life. The impact of these words comes into force when you read them four times with different inflections on the verbs. "All you can do is all you can do." Try it, and you will see the strength in the motto (daledawn).

God can and will use you to glorify Him. He wants you to be useful to Him. Therefore, serve Him and love Him with all your heart, with all your strength, and with all your soul.

Romans 11:29

*For the gifts and the calling of God are irrevocable.*

## PRAYER

Lord, my God, thank You for being such a mighty and awesome God. When the world would cast us aside for our weakness and uselessness, give us strength and power to work for You. What a blessing it is from You to be useful to You and Your glory. Take me home when You are done. Let me be able to say I fought the good fight and ran the whole race, not out of pride for anything but for serving You. Amen.

## CREDITS AND/OR INSPIRATION

The story of the cracked pot pricked my heart, reminding me of this verse:

2 Corinthians 12:9—*And he hath said unto me, My grace is sufficient for thee: for my power is made perfect in weakness. Most gladly therefore will I rather glory in my weaknesses, that the power of Christ may rest upon me*

daledawn. "Art Williams— AL Williams Founder—The Coach—Prime America—Must See Videos," Pure Motivation. April 18, 2020, https://puremotivation.com/artwilliams/.

Goodreads. "John Wesley Quotes." Accessed April 30, 2025. https://www.goodreads.com/quotes/12757-do-all-the-good-you-can-by-all-the-means.

Zac Poonen. "The Broken Pot." Word4life. Accessed March 11, 2023. http://word4life.com/brokenpot.html.

# Surprise!

## CONCEPTS

This concept may never have occurred to you or those who hear this. It might even be a paradigm shift for some people to realize that God is good to them.

## PURPOSE

This is the gospel that God is good and the One who gives good gifts for His glory and purpose. To realize and internalize this truth makes one humble and grateful. These attributes are where people meet God, love Him more, and glorify Him with thankfulness. The Good News is His gift of His Son, Jesus, and eternal salvation is the greatest gift of all.

## SCRIPTURE BASE

1 Chronicles 16:34, James 1:17, Ephesians 2:10, 1 Timothy 4:4, Romans 8:28, Philippians 2:13, 1 Corinthians 2:14, Lamentations 3:25, Romans 6:23

## BACKGROUND

People tend to view themselves and others with unique talents and gifts as attributes they were lucky to be born with or earned independently. These are lies of satan and lead to hubris and pride. Unless people come to know where their gifts are from, they will be less inclined to thank their Maker for them. Gratitude is the attitude God wants in each of us.

Consider all the musicians, athletes, authors, and movie stars who could have done so much more with their lives if they had given thanks, knowing their gifts and physical attributes came from God. It staggers the mind when you realize how God gives and takes away.

## SPUR

Have you ever received a gift and didn't know where it came from or why? Then later you find out who gave it the gift. Were you surprised? Did it mean more to you to know who gave you the gift? Knowing it came from them, did you feel more love or affection for the giver?

All, and I mean *all*, gifts and good things come from God. Even the ones others gave you or you received, unaware of where they came from. Thank God for those gifts, but also thank Him and love Him more for knowing that He gave each of us excellent gifts.

I am being repetitive purposely—because God is good all the time, and all His gifts are good too. Knowing and accepting that truth should make us even more thankful and more in love with the One who gives us everything. Be grateful, especially for knowing who our giver is. Where our salvation comes from and who our God is.

1 Chronicles 16:34

*O give thanks unto Jehovah; for he is good; For his lovingkindness endureth forever.*

What if you didn't know Jesus? What if you have never acknowledged God? Maybe you are one of those folks with a God-given gift of talent, beauty, skill, ability, knack, or intelligence that socially lifts you above others without those gifts. People always told you that you were God's gift at something. All this time, you thought you were just lucky. You didn't thank anyone because there was no one to thank. You thought your parents had good genes. You might be right about that, but who gave you your parents? You make up all kinds of reasons for your ability that no one else has. You're simply better than the rest. Lucky you! You might be one of those who lean into themselves and say, "I'm self-made. I deserve all this because I worked hard at it."

You might have a point, but who gave you the drive? The inspiration? The desire? Did your folks teach you? Did you have a good teacher or coach? Think about it. It all came from God. Every bit of it. Did you decide where you were born, what color you are, who your parents are, where you went to school, and who your examples were? Nope, none of that. God's sovereignty did all that.

James 1:17

*Every good gift and every perfect gift is from above, coming down from the Father of lights, with whom can be no variation, neither shadow that is cast by turning.*

Ephesians 2:10

*For we are his workmanship, created in Christ Jesus for good works, which God afore prepared that we should walk in them.*

Now, for the flip side. How do you judge all those who aren't as fortunate as you? Were they born under an evil star? Are they not as intelligent, pretty, strong, talented, or rich? It sucks for them, huh? What conceit! Right there is the type of unrighteous pride that God hates. He's the giver of life; you can't take the credit for yourself while spewing judgment upon others. God doesn't make trash lives.

1 Timothy 4:4

*For every creature of God is good, and nothing is to be rejected, if it be received with thanksgiving.*

Romans 8:28

*And we know that to them that love God all things work together for good, even to them that are called according to his purpose.*

The last thing I want to point out is that maybe God hasn't gifted you or someone you know with a realized talent *yet*. He wills and provides skills in His time when His Spirit fills those upon accepting Jesus as Lord and Savior. He promises that. He wants you to serve Him and will provide you with the talents to do that. I'm not saying He will turn you into a superstar, and you'll become rich and famous; I'm saying He will give you what He wants you to use to glorify Him and provide you with a complete and blessed life.

Philippians 2:13

*For it is God who worketh in you both to will and to work, for his good pleasure.*

Whether you feel you are gifted or ungifted, talented or talentless, God's perfect sovereignty makes everything suitable, and He is there waiting for you to choose Him. He has already chosen you; now, you must accept Him. Without Him and the Spirit you receive, you'll never understand what greatness He has in store for you. Those blessings come through Him now on this earth and for eternity in heaven. Accept the most precious gift of all, Jesus.

1 Corinthians 2:14

*Now the natural man receiveth not the things of the Spirit of God: for they are foolishness unto him; and he cannot know them, because they are spiritually judged.*

Lamentations 3:25

*Jehovah is good unto them that wait for him, to the soul that seeketh him.*

That's all You, Lord. Praise Your Holy Name, the giver of our life and eternal salvation. Name a more excellent gift that can be given than that.

Romans 6:23

*For the wages of sin is death; but the free gift of God is eternal life in Christ Jesus our Lord.*

## PRAYER

Lord God, what a mighty God You are! I praise You, Lord, for every good thing in my life and the lives of those I love. You alone are good. Thank You for loving me, for Your Word, and light in my life. Thank You for Your sovereign power that guided and blessed me before I was born. I owe everything to You. Amen.

## CREDITS AND/OR INSPIRATION

I become disheartened when I see the lives of celebrities and famous people wasted because they do not have Jesus or His indwelling Spirit. We constantly read news reports about people who worship satan or destroy their lives with drugs, sex, power, or the love of money because they don't realize the very talent they misuse and abuse came from God. I can't help but believe that if they only knew and were grateful to their Creator for what He has given them, their lives and ours for knowing them would be brighter and more fulfilling.

# Take Your Pick

**CONCEPTS**

God, through His Word and us, accomplishes what He intends. God's sovereignty is manifested either by divine intervention or the leading of the Spirit. He creates and changes man's destiny through man's free will. Other times, His will changes our destination by opening doors that no one can shut and closing doors only He can open.

**PURPOSE**

Often, we intend to do one thing, and the outcome is another. I love those stories people tell about how their lives were changed instantly. God's sovereignty reigns in our lives. Sometimes, we accept it; other times, we fight it. Then, there are times when we have no choice in the matter. People should consider when God makes a different pick for our future. It isn't good luck or bad luck; it's God. Christians should expect His will and prepare to accept His will.

**SCRIPTURE BASE**

Proverbs 16:9, Isaiah 55:11, Revelation 3:7, Psalm 73:28, 2 Samuel 7:28

**BACKGROUND**

Consider Mary and Joseph's story in the Bible. They intended to get married and live happily ever after. Then God, through His messengers, changed their lives in ways they could not have imagined. God has a way of getting His way through changing our ways. Maybe you have a story you could insert in place of mine.

## SPUR

You can take your pick on anything, but the Lord gets His way when you have given your life to Him. If you have earnestly told the Lord that your life is His to use, hang on! You better mean it because He will use you for His glory and your blessing.

Think of a time when you had plans to do one thing, and God took control and changed your plans. I'm talking about life-changing plans. Maybe something happened that you didn't expect or was entirely out of your control. A list of possible life-changing events would be too numerous and unique to record. But if one or more happen to you, you'll know.

The change He set into my life altered my entire life's path. Becoming a chef was my life's ambition. I liked cooking and preparing food, baking, and fry-cooking. I was good at it because my first several high school jobs were cooking short orders at restaurants. I desired to become a chef by attending a local culinary college in my town. It was a well-established vocational school, and some excellent chefs were found there. While attending there, my grades and progress allowed me to look forward to a bright future doing what I enjoyed. Then, the bottom fell out. Life-changing news came to me in the mail that required me to leave the program three-quarters through the course.

My instructor was a master chef, an older man who retired from the Navy as a chef on battleships and aircraft carriers. He served seamen of all ranks and became the Officer Quarters' master chef. He was challenging, motivational, and an excellent teacher. When I showed him the induction (draft) notice I received in the mail, he told me that maybe I could become a cook in the military. The education of my choice was no longer an option. The following months of military school prepared me for the Vietnam War, and the Air Force seemed to have plenty of cooks. What God and the military turned me into was utterly different. I was totally out of control of my life.

83

Non-Christians say that's what you can expect when life happens. They're not wrong—it is life, and if you are a child of God, it is a life He has called you into for a purpose. His purpose. You may or may not believe God has that kind of control or that He would do—whatever it was—to change your path. Be assured that God is sovereign and in control of you and everything else around you.

My blessing is to be able to look back over all those years. Knowing that God steered my life and created the tests and tribulations, experiences, and situations that molded my character as I grew into manhood increases my faith. God made and shaped me like clay to be the man He wanted. I was to serve Him as He willed for His purpose. It is a blessing to me to see how His hand has shaped and crafted my life. I know God still has control of me, and my life continues without fear as His will is the best for me.

It is possible that God hasn't drastically changed your life in the manner described above. However, that doesn't mean He won't. It could all change tomorrow. That's what this Spur is all about. When you give your life to Jesus and walk in the Spirit, you must expect that God's will for you might differ from your plans. When you plan for your life, I pray that you are attuned to God's will and that your life path is synchronized with His.

It would be remiss not to mention those little changes in our plans that God does to provide an experience, make a divine appointment, or give you a blessing. Those times might be another Spur entirely, for God is sovereign over your whole life, including your day-to-day experiences.

## PRAYER

God, Father, and Sovereign Lord of all the earth, bless us with Your countenance and favor. Use us to be Your hands and feet to accomplish Your will in our lives and the lives of others. Guide us, Holy Spirit, wherever we walk with You. Keep us from temptation and deliver us from evil. We ask these things in Your heavenly name, Jesus. Amen.

## CREDITS AND/OR INSPIRATION

As a Christian, it is hard to comprehend what it would be like without God. Sit in prayer and contemplation and reflect on what God has done for you. Thanksgiving becomes the attitude of gratitude for Jesus, who saved you and gave you all good things. That concept is inspirational right there.

# The Old, Old Story

## CONCEPTS

People who have been in ministry for years think they must do something new, fresh, and fashionable. The truth is that nothing can be preached or taught about the true gospel story that gets old, worn out, or out of style. God is the same today as yesterday, and though you might know the story well and have heard it taught and preached a thousand times, there might be one person out there being called to hear it for the first time. They might even need to hear it again for it to take hold of their heart and spirit as they are being called in that hour to believe. Isn't that what we do? Isn't that the very heart of every ministry?

## PURPOSE

We are to fulfill our calling as ministers. We don't call people to Jesus. We don't change people. We don't save people. The Spirit of God does all of that. We are to teach (tell) and preach the gospel to those God sends to us for the opportunity and divine appointment.

## SCRIPTURE BASE

1 Corinthians 15:1–4, 2 Timothy 1:8–11, John 3:16–21

## BACKGROUND

The following are three quotes from famous Christian men who inspired the writing of this Spur. The Spirit of God is the true inspiration. Praise Him!

If the presence of God is in the church, the church will draw the world in. If the presence of God is not in the church, the world will draw the church out.

Charles Grandison Finney

The motto of all true servants of God must be, "We preach Christ, and Him crucified." A sermon without Christ in it is like a loaf of bread without any flour in it. No Christ in your sermon, sir? Then go home and never preach again until you have something worth preaching.

Charles Spurgeon

Ministers often preach about the Gospel instead of preaching the Gospel. They often preach about sinners instead of preaching to them.

Charles Grandison Finney

## SPUR

*Tell Me the Old, Old Story* is a famous and well-known hymn by Katherine Hankey in 1866. She wrote the poem, but William Hovard Doane set it to music (Wikipedia Foundation).

I often sang this song during my youth in the church. Today's praise and worship songs do not carry the same fervor for me. The following words reveal the essence of why and how we need to teach the gospel (1 Corinthians 15:1–4). I can't write this Spur any clearer and more concisely than this lovely poem and song.

> *Tell me the old, old story.*
> *Of unseen things above,*
> *Of Jesus and His glory,*
> *Of Jesus and His love.*

*Tell me the story simply,*
*As to a little child,*
*For I am weak and weary,*
*And helpless and defiled.*

*Tell me the story slowly,*
*That I may take it in,*
*That wonderful redemption,*
*God's remedy for sin.*
*Tell me the story often,*
*For I forget so soon;*
*The early dew of morning*
*Has passed away at noon.*

*Tell me the story softly,*
*With earnest tones and grave;*
*Remember, I'm the sinner.*
*Whom Jesus came to save.*
*Tell me the story always,*
*If you would really be,*
*In any time of trouble,*
*A comforter to me.*

*Tell me the same old story.*
*When you have cause to fear*
*That this world's empty glory*
*Is costing me too dear.*
*Yes, and when that world's glory*
*Is dawning on my soul,*
*Tell me the old, old story:*
*Christ Jesus makes thee whole.*

Refrain: *Tell me the old, old story,*

*Tell me the old, old, story,*

*Tell me the old, old story,*

*Of Jesus and His love.*

Most Christians know the song, but when did you last read all the verses? These are the basics. How often are they preached? Everyone thinks they are over-preached. I contend they are not. The gospel is under-preached. Proclaiming the Good News of Christ's saving grace is why we are here (2 Timothy 1:8–11). Tell me the old, old story is ironic in the fact that the story never gets old. Jesus Christ, our Lord, is the whole story.

John 3:16–21

> *For God so loved the world, that he gave his only begotten Son, that whosoever believeth on him should not perish, but have eternal life. For God sent not the Son into the world to judge the world; but that the world should be saved through him. He that believeth on him is not judged: he that believeth not hath been judged already, because he hath not believed on the name of the only begotten Son of God. And this is the judgment, that the light is come into the world, and men loved the darkness rather than the light; for their works were evil. For every one that doeth evil hateth the light, and cometh not to the light, lest his works should be reproved. But he that doeth the truth cometh to the light, that his works may be made manifest, that they have been wrought in God*

**PRAYER**

Lord, God and Father, let us not forget. Let us always remember who, what, and why we praise the holy name of Jesus Christ, for You alone are worthy. Your story is eternal and gives life to those who hear it. Your story gives us faith, comfort, strength, and assurance. Without You, we are nothing, but with You, we are saved to eternal life. I need that reminder daily, and I pray that others hear the truth. Thank You, Lord. Amen.

# CREDITS AND/OR INSPIRATION

I'm underwhelmed with the constant conversations I hear about what we must do to grow our fledgling attendance within our churches. "They just aren't what they used to be." We aren't what we used to be! I can't help but consider that, collectively, we've tried everything with anemic results except the thing most think won't work. If we devote ourselves to the basics of Christianity, the very roots of our religion, I feel we will all (nationally) experience revival.

AZQuotes. "Charles Grandison Finney Quotes," Accessed March 10, 2022. https://www.azquotes.com/quote/1380354.

AZQuotes. "Charles Grandison Finney Quotes," Accessed March 10, 2022. . https://www.azquotes.com/quote/1373424.

AZQuotes. "Charles Spurgeon Quotes." Accessed March 10, 2022. https://www.azquotes.com/quote/703855.

Wikipedia Foundation. "Tell Me the Old, Old Story." Accessed April 5, 2025. https://en.wikipedia.org/w/index.php?title=Tell_Me_the_Old,_Old_Story&oldid=1200804523.

# Unbelievable?

## CONCEPTS

Man's original sins were disobeying His commands and not accepting God's words as the truth. The original sin is still a primary sin today. Discounting and denying the power or Word of God by explaining away miracles and biblical stories is a slippery slope that has invaded our society, even our religious doctrine and discipleship training.

## PURPOSE

Many stories in God's Word are described as fantastic. Some stories are hard to consider believable, even by Christians. Right there, that's the problem. Satan had Eve doubt God's word and commandments, leading her and Adam to sin. Disbelief is a lack of faith. In this case, it led to sin and the downfall of man. This is our battle as Christians and as disciples leading others to Christ. Are you ready for the hard questions about believing in God's Word? Can you defend God's Word when you encounter others who disbelieve? This Spur is about what attacks our faith as Christians, not the story of Adam and Eve.

## SCRIPTURE BASE

James 1:5–8, Proverbs 2:6, Genesis 3:1

## BACKGROUND

Do you know the simple story of Adam and Eve in the Garden of Eden—the fall of man? First of all, it's not as simple as it reads. I believe the story in its entirety. Read Genesis 3 to refresh your memory of man's downfall through a lack of faith to believe God's Word.

## SPUR

According to *The American Heritage Dictionary,* the definition of *fantastic* is: 1) based on or existing only in fantasy, unreal; 2) strange or fanciful in form, conception, or appearance; 3) unrealistic, irrational. Interestingly, we always use the word fantastic in the context of favor toward a concept, place, or object. The Grand Canyon was fantastic. That banana split was fantastic. That story about Noah's ark was fantastic. Be careful of what you say and what you mean.

Recently, I was studying for an adult Sunday school lesson, and the study guide was a published text from a widely used and famous curriculum for churches all over America. In the passage John 5, Jesus performed a miracle for a lame man who couldn't get into a pool before others because he was crippled. The study text the class members read explained away the story in the Bible's King James Version (KJV) that the pool probably had a spring under it that caused the water to stir occasionally. But the biblical text said the reason the pool stirred was that an angel stirred the pool, and the first to enter the pool, called Bethesda, was healed upon being stirred. The lame man lay beside that pool for thirty-eight years. Read John 5:5 for yourself in the KJV or NKJV. Do you suppose all these people around the pool were there because they might get healed or that they knew if they were the first in the pool, they would be healed? How was the pool stirred? What did the Bible say? The story goes on with Jesus asking the man if he wanted to walk and then merely telling the man to stand up and walk, and he was healed. Was this a miracle of Jesus' power, or was the guy just lazy all along? Test yourself. What do you think is the truth?

A deeper dive into this dichotomy of why some texts relate how an angel stirred the water to cure the sick and lame is a distraction from this Spur. The miracle is what Jesus did. However, discounting that other well-known and established biblical accounts contain angel stories leads some to doubt the Bible, which is always dangerous.

The study guide for this Sunday school lesson was written for the teacher, and it contains in-depth explanations as to why there might be conflicts in God's Word about this story. Some other Bible versions leave the reference about the angel stirring the water out of their text. Therefore, the writers of the teacher and student guides came up with their own interpretations. The point? I felt uncomfortable that the study text wanted the instructor to explain away how God used an angel to perform miracles. The story, written in the Word of God, has endured for about two thousand years.

Recently, my wife and I took a brief vacation and drove to Kentucky to visit and tour The Ark Encounter and The Creation Museum. If you ever get a chance to go, I highly recommend it. Within both the Encounter and Museum, the authors displayed many examples where the Bible says one thing and the world or science explains something else. Science often supported the biblical event; other times, it seemed too fantastic. You can research their websites or go to the Answers in Genesis YouTube channel to find several other supports about the Bible vs. science. They will help you change the fantastic into the awesome.

The point of this Stem is this. Question whenever you hear anyone "splain" away biblical accounts to the stories written in God's Word. Consider the stories of the six days of creation, Adam and Eve, Noah's ark, Moses parting the Red Sea, talking donkeys, stirring waters, casting out demons, raising the dead, healing the blind, the resurrection of our Lord, etc. Whenever someone thinks it's fantastic, tell them it's NOT unbelievable. Have faith to believe God's Word. Where do you stop if you don't believe one story over another? Will you cherry-pick what to believe in the rest of God's Word? James says in 1:5–6:

> *But if any of you lacketh wisdom, let him ask of God,*
> *who giveth to all liberally and upbraideth not; and it shall*

*be given him. But let him ask in faith, nothing doubting: for he that doubteth is like the surge of the sea driven by the wind and tossed.*

Don't be that person, or your faith becomes suspect. God's Word is the beginning of wisdom. Proverbs 2:6 says,

*For Jehovah giveth wisdom; Out of his mouth cometh knowledge and understanding:*

Satan spoke to Eve. He made her doubt God's words and commands. We are no different. The moral of the story is a question of faith. Do you believe it? Genesis 3:1 is a simple question of satan to Eve, but it set off man's downfall.

*Now the serpent was more subtle than any beast of the field which Jehovah God had made. And he said unto the woman, Yea, hath God said, Ye shall not eat of any tree of the garden?*

The story is the best example of a slippery slope. Eve doubted God's command through satan's pull on her desire to be like God, to know good and evil. When we believe someone's explanation that contradicts God's Word, we slide down that same slippery slope.

## PRAYER

Lord, God and Father, thank You for revealing how easy it is to doubt or try to explain in human terms what we can't understand. Speak to us through the Spirit to know Your works as a mystery and help us to understand and accept how powerful and capable You are. With all that, help us understand that our ways are not Your ways, and Your will is far above our imagination. We praise You for the mighty God You are. Thank You for loving us and giving us all good things. Amen.

## CREDITS AND/OR INSPIRATION

John 5:1–17 (NKJV), the story of Jesus healing a lame man by the pool of Bethesda. The Spirit of God revealed to me the number of ways nonbelievers try to dismiss or minimize the power of God.

*American Heritage Dictionary, The*. "Fantastic." Harper-Collins Publishers, 2022.

"Answers in Genesis." YouTube channel. Accessed March 31, 2023. https://www.youtube.com/@answersingenesis.

# A Close Call

## CONCEPTS

Too often, we choose to forget our mortality and how fragile our lives are. We forget that everything can change very quickly, and we need to prepare for the unexpected and the eventual.

## PURPOSE

It is seldom that you hear a sermon preached like this. People don't like to face their mortality, and many do not enjoy the possibility of death on Sunday morning. They should. Not every Sunday, but just on the Sunday they might meet their Maker at the next green light on their way home.

## SCRIPTURE BASE

Matthew 28:19, Luke 14:23, Psalm 118:17–29, 1 Thessalonians 4:13, 1 Timothy 2:3–4, Luke 15:7

## BACKGROUND

The experience related to this Spur is personal. I worked for years in a motorcycle ministry that catered exclusively to motorcycle accident victims in my home area. We had so many casualties and deaths in our area that it was hard to keep up with them at times. Our goal was to visit, pray over, witness, and aid financially within our ability. We garnered prayer from devoted prayer warriors nationwide via the internet. The ministry is called BikerDownLiftedUp.org, and it is a ministry of prayer. Use it as an example of this author or substitute it with your experience.

## SPUR

Before and since I met my wife, I was a motorcycle enthusiast for fifty-some years. Back then, that is what you would have called me unless you saw me riding on the street with my colors, and then you would probably have called me a biker.

For fourteen years, until as recently as 2018, I was a Christian biker and belonged to Heaven's Saints Motorcycle Ministry. I am no longer a biker. I have quit riding, and though I still desire to ride, I cannot ride safely for reasons resulting from a motorcycle accident I sustained in 2005 but mostly my age.

One week, while studying the book of James for Sunday school, I became convicted by God's Holy Spirit. As a teacher in Sunday school, the blessing is learning more than your students because you must be prepared to teach and answer questions. All teachers and preachers know this. James and the Holy Spirit inspired me, and I felt the call to go out on faith to work as a home missionary to a lost world of bikers. I felt then, as I do now, that we are all called as Christians to *Go Out* as written in Matthew 28:19 and spread the gospel.

I felt drawn to the motorcycle biker ministry because most of those sinners do not come looking for Jesus or seeking Him in buildings or sanctuaries like most of our churches, and I lived closely in that circle of bikers. Bikers have a code lived by and understood only by other bikers. It is a code I knew well and respected.

Luke 14:23 says those He invites are found out there on the highways and in the hedges, and we must compel them to come in so God's house might be filled.

Heaven's Saints is a thirty-five-plus-year motorcycle ministry founded by a former Hells Angel, Barry Mason. Because of a praying mother and his trials and tribulations, he became a new man when Jesus came into his Life (Mayson and Marco). As a result, he founded a motorcycle ministry, and it is this organization I joined those many years ago that ordained me as a minister. Since then, I have actively served alongside other Christian biker organizations, sharing our faith in Jesus with those who will not set foot in a church to hear His Word.

Ten years ago (at the time of this writing), I was called to another ministry named BikerDownLiftedUp. BDLU is a 501c3 nonprofit organization. The mission of BikerDownLiftedUp is prayer, ministry, and financial support for motorcycle accident victims and their families.

Psalm 118:17–29:

> *I shall not die but live, And declare the works of Jehovah. Jehovah hath chastened me sore; But he hath not given me over unto death. Open to me the gates of righteousness: I will enter into them, I will give thanks unto Jehovah. This is the gate of Jehovah; The righteous shall enter into it. I will give thanks unto thee; for thou hast answered me, And art become my salvation. The stone which the builders rejected Is become the head of the corner. This is Jehovah's doing; It is marvellous in our eyes. This is the day which Jehovah hath made; We will rejoice and be glad in it. Save now, we beseech thee, O Jehovah: O Jehovah, we beseech thee, send now prosperity. Blessed be he that cometh in the name of Jehovah: We have blessed you out of the house of Jehovah.*

*Jehovah is God, and he hath given us light: Bind the sacrifice with cords, even unto the horns of the altar. Thou art my God, and I will give thanks unto thee: Thou art my God, I will exalt thee. Oh give thanks unto Jehovah; for he is good; For his lovingkindness endureth for ever.*

After someone has survived a severe motorcycle accident, visiting them allows me to witness to the victims and sometimes to family members who have just experienced a "close call."

I, too, have had motorcycle accidents, and though none have been as severe as the victims I visited in the hospital, each accident I endured was, no doubt, also a close call.

Many people we meet have had close calls. Have you ever said or heard others make statements like these:

"IF only I had been ... a minute earlier, a second later"

"IF we had gone left instead of right"

"IF it had come half an inch closer"

"IF I had taken that ride or gotten on that boat"

"IF I had not looked that split second in that direction"

Or IF, IF, IF ...

I know we all have IF stories like that. At the end of the story, IF we have a mind to think of it, we amaze ourselves and wonder, by the grace of God, that person could have been me, or God kept me from the worst of what it could have been. IF you are NOT thinking and thanking God like that, you should.

## HE SAVED YOU!

Everyone can identify and know what you are talking about with these statements. These examples are universal life experiences.

I can assure you that I heard many of those stories after being in a ministry for downed bikers for several years. So many reports include statements like "if that nurse had not been there driving along the same road on vacation" or "if I had crashed ten more feet down the road" or "if we would have left just one minute before" or "if I had not looked in my rearview mirror at that very moment. IF, IF, IF… and I believe every word from those survivors. Some stories I can explain as God's providence, but others were absolute miracles. I see miracles all the time, and I never take away from God what no one can explain.

Western North Carolina is a type of Mecca for motorcycle riders from all over the United States. Being so popular, it is also "Accident Central." Mission Memorial Hospital in Asheville, NC, is one of the Southeast's biggest and best trauma centers. The reason there are so many accidents in Western North Carolina is simple. The area features some of the most beautiful scenery in the world. Because of all the stunning mountains and twisty roads, people come from around the United States to challenge their skills. They ride Deal's Gap and the Dragon's Tail, the Blue Ridge Parkway, the Rattler, Rabbit Skin, Cherohala Skyway, and many other named stretches of road that bikers love to ride and test their skills or, sadly, search their limits. Usually, nine guys come to the area from some flatland country called Florida or Pennsylvania. Eight go back home to work and family. The other rider is laid up in Mission Hospital, wondering about that big question. Why me?

Far too many people have looked up at the ceiling in pain, with that question on their minds. Fortunately, they are the ones who did not suffer the worst. A minister never wants to become morbid about it; instead, he must stay compassionate for those who are hurt. Never become numb to continually being amid those faced with tribulation and need to call on a Savior who can help with His divine grace and mercy. The mission of BikerDownLiftedUp is to lead them to Jesus and His strength, comfort, and healing, both physically and spiritually. Sometimes, God provides an opportunity to help them eventually answer that ultimate question they all ask. WHY ME? Ask them if they think they have had a close call when they ask that.

Have you ever had a close call?

Have you ever had a close call with death?

That is what a close call means to many of us. But, has the angel of death ever knocked on your door sometime and nearly called you away?

There are many ways we face death. Again, I do not mean to get all doom and gloom. It is not a favorite topic for most people. But we see it all the time, don't we? We do not like talking about it much. We even take it for granted sometimes. We cheapen what death is.

Like on TV or in the movies, we see people getting killed or murdered and amuse ourselves with the story, the drama ... even the comedy. We joke when the hero kills hundreds of bad guys and saves the world.

How many kills did you count? Do you know what movie has the most kills in it? Someone has kept count. The actor, writer, producer, and director Mel Gibson is best known for the number of ways a director can film, in complete detail, a person being killed in battle or by nature.

We get all enthralled by the plot, the means, and the impact on the lives of those in the story. Sometimes it excites us, and sometimes it tears our eyes. Sometimes it is very unpleasant.

Have you ever watched those crime drama documentaries about the murder of someone who overdosed or become enthralled with the autopsy of some celebrity and how they died? The mystery of their last hours. I have heard more passion from a backyard mechanic working on his truck.

Do those shows bring you to face death? Or were you bored with the details or disgusted with how people just threw away their lives on dangerous living, drugs, vanity, or lust? Amusing, isn't it? How can we watch sin so unfazed these days?

I heard a statement on a news broadcast the other day that rings true. "What was once shunned and hidden in the dark alleys is now openly displayed in our living rooms and broad daylight on Main Street."

Dramas and movies about the tragedies of war and catastrophes of nature are sometimes entertaining; they might even be accurate and historically relevant, but rarely do they draw us face-to-face with our mortality.

Let us talk about real life and death that are relevant to us. Personally. Tragic deaths and tragic stories of death. The ones we read about—are you moved by the deaths you hear about on the news? The car accidents, shootings, murders, tree fallings, drownings—I mean even with all the deaths from hurricanes or tornadoes, floods—or those who lost their lives in the California fires. What about all those who died of COVID-19? Did any of those deaths come close to you? Did you know any of the victims? Do you have family or friends, or even a friend of a friend who was affected by one of those kinds of tragedies? Did any of those deaths touch your heart?

My son and his family escaped the dangerous onslaught of a recent storm. They were in a remote beach house on the Outer Banks of North Carolina. But, IF they had not heeded the potential danger, and IF they had not listened to the warnings, and IF they had waited just another hour before they left while the tide and storm surge was rising, if they would have stayed in and been swept away by the storm, or if they could not have found gas … IF … IF … IF.

We all have someone we love, and when we see them faced with death, we think about the separation that will come from the death of a loved one, even if it is ourselves. It makes most of us sad to think about that.

And now we are getting close to home. The death we face in life. The most intimate kind. Actual death, the kind that impacts us personally. Sometimes, we face death when it involves a close friend, a loved one, a family member, or someone we knew at work or school who was here one day and gone the next. A classmate, military buddy, or an old friend or relative you grew up with. We know people who have had a close call, an accident, or hospitalization due to an illness of some kind. You know that whoever that person was, they faced death. Some of us may be facing death right now.

So, how do you face death? Maybe we need to realize we are all faced with death every day. God makes no promises to us for tomorrow.

1 Thessalonians 4:13 says,

> *But we would not have you ignorant, brethren, concerning them that fall asleep; that ye sorrow not, even as the rest, who have no hope.*

I have hope. My hope is in Jesus. That is how I face death with hope. Do you have hope? What is your hope?

We have biblical examples of facing death, and one of the best is how Jesus faced death.

I believe He saw it wherever He was, wherever He went. He saw it all around Him. He talked about death as much as He spoke of life. And like us, when He faced His death, He showed us much about Himself through the Word, left for us to see how to face our death. He prayed in the garden of Gethsemane.

Jesus faced death because He knew what death was all about. He knew exactly how He was going to die and what He would suffer. And like Him, some of us no longer fear death as much as we fear just how we might die or how we might suffer.

He loves us, and He grieves with us when we grieve death. The story of Mary, Martha, and Lazarus, when Jesus wept, tells us that He grieves. He shares with us when we grieve, and He is there to comfort us with His peace. He is a compassionate God. But He also grieves when He knows someone dies and will be separated from Him—forever.

Jesus knows all there is to know about death. As God, He knows everything about us. His plans for us and His grace to give us are holy. He is already standing there to welcome us home or condemn us to eternal death once we cross that bridge.

A close call. Can you remember the one you had? A close call? A close call to this life? A close call to injury? Or a close call where your life on earth could have gone either way? But, by the grace of God, He saved you from certain death.

Think about that briefly because I am about to give you another close call. This invitation is a different kind of close call.

A close call from Jesus. A solemn close call. Have you ever had a close call from Jesus to life? Are you listening?

Maybe you are sitting there thinking of your close call with death or have had enough close calls with death to know that you need an invitational call to life.

Life everlasting. Did you ever think for a moment after that close call with death, about where you would go if you answered that close call with your life and died? Do you know? Are you sure? How would you like to put that concern aside and consider a close call with living instead?

Those are the questions I get to ask people I meet in the hospital who look up at the ceiling and ask, "Why me?"

But the question is valid for everyone.

How would you like to answer an eternal question with an everlasting answer?

Your answer must be—I know Jesus, and He knows me. That is more than hope.

I have victory over death right now, and you can too. The answer is life everlasting.

What a beautiful concept … a wonderful reality to know I am not going to die. Oh, my body will, and I might suffer the pain of leaving the body, but me … the guy in here. I am only going to change addresses. I am going from this earthly address to my permanent home address in heaven.

Do you ever ask a Christian, "*How do you know* you're going to heaven?"

I know because I am possessed by the one who owns the keys. The one who knows all about death and has defeated it. He has told me in His Word that He has prepared a place for me in heaven.

You see, I have reservations. Like season tickets to seats in the stadium, I know I have assigned seating when I get there, and I am not worried about it. Just like when I call ahead and make reservations at my favorite diner, I will have a seat at a table at the appointed time.

What peace you have when you can walk by that line or right by all those others seated and walk up to the *maître d'* and give him your name and have him look in the book and say, "Right this way, sir," and you go and sit down at the table. Even better. I love going where they know who I am, have my seat, and lead me straight to my reserved spot. My reservation is secure because I have already answered His close call.

That is my hope and my faith— in Jesus.

Maybe you know this story already. Perhaps you have felt that tug on your heart from the one who makes the invitations and reservations. Do you want to be seated at His table? Would you like reservations for eternity in heaven?

Can you afford to turn down a close call, knowing that you might have to answer the next close call without reservations? IF anyone here has never responded to Jesus' close call on your life today, I am praying that you will answer the close call that Jesus is making for you right now. Jesus will make you eternal reservations; all you must do is answer His call.

He is calling you to come close to Him.

Jesus loves us, and it pleases all of heaven when we accept Him, for we will be with Him forever after. Therefore, He wants all to be with Him.

1 Timothy 2:3–4 says,

> *This is good and acceptable in the sight of God our Saviour; who would have all men to be saved, and come to the knowledge of the truth.*

Luke 15:7 tells us,

> *I say unto you, that even so there shall be joy in heaven over one sinner that repenteth, more than over ninety and nine righteous persons, who need no repentance.*

**Pray this prayer**:

*"Yes, Lord, take me.* When death knocks on my door, when I face death, I want You, Jesus, to answer it for me and defeat it. Give me victory over death. Enter me with Your Spirit, the same Spirit that gave You victory over death and raised You from the grave. I want that! Forgive me of my sin, live in me, possess me, and when I face death, fill my reservation and take me home."

If you can say that in your heart and mean it, He will. He will. He is faithful, and He will.

Will you? Will you answer Him and this close call? All you need to do is call Him back. Call on the name of Jesus, and He will save you. IF you want to make a reservation for heaven, call on His name. IF you will, He will answer, IF, IF, IF. Make some reservations.

## PRAYER

Dear Lord, God and Father, with tears, I request that You inspire those who read and hear this message to repent and draw unto You before it is too late. I pray that each soul might realize how precious Your gift of life is and how You control every breath we take. Invite those who do not know You today to bring their life to You and give You their devotion and purpose for living. Amen.

## CREDITS AND/OR INSPIRATION

All credit and glory go to our Lord and Savior, Jesus, for the biker ministries He has blessed me to serve.

Barry Mayson and Tony Marco. *Fallen Angel: From Hell's Angel to Heaven's Saint.* Doubleday, 1982.

# What Motivates You?

## CONCEPTS

The various forms of pride in humans are satan's sneakiest sins. Pride creeps into our lives, minds, and hearts in many ways. Trying to parse good and evil when we seek glory for ourselves or others is brutal and often spiritually unhealthy. The good ones can turn nasty and become sins. These are sins we rarely account for, and often they are sins of omission because we don't even consider them, ask for forgiveness, or repent from them. Yet they hurt our relationship with our Lord. Consider this in your next prayer time.

## PURPOSE

From childhood, we are motivated to_____ whatever, you name it. Who motivates us? Motivation comes from parents, peers, teachers, pastors, enemies, coaches, drill instructors, bosses, spouses, family, children, work associates, competition, self, and God's Word. All of these motivators can be good. Some can be bad, and some are both good at times and bad at others. Pride, pleasing man, and pleasing ourselves are motivating issues we must address according to God's Word.

## SCRIPTURE BASE

Colossians 3:2, Deuteronomy 8:17–18, Proverbs 16:2, Proverbs 8:13, Romans 12:2, Matthew 6:1, Psalm 139:23–24, Philippians 4:20

## BACKGROUND

I sincerely doubt I am the only one who has trouble when I pause to consider my motivations before I embark on a project or even while I'm in the middle of one, especially ministry projects. Many people don't even pause to consider it, but that is precisely what we need to do. We need to test ourselves on why we do what we do. Are we in God's will? Are we humble enough to give God glory in all we do?

## SPUR

What drives you to do what you do? Let's begin with a few questions, and you will soon figure out where this Spur is headed.

- Do you volunteer to serve so you will become noticed or recognized by others for your work?
- Do you want others to congratulate you on your completed job?
- Are you looking for a promotion when you strive to outperform your competition?
- Do you enjoy being on stage for the applause and cheers of the crowd?
- Do you speak or perform so that others will praise your ability and talent?
- Do you dress for success or to attract the looks of others?
- Do you tell stories of success and boast of your experience and achievements so others will look up to you?
- Do you drop names of notoriety or of influential people you have worked with, related to, or met so others will consider you their peer or to become more popular?
- Do you seek recognition, congratulations, or aggrandizement after leading a successful project?
- Do you seek leadership roles because you want to be in charge?
- Do you want others to look up to or idolize you to make you feel good?

Get it? One or more of those might have hit you between the eyes. You have already begun to rationalize with "What's wrong with that?" The answer to that question depends on why you do it.

Colossians 3:2

> *Set your mind on the things that are above, not on the things that are upon the earth.*

Can you define the following words: *pride, arrogance, narcissism, egotism, conceit,* and *vanity*? I can with one word ... sin. Do any of these sins cloud your judgment? Do any of these sins separate you from God as you become your idol? These are dangerous grounds, and satan uses these sins to slip in the cracks of our mentality and thought processes. You may get praise, make more money, get a raise, applause, or recognition for your talent, looks, performance, or work. But is that why you do it? That's the tricky question for yourself. Here's why.

Deuteronomy 8:17–18

> *And lest thou say in thy heart, My power and the might of my hand hath gotten me this wealth. But thou shalt re-member Jehovah thy God, for it is he that giveth thee power to get wealth; that he may establish his covenant which he sware unto thy fathers, as at this day.*

Ever since we were very young, the world has drilled these attitudes into our heads. You've been told you need to compete, you must get the prize, you have to be first, and you have to be better than the next person. Ever feel that pressure from your parents, peers, coaches, or teachers? We all have it at some point in our lives. We see it as encouragement and love from those who want us to succeed and produce. To become the best we can be. But then, the praise becomes a drug, the desire to receive it becomes our addiction, and soon the talents and gifts we received from God to glorify Him get lost in even thinking about Him at all.

Proverbs 16:2

*All the ways of a man are clean in his own eyes; But Jehovah weigheth the spirits.*

Related story: Remember Whitney Houston? One of the most talented voices people have ever heard. Her story is tragic, but she falls right into this narcissistic kind of pride and gets sucked down by satan. An entire world watched as she rose to heights unseen before her time and then self-destructed and died from a drug overdose. She used her God-given talent and beauty at the beginning of her career as a Gospel singer, glorifying Jesus. Then came fame, money, pride, more fame, and ultimately, death. How did she lose her way? Her story is on LiveAbout.

How do we unload all this programming? We have all received it, but has satan reinforced it into self-destructive pride? Note that God hates pride and those who become haughty in serving Him.

Proverbs 8:13

*The fear of Jehovah is to hate evil: Pride, and arrogancy, and the evil way, And the perverse mouth, do I hate.*

The gifts He gave you are meant to glorify Him, not you. He deserves all the praise because, without Him, you are nothing. He is first, every time, and you must keep Him first in every aspect of your life. Remember …

Matthew 22:37

*Thou shalt love the Lord thy God with all your heart, with all your soul, and with all your mind.*

You may think you should quit all that work, performance, ability, reward, acceptance, and praise. Not at all. You can be all that and humble too.

Romans 12:2

> *And be not fashioned according to this world: but be ye transformed by the renewing of your mind, that ye may prove what is the good and acceptable and perfect will of God.*

Your humility can show through, and you will receive even more blessings. God gives all good things, and everything He gives you is good. Give God the credit. Glorify Him in all that you do and the reason for doing it. Praise Him! Shout to others for what He has done for you and how He has blessed you. He gives success; you didn't earn it. He provides. We have heard this many times in our Christian discipleship education. Remember that the shining glory belongs to God whenever you embark on a project that will thrust you into the spotlight.

Matthew 6:1

> *Take heed that ye do not your righteousness before men, to be seen of them: else ye have no reward with your Father who is in heaven.*

We motivate others when we continually give praise, adulation, and rewards to others around us. We are supposed to. But are we complicit in making them eager for the attention and wrong reasons? Let's pray we are not. We want to lift up others, and we should like to promote those around us and remind them to give credit where credit is due. We motivate and encourage our children, friends, and fellow workers. Shape your praise of others in a way that reminds them it is God who blesses them for having made the achievements or done so well in their performance. We can do our part to remind ourselves and others we love that God is first in all our lives.

## PRAYER

Lord, God and Father, today I pray that You would show me where my heart is when it begins leaning toward the wrong motivations. Lord, I ask that You remind me and prick my heart when I motivate others to think wrongly about themselves or others. Guard me against these sins and lies that satan whispers in my ears or when my tongue gets out of control. I don't want to be this kind of sinner. Thank You, Lord, for knowing I can ask You for anything in Your will, and You will grant it. Grant these to me today and forevermore. Amen.

Psalm 139:23–24

*Search me, O God, and know my heart: Try me, and know my thoughts; And see if there be any wicked way in me, And lead me in the way everlasting.*

## CREDITS AND/OR INSPIRATION

My Lord and Savior, Jesus Christ, sought glory for our Father, God, in obedience unto death.

Philippians 4:20 *Now unto our God and Father be the glory for ever and ever. Amen.*

LiveAbout. "The Whitney Houston Story." Dotdash Meredith.2009. https://www.liveabout.com/whitney-houston-biography-3245298.

Sager, Jessica. "Whitney Houston's Tragic Real-Life Story." NickiSwift.com. Updated February 3, 2023. https://www.nickiswift.com/82552/untold-truth-whitney-houston/.

# I Ain't Skeered

**CONCEPTS**

As Christians, the Bible tells us in Matthew 5, Jesus' Sermon on the Mount, to be timid and meek. This is true. The Bible also tells us to be bold and courageous. Use your concordance, and you will find many references. How do we balance these concepts that seem to disagree? First, we must recognise that there is no disagreement. God's Spirit is power; that Spirit is the same One within us as believers. When to use each is wisdom. Knowledge of God's Word is the beginning of wisdom.

**PURPOSE**

People need hope; they need to build faith when they face tribulations. They need to know how to approach God in prayer and live a life of faith daily. When people realize who God is and the power He has to support and save, they will be ready to be used by God for His purpose.

**SCRIPTURE BASE**

2 Timothy 1:7, Hebrews 11:6, James 1 2–4, 1 Samuel 17:34–35, Philippians 4:13

**BACKGROUND**

Consider the life of Jesus and what He faced every day of His recorded ministry. Right up until His death on the cross, Jesus was tempted. He knew what was coming, much more than we ever know, but He faced everything with strength, power, faith, prayer, and action. His example is our example. He sometimes failed to accomplish what He wanted, but it didn't stop Him. His life is what

He calls us to do when He tells His disciples we must pick up our cross and follow Him (Luke 9:23, Matt. 10:38).

## SPUR

2 Timothy 1:7 NLT says, *God has not given us a spirit of fear and timidity.* The Bible also says, *Without faith, it is impossible to please God* (Hebrews 11:6). Together, these verses make bold warriors for Christ. So don't get involved in anything that doesn't require you to use your faith. The key to momentum is always having something to look forward to and depend on God. You either venture or you vegetate.

Then, there come the storms of our life. Jesus deliberately sent His disciples into a storm (Mark 4). Why? To develop their faith and show them they could get through anything with Him on board! God will keep exposing you to difficult situations because He knows it's the only way your faith will grow.

James 1:2–4

*Count it all joy, my brethren, when ye fall into manifold temptations; knowing that the proving of your faith worketh]patience. And let patience have its perfect work, that ye may be perfect and entire, lacking in nothing.*

Nineteenth-century American preacher and abolitionist Phillips Brooks wrote,

Do not pray for easy lives. Pray to be stronger men. Do not pray for tasks equal to your power; pray for power equal to your tasks. (AZ Quotes)

You don't tap into God's resources until you attempt something that seems humanly impossible. That's when you discover: *I can do all things in him that strengtheneth me*

116

(Philippians 4:13 ). That's the power of God. His power is not to be misused or abused but within His will.

All progress involves risk. You can't grab the golden ring on the merry-go-round if you don't stretch out from your seat on the pony. Progress consists of overcoming fear. One day, when David was tending his sheep, *there came a lion* (1 Samuel 17:34–35). But in God's strength, he defeated it, plus a bear and later a giant called Goliath. That lion was just an opportunity in disguise. If David had wavered or run away, he'd have missed his chance to become king of Israel. So, when a lion of fear comes into your life, recognize it for what it is: an opportunity from God to rise up in faith and conquer it.

Prayer Point: Pray for anyone going through a difficult time. Ask them to see their time of tribulation as an opportunity to experience God's strength. That can be tough for a nonbeliever with no faith, but for a mature Christian, it is precisely what they need to hear from God's Word.

Taking action and ministering to others for God is a reason to be bold and pray in faith for Jesus to give you the power to glorify Him. Responding in prayer and having faith that God will save you from your current situation or tribulation are two sides of the same coin. They both lead to depending on God for His strength and power. This is the definition of a mature Christian: to know God will never leave you or forsake you.

## PRAYER

Great God Almighty, whom do I have to fear? You are my God. Give me the boldness to use the gifts You have blessed me with to glorify You in all I do. Help me step out in faith to show Your light so others can see and believe. Regardless of where I am and what is happening in my life, give me the power to be a witness to You. Amen.

## CREDITS AND/OR INSPIRATION

AZQuotes. "Phillips Brooks Quotes." Accessed April 30, 2023. https://www.azquotes.com/author/1975-Phillips_Brooks.

John Mason. *Believe You Can: The Power of a Positive Attitude*. Baker Publishing Group, 2020, 167–168.

# An Old African Proverb

## CONCEPTS

Many people decline to participate in ministry because they feel they have nothing to offer. They are not speakers, teachers, leaders, or educators, and they do not think they are a vital part of the body of Christ.

## PURPOSE

This Spur emphasizes how important each of us is to God. God takes what seems small and insignificant and makes it great in His Kingdom. Everyone can participate in glorifying God and become active in using the gifts God has given or can prepare through faith to receive the gift God has in store for them.

## SCRIPTURE BASE

2 Kings 4, 1 Samuel 17, James 3, John 4, Luke 10, Mark 12, John 6, Luke 19, Matthew 5:16

Each set of verses highlights how the Lord uses those to do His will when called: Matthew 5:16, Matthew 13:31–32, Matthew 17:20, Mark 4:3, Mark 6:41, Luke 13:19, Luke 17:6, 1 Corinthians 7:7, 1 Corinthians 12:4–11, James 1:17, 1 Peter 4:10–11, Romans 12:6–8

## BACKGROUND

Jesus references the tiny mustard seed in several places. The gospels contain his parables and mention what the Kingdom of Heaven is like. There are also references to how much faith we need to accomplish His will. The mustard seed and the *yud*, or *yod* in Hebrew, are both small but extremely important. So are all of us. God will use you if you are willing by faith to serve Him. He has done so much for us; we should want to do good works for Him as He had planned for each of us before time began.

## SPUR

Have you ever wondered why God made things that seem so useless? I mean, we could do without a few bugs. Take, for example, the mosquito. Why did God ever make the mosquito? I wish Noah would have stopped them right on the boat. So, what good are they anyway? Has any scientist, biologist, or entomologist defended the necessity of mosquitoes? I doubt I would believe them if they thought of a good reason.

Well, the reason God made mosquitoes might be the biggest lesson of your life today.

An old African proverb goes like this: "If you think you're too small to make a difference, you haven't spent a night trying to sleep in a room with a mosquito" (Indian in the Machine).

Can you identify with that? Which part? Thinking you are too insignificant or maybe trying sleeping in a room with a mosquito?

The principle is the same, whether you are thoroughly annoying or helpful beyond measure; being small or insignificant does not mean you do not make a difference. The Bible is full of inspiring stories about one person who became a genuine voice of truth. Or one person whose kindness saved a life. Each person matters when doing the will of God.

- A small jar of oil. 2 Kings 4.
- David, a young boy, kills a giant, Goliath. 1 Samuel 17.

- Think of a large ship steered by such a small rudder; it is the same with the tongue. James 3.
- The woman at the well. John 4.
- The Good Samaritan. Luke 10.
- The widow gives two copper mites. Mark 12.
- Jesus feeds thousands with five loaves of barley and two fish given by a small boy. John 6.
- A small man in a tree. Zacchaeus. Luke 19.

Our very beginnings in life and growth begin small and get bigger with time. How about you? Do you think you are too small or insignificant to make much difference? God's Word says explicitly that you are wrong.

God is big, and we often think of Him in His grandiose state more than we consider Him in small things like a mustard seed or a *yud*. What's a yud, you ask? The yud is the tenth and smallest letter in the Hebrew alphabet. It is a small mark that looks like the English version of an apostrophe. The difference in what it means in Hebrew is much more critical.

The yud has historical significance because it is the precursor of the Roman letters *Ii* and *Jj*. Note that both have a dot above the lowercase letter. The yud also has a parallel in the Greek alphabet—the *iota*. In this case, the iota is also the tenth letter and means ten. Iota and jot are synonymous. Hence, the phrases "not one iota" or "not one jot or tittle" have become associated with the smallest dots or marks written on parchment (Raskin).

What makes the yud so powerful? The yud is significant because it is noted in brief as the power of God. In Hebrew, it is the first letter in Yahweh or YHWH. The name of Jesus begins with a yud, as does Jerusalem and Israel. Could it be a coincidence? How is it that the smallest of letters is the beginning of the greatest of words?

121

Let's look at some small things that Christians do. We are at our best when we encourage one another. Examples are those who visit church members and family members who are sick or injured or help feed those who need a meal. How about writing notes or sending cards to those who are shut-in, jailed, on missionary trips in faraway lands, military members on overseas duty, missing members from the church, acknowledgment of an accomplished life event, or grieving over a lost loved one? These trivial things are not trivial at all. They mean so much in the life of a church and the encouragement of members. People who do these things tirelessly are gifted and talented.

The congregation and staff should never slight the menial workers and volunteers, often taken for granted for work done behind the scenes. Many times, only the talent gets the applause or mention. How about the janitor, the greeter, the maintenance team members, the technical team, the security team, and nursery volunteers? Do not ever forget the cooks. These people need to be encouraged too. Every member of the body of Christ has a place to serve God.

He has given you gifts to use, and He will appoint you to glorify Him by doing things He has planned for you, big or small. What you need to do is be available to Him and His calling. So, dwell on this word from God today in Matthew 5:16:

> *Even so let your light shine before men; that they may see your good works, and glorify your Father who is in heaven.*

Might I add ... no matter how small you are.

## PRAYER

Lord, God and Father, though I am weak, You are strong. I praise and thank You for reminding me that You are always there to lean on when I feel small and insignificant. I know that You are great, and You lead and guide me. You are my strong tower and hold me in Your mighty right hand of power. Thank You, as You remind me, no one can stand against me when You are for me. What a mighty God You are. Amen.

## CREDITS AND/OR INSPIRATION

Biblehub.com. "The Mustard Seed: A Sermon for the Sabbath-School Teacher." Accessed August 3, 2022. https://biblehub.com/sermons/auth/spurgeon/the_mustard_seed_a_sermon_for_the_sabbath-school_teacher.htm.

Indian in the Machine. "If You Think You're Too Small to Make a Difference, Try Sleeping in a Closed Room with a Mosquito." Posted by Ricardo Peterson Kuthumi. January 14, 2010. https://indianinthemachine.wordpress.com/2010/01/14/if-you-think-youre-too-small-to-make-a-difference-try-sleeping-in-a-closed-room-with-a-mosquito-african-proverb./

Raskin, Rabbi Aaron L. "Yud: The Tenth Letter of the Hebrew Alphabet." Chabad.org. Accessed April 30, 2025. https://www.chabad.org/library/article_cdo/aid/137082/jewish/Yod.htm.

# Better Teachers

## CONCEPTS

Churches, especially church leaders, must have a heart for the lost and love one another. The community will know you as a Christian if they see your love for them.

John 13:35

> *By this shall all men know that ye are my disciples, if ye have love one to another.*

## PURPOSE

This Spur is written to encourage church members and ministers to follow God's commission and commandments to make disciples and love one another.

## SCRIPTURE BASE

John 13:35, Matthew 9, 1 Timothy 2:3–4, Matthew 28:19, Mark 12:30-31, James 2: 1–9

## BACKGROUND

My young family and I joined a church that created its deaconship by filling it with influential men of the county, rich men, and long-time church owners/operators. These men steered, and the congregation followed, as did the residing hireling under-shepherd. During a concerted effort to reach out to the surrounding community, the pastor bravely assigned pairs of church members to visit local trailer parks and low-income housing areas. I was paired with an influential local school board member. After visiting a few people and one double-wide park trailer containing a beautiful young family, my partner decided he had had enough cold calling. He said there was no future in getting these people to join our church. His reasoning was, "They don't have any money to give, and most are no-talent losers with needy little kids." He said these words I'll never forget: "These are not the people we want in our church. They are a drain on us." I left that church within weeks of that discussion. For many years, that church struggled and suffered pastor after pastor.

## SPUR

There are a plethora of studies on the improvement of education. For over a hundred years, master's degree thesis studies, doctoral dissertations, and books about school improvement have abounded. Repeated studies and statistics proved the same thing. If you want to improve teaching in the classroom, improve the teachers who do the teaching. More money isn't the answer, and neither is technology. You don't need more teacher assistants or better principals. Though they might all help, the most significant impact comes from having a better teacher. Studies about years of experience, new teachers versus veterans, expensive school graduates, money increases per child in the classroom, etc., show that no factor comes close to the conclusion that better teachers improve schools. So, the question is, what makes a good teacher? Again, the typical findings are that good teachers love to teach and want to impact their students positively. More importantly, each student feels accepted and encouraged to learn.

You cannot teach how to love students or create that desire for any teacher who doesn't have it. Individually, teachers who have it can lose it, and others can start without it and gain it over time. Unfortunately, school systems and boards of education think that all it takes is throwing more money at the teacher problem if their school needs improvement, but they are reluctant to throw more money at the teacher. Sound familiar? Administrators continually make the mistake of thinking staff development, the flavor-of-the-month programs, in-classroom techniques, and even better students are the keys to school improvement. None of it comes close in comparison to better teachers. Does more money make a better teacher? Not often, but it might buy a better teacher.

The parts of this discussion about teachers also translate to preachers and pastors. Take that any way you want to. Teachers don't like to hear it either.

So, you ask, what makes a church thrive? What makes a church thrive is the same thing: adding a good infusion of the Spirit of God to the mix. There is no greater love for one another or a congregation than the love infused with God's Spirit.

Let me start over. People will not care for what you say until they know how much you care. The best churches I've ever been part of are those where most in the congregation show one another genuine love. That love begins with God and is poured upon the congregation by example. The congregation's best example of love is Christ. He is the example for the pastors, leaders in their church, and one another. This is all very biblical.

If that kind of love is lacking in your church, revival needs to begin from the pulpit. Sometimes a member or a visiting pastor can bring revival or start an outpouring of Spirit that brings revival, but it should be in the pastor's job description, and if it is not, I pray it already dwells in the church DNA. Your church can have a good music program, lights, talented musicians and singers, a beautiful building, and if you don't have love, all you might have is showtime on Primetime Sunday morning. God is love, and worshipping and glorifying Him should always be Primetime.

Jesus' love for those He ministered to is not the average Sunday morning churchgoer we see today. Jesus' healing power brought all types of people to see Him and hear His words. Our modern-day

126

churches don't often seek the kind of people Jesus sought. He said He came to heal the sick (sin-sick), not the righteous, who don't need Him. Matthew 9 says He loved the unlovely and was reviled for caring about those He sought to save.

How hard is it to love the unlovely? These are the people churches shy away from and neglect to minister to or even approach. The ugly, scarred, toothless, old, alone, sick, young and restless, druggies, tattooed, pinned with studs and earrings, smelly, drunk, nasty looking in dress and style, street people, gay, evil-looking, homeless, mentally or physically challenged—add a different skin color or a language barrier to any of these for multiplying effects. After all, what good are they to your church anyway? Recognize that they are likely burdensome and have no resources or talent, baggage, and many needs. Can you see them, or are they so far out of sight you don't even want to think about them?

1 Timothy 2:3–4

*This is good and acceptable in the sight of God our Saviour; who would have all men to be saved, and come to the knowledge of the truth.*

Matthew 28:19

*Go ye therefore, and make disciples of all the nations, baptizing them into the name of the Father and of the Son and of the Holy Spirit.*

We are not defined by our worst or our best. Our God defines us. The last time I looked up the definition of *all*, it meant all, everyone, everywhere. Preachers and pastors, under-shepherds, deacons, ministers, and laypeople who believe in God, Jesus, the Holy Spirit, and the Word must know and prioritize the great commission (Matthew 28:19). They must also prioritize the greatest commandment to love the Lord your God with all your heart, soul, mind, and strength. And they should live by the second most important commandment: love your neighbor as you love yourself.

Mark 12:30–31

*And thou shalt love the Lord thy God with all thy heart, and with all thy soul, and with all thy mind, and with all thy strength. The second is this, Thou shalt love thy neighbor as thyself. There is none other commandment greater than these.*

So, the essence of this Spur is in James 2:1–9. I cannot add to it or subtract from it. I'd love to say it better than this, but James, the half-brother of Jesus, says it best:

*My brethren, hold not the faith of our Lord Jesus Christ, the Lord of glory, with respect of persons. For if there come into your synagogue a man with a gold ring, in fine clothing, and there come in also a poor man in vile clothing; and ye have regard to him that weareth the fine clothing, and say, Sit thou here in a good place; and ye say to the poor man, Stand thou there, or sit under my footstool; do ye not make distinctions among yourselves, and become judges with evil thoughts? Hearken, my beloved brethren; did not God choose them that are poor as to the world to be rich in faith, and heirs of the kingdom which he promised to them that love him? But ye have dishonored the poor man. Do not the rich oppress you, and themselves drag you before the judgment-seats? Do not they blaspheme the honorable name by which ye are called? Howbeit if ye fulfil the royal law, according to the scripture, Thou shalt love thy neighbor as thyself, ye do well: but if ye have respect of persons, ye commit sin, being convicted by the law as transgressors.*

## PRAY

God and Father, I pray this Spur touches the hearts of those who read and yearn to build a fellowship with these priorities. Lord, I wish not to offend. I pray to encourage those not to fear but to be courageous, lead in strength and compassion, love tirelessly, and gather or build a church membership that desires Your will. Give them Your eyes to see, love the unlovely, and gather those who fall through the cracks of other fellowships that can't or won't see them. Lord, give those who hear Your Word the power to stand in the gap and complete Your will. Amen.

## CREDITS AND/OR INSPIRATION

My inspiration is based upon good friends with the talent to love the unlovely better than any other Christians I've ever met.

# Appointing Your Days

## CONCEPTS

The Bible has everything we need to learn to live. No one handed us a user guide on life after learning to read. The Bible is just that.

## PURPOSE

People need to think of their future and find guidance to live toward that future. God has a plan for each of us to glorify Him. Would it not be reasonable to research what that plan is?

## SCRIPTURE BASE

Psalm 90:12, Job 28:28, Psalm 119:105, Romans 8:28, 1 Corinthians 2:9, Matthew 25:23

## BACKGROUND

I have been out of control for most of my life, figuratively, off the chain. Not knowing what would happen next because I had not planned, I had not asked or prayed for a future aligned with what God wanted. I had no idea He steered me by doors of opportunity, walls I could not get around or through, circumstances beyond my control, and people He placed in my life to mentor and advise me. I never realized I was out of control until I realized He had always been in control of my life. God nursed me and led me by the hand until I could see His lamp to my feet and light to my path. God's Word is that lamp and light in Jesus.

## SPUR

Psalm 90:12 says, *So teach us to number our days, That we may get us a heart of wisdom.*

Did you know that praying for wisdom is within God's will? It is always important to pray in the same direction God wills. Why? Because praying against God's will is wasting your breath. (That is, if you pray aloud.) God wants us to walk with wisdom, and He wants to give us understanding. His Word is full of wisdom; the more we read and heed it, the wiser we become. Job 28:28 says, *And unto man he said, Behold, the fear of the Lord, that is wisdom; And to depart from evil is understanding.*

However, what does it mean to "number our days"? When read in Hebrew, the words used have much more context than what we read in English. For example, *manah* in Hebrew means more than "number" in English. Translated in context, it means to appoint or prepare. The story of Jonah used the same word when God prepared those things that became such a problem for Jonah to teach him the lesson God wanted him to learn (Cahn). He does the same with us. Do you genuinely think the morning when you had so many plans ahead for your day that the flat tire you had was a fluke? It changed your plans; it made you zig when you were in the middle of your zag. I believe there is a reason for those unplanned zigs, and now, after years of experience, I can see those divine changes when I had no control as acts of God to show me something I might not have experienced without His intervention.

We know we have a certain number of days in our lives—God already designated them. So, what can we do to prepare or appoint our days? The pat answer is to read God's Word and pray daily for Him to show you His way to your day. It is precisely what Psalm 119:105 says, *Thy word is a lamp unto my feet, And light unto my path.* You can't see the Light if you don't read the Bible.

That is a question of the ages. Many philosophers and theologians have discussed this question, and the answer is simple. We make it complex. How does one prepare for days that are yet to come?

God brings good things to those who believe. Now and in the future. Romans 8:28 says, *And we know that to them that love God all things work together for good, even to them that are called according to his purpose.*

You say, the future? Yes, your eternal destiny. We all have one. "Death is only the beginning" is a famous movie quote from *The Mummy* (Lillegjord). The intent of the quote was devised to be scary. It is, if you think about it. The truth is that our eternal future without Christ is pretty frightening. His future for those who believe in Him is beyond our wildest imagination. You must love the song "I Can Only Imagine" by Bart Millard (Turner). I am not sure, but I think Bart may have been thinking about 1 Corinthians 2:9, where the Bible says, *But as it is written, Things which eye saw not, and ear heard not, And which entered not into the heart of man, Whatsoever things God prepared for them that love him.* To paraphrase, "You have not got a clue what good things God has for those who believe in Him." He wants a life for us that glorifies Him and blesses us. We only need to seek His face, trust Him, and obey His Word. Have faith to know God will do the rest unto your eternal rest.

I am sure Bart wants to hear the same thing as you, and I want to hear from God as it says in Matthew 25:23, *"Well done, good and faithful servant"* (Turner).

Are you prepared for your future?

**PRAY**

God, each day, I ask for Your divine wisdom. Show me the way of the Lord, and inspire me to know Your will in my life. May

I bless You, Lord, with faith to complete the race of life well and join You eternally in peace only You can give. Thank You, Lord, for choosing me to be Your faithful servant; forgive me when I fail You in that service. Amen.

## CREDITS AND/OR INSPIRATION

Jonathan Cahn. "Appointing Our Days: Part 1." The Creator's Calendar. Accessed April 30, 2025. https://www.thecreatorscalendar.com/appointing-our-days-part-1/.

Kacie Lillegjord. "10 Best Quotes from the Mummy." Screenrant. June 1, 2020, https://screenrant.com/the-mummy-best-quotes/.

Wikipedia Foundation. "I Can Only Imagine (MercyMe Song)." Last Edited on April 20, 2025. https://en.wikipedia.org/wiki/I_Can_Only_Imagine_(MercyMe_song).

# Sacrifices That Please God

**CONCEPTS**

To a modern-day Christian, the word *sacrifice* can sometimes get lost in the Old Testament (OT) and New Testament (NT) use. This Spur recognizes what Jesus did for us and what we can do in appreciation that is acceptable to God. Like Christian works, sacrifice is nothing we have to do, but we should do to live out our love for Christ.

**PURPOSE**

As Christians, we can recognize how to please God through our actions of sacrifice in recognition of Jesus' sacrifice.

**SCRIPTURE BASE**

Psalm 89:30–37, Matthew 9:13, Hebrews 13:15, Hebrews 13:16, Proverbs 21:3, Luke 21:3, 1 John 3:16, Romans 12:1–2, John 15:12

**BACKGROUND**

While researching the origins of what and why sacrifices were made unto God, I realized that history is relevant, but living a life of sacrifice is much more critical to our lives as Christians.

**SPUR**

The word *sacrifice* means different things to different people. Being nouns and verbs, our modern-day definitions of sacrifice relate to everything from an outfield fly ball to giving up something valuable for something else deemed more useful or desired.

The OT defines a sacrifice, its beginnings, and why it was needed. Genesis, Exodus, and Leviticus are the primary sources defining sacrifice as well as describing when and how it was performed. Each book tells the essence and details of sacrifice as handed down to Moses by God as law. The OT points to the Messiah and His sacrifice, but with few exceptions concerning the OT law, the NT is entirely about Jesus and His perfect sacrifice.

So, what became relevant to my study was what the Bible says about the sacrifices we can make that please God.

To be clear, God is always faithful. There is nothing you, as a believer can do to make Him love you any more or less. Psalm 89:30–37 tells us that God may punish us for our transgressions but will never take His love from us. God's covenant of grace is a promise. It is a promise you can lean on even in your darkest hour of disgrace and sin; He will cover you in love everlasting.

Though some theologians divide the Scripture to mean that the writing in Psalm 89 refers to sinning that requires a sacrifice for forgiveness, I can't entirely agree. I think it simply says that the penalty for disobeying God's commandments and statutes will bring the punishment of consequences. Those consequences might be pain and suffering. The psalm did not say death. (See verses 31–32.) Furthermore, God continues with His assurance that He will never break His covenant regardless. God's faithfulness and love are eternal for those whose names are written in the Book of Life.

Suppose I can explain salvation concisely for the sake of this paragraph. The NT tells how Jesus died on the cross to redeem us from the penalty of sin by paying the price for our sins through His perfect sacrifice—once and forever. Grace is a gift to all who accept Jesus' sacrifice through free will. There is no argument here, but even though our sins are forever forgiven, our consequences for sin may not be. Our suffering for consequences should not be confused with the sacrifice needed to forgive our sins. Jesus made the sacrifice, and no other is required. Consequences of our sin may come due not in the next life but possibly in this one. You may disagree with me, and that's okay. What is essential for all of us to agree on is that Jesus paid it all, and His sacrifice is the only sacrifice that secures our future and eternity with Him.

With that in mind, let us discuss what pleases God in our response to Jesus' sacrifice for our sake.

Matthew 9:13

> *But go ye and learn what this meaneth, I desire mercy, and not sacrifice: for I came not to call the righteous, but sinners.*

This verse should be written in red letters for Jesus is speaking about what he prefers and desires. He desires mercy over sacrifice. In context here, Jesus is saying that those around Him who practice OT law by sacrificing animals and such for their sin are not the reason He is here. He is here to give mercy to sinners. How does this fit with the theme of this Spur, you ask? Jesus is our example. We should also desire to show mercy to those who sin against us. Forgiveness to those who have wronged us does not require us to forgive them if they ask us to or even after they make it up to us. We should forgive them, period, because that is merciful and Christlike. To do that would please God.

Hebrews 13:15

> *Through him then let us offer up a sacrifice of praise to God continually, that is, the fruit of lips which make confession to his name.*

Some who read this might not understand what the sacrifice is. How does praising God with the fruit of our lips while confessing His name become a sacrifice for us? It combines the law in Leviticus and a reference to Cain in Genesis, who brought fruit to God as his sacrifice. Levitical law states that we should continually give God praise, thanks, and adoration; the sacrifice is burnt offerings. Cain offered his crop's first fruits to God as an offering. The writer of Hebrews says we should give the fruit of our lips in constant praise, thanks, and adoration as our offering. Therefore, to praise God with our lips in prayer or song is an acceptable sacrifice unto the Lord. It doesn't cost us too much, but I'm confident we do not do it enough.

Hebrews 13:16

*But to do good and to communicate forget not: for with such sacrifices God is well pleased.*

Proverbs 21:3

*To do righteousness and justice is more acceptable to Jehovah than sacrifice.*

Being a do-gooder may not be high on anyone's list these days, as our peer group of the world says just the opposite. "Get it while you can" would align more with the world. The writer of Hebrews says, "Hey, don't forget it. Be a do-gooder, and to do so will please God." To do that every day for someone like me would be a sacrifice. I'm blessed to know a few do-gooders, and I know it is not only their way of life, but they're also exceptional at it. I contend that these people are spiritually gifted and talented to be do-gooders. Proverbs says plainly that doing right and seeking justice is more acceptable than sacrifice. Again, do good.

Luke 21:3

*And he said, Of a truth I say unto you, This poor widow cast in more than they all:*

I think many people can relate sacrifice with our financial giving and tithing. Much is expected from those who have been given much, but to give until it hurts? Notice that this is not a biblical reference, as I can find none. Jesus says here in the familiar story of the widow's mite that giving all you have as she did is truly a sacrifice. Was He pleased with what she gave? The story bears out that He is pleased by making her simple, poor gesture an example for us all to read about for nearly two thousand years. God sees what's in the heart and is unconcerned about what's in the wallet. He knows what's in both.

1 John 3:16

*Hereby know we love, because he laid down his life for us: and we ought to lay down our lives for the brethren.*

Few people like to consider the sure-fire sacrifice of laying down their lives for another. Yet, several Christians I've known throughout my military career as a war veteran knew and understood we might have to cover the check we wrote when we enlisted. Those who volunteered realized the magnitude of the blank check we had written when we signed the enlistment and raised our right hand in allegiance. In surrender, our lives were available to our country, family, friends, and fellow service members. Many have given their lives on the battlefield and in civil service as genuine heroes. I'm confident we can all recall a few of those heroes today. John says it is out of our love that we sacrifice ourselves for another. Love is the key to all sacrifice. God so loved us He gave His only Son.

Romans 12:1–2

*I beseech you therefore, brethren, by the mercies of God, to present your bodies a living sacrifice, holy, acceptable to God, which is your spiritual service. And be not fashioned according to this world: but be ye transformed by the renewing of your mind, that ye may prove what is the good and acceptable and perfect will of God.*

These verses may be the best known for what a pleasing sacrifice is to God. Paul minces few words about what we should give to glorify and please God. The oxymoron of the verse would sound strange to the ears of the people of that time, which makes it even more astonishing that he wrote it. A sacrifice is usually something killed or given to be burnt, not living. Paul's description here would represent a paradigm shift in how people in those times thought of the word 'sacrifice'. Applying it to themselves and staying alive would generate some mental athletics and, in many ways, still does today.

Paul is telling us quite plainly to live a holy life *in all that we do* as a spiritual service to God. We are to life-walk with the Spirit we are possessed of and be contrary to the world around us. Paul, a confessed sinner himself, knows this is no easy task and says this is our sacrifice to live in this way, giving ourselves wholly unto God.

John 15:12

*This is my commandment, that ye love one another, even as I have loved you.*

In Jesus' words, this verse is short but sweet. It is the capstone of all the previous ones and many more not listed. All of the above verses are embroidered in God's hand with a golden lining of love, or we couldn't do it, or wouldn't do it. Without love, we are nothing. God's love is everything; through us, it can do anything.

## PRAYER

Lord, God and heavenly Father, I praise You alone for being an awesome God. I want to please You and bless You in what I think, do, and say. Lord, show me where I offend You; show me the evil in my heart that keeps me from living the sacrificial life You have asked me to give. Please give me more faith and strength to be that each day of the rest of my life. Amen.

## CREDITS AND/OR INSPIRATION

The research into sacrifice began as a quest to understand what biblical sacrifice was all about. In that study, I found that the historical details of sacrifice were not as important as the divine sacrifice of Jesus and what I owe to Him for what He did for me.

# Too Bad

## CONCEPTS

Many people think they can never be good enough to become a Christian. They can't accept Christ because they are too sinful and evil. These people do not understand the concept of grace or the faithfulness of God to save them from their sins through Jesus and His infinite power.

## PURPOSE

Someone in your church may think they are worse than those I'm telling you about. This story might convince them that it doesn't matter how bad they have been; Jesus is faithful to forgive.

## SCRIPTURE BASE

The story of Saul to Paul. Read Acts 9 on the road to Damascus and 1 Timothy 1:12–17, where Paul gives his testimony.

## BACKGROUND

I served as a minister in a Christian motorcycle ministry for several years. In that time, I heard and met both men and women with horrendous backgrounds and histories—some who found Jesus and got out of their snake pits of outlaw biking and some who didn't. I can tell you that during this time, I heard testimonies that bothered me. Some of those testimonies sounded like they were bragging about how bad they were. Others who spoke of their past were truly broken and ashamed of their sin and life before meeting Jesus. The best testimonies I heard were from those who lived so close to hell that they understood how much forgiveness and grace they received and were eternally grateful they accepted Jesus.

## SPUR

The motorcycle ministry is not for wimps or light Christians. Most of the best leaders I met came from backgrounds of ex-cons, enforcers, rapists, drug dealers, addicts, pimps and prostitutes, alcoholics, thieves, and murderers—I have known more than just a couple of every one of these. Bad men and women. Some of these people are still my good friends and brothers in Christ.

I knew one guy, now deceased, who was determined that when he died he was going to hell, find satan, kick his butt, and take his job. His testimony convinced me he would have tried, and I believed him.

This man was a big, ugly, mean-looking biker. He was all of 280 lbs. of solid bulging rock. After beating a man to death in a bar, he spent six years in prison for second-degree murder. He became an enforcer in an Arizona state prison for the ABs (Aryan Brotherhood). He told us of the wicked things he did to strip away the few things you could take from someone in prison, including their pride, dignity, and self-worth. He made them do unspeakable things at the threat of their life or in fear of more pain. After his time in prison, he was an enforcer for an Arizona biker gang, and he did what he had learned in prison to the gang's enemies. Ultimately, he became so dangerous and out of control that his own club was afraid of him and decided to kill him. During a party night of drunken stupor, those who wanted his life nearly killed him, but he escaped to find refuge in the only place they would not look for him: a church. His story ends with accepting Jesus as Lord. He became a humble servant and leader of a large Baptist church in South Carolina. His motivational speaking brought many people to Jesus. A few years after

I met him, he died of liver cancer, but his testimony will always be in my heart. I'll see him again, I'm sure.

There was this other guy who was indeed a monster. He was intelligent, well-educated, and came from a good family; he thought he was next to become a bigwig in his field. He was a really intense guy. He was powerful and used the law to be an enforcer. He persecuted those who were his club's sworn enemies. He chased them down, smoked them out, arrested them, and watched while they were beaten to death, thrown into prison, tortured, and killed. He was, and he admits he was, an evil man.

In the depth of their wickedness, both these guys I know of or have met came to Christ.

The last guy is written about in the Bible. I'm going to tell you this guy's story. He called himself chief of sinners. Read the story of Saul on the road to Damascus in Acts 9. Then read 1 Timothy 1:12–17, which is Paul's testimony.

The following is a typical sermon from a biker preacher to a biker audience.

Some of you think you're too bad to be saved from sin. You might think that before God, Jesus, or the local church could accept you, you'll have to change first, and you know you can't. You're too bad to change so you can be accepted and loved by decent people. Some of that is right. That's because you can't change on your own. You can't stop the drugs; you can't stop the bad habits; you can't lose your partner or your friends or your job for Christ. You're right! You can't do it, but the power of God's Holy Spirit can.

What's stopping you? If the worst bad men you have ever known can sell out to Christ, give it up, and humble themselves before God, then maybe you're not so tough after all, because they were tough. The light they showed with the love of Jesus was their heart, as bright as a welding torch. Why? Because every one of them knows just exactly what God saved them from—hell. They were close enough to feel the burn. He saved us all from death. The Bible says sin is death, and Jesus washed all my sins away just like He did for those guys, and He can do so for you. Right now. Take that step toward Him. Do you want life? Eternal life in heaven? Or do you choose another day on the highway to hell? We will all bow to Him one day. Me? He knows my name, and I'm going with Him. If He doesn't know your name—well, let me put it to you this way: It's hell without Jesus. Choose this day whom you will serve. We are here to lead you to Him, but you must step up. Listen to your heart. Let God call you home.

## PRAYER

God and Father, I ask You to stir the hearts of the pastors and preachers who read this Spur to use it. Inspire them and prick their hearts for the lost. Show them a side of people who feel too deep in sin to accept You as Lord. Show them to reach out to the vilest and wicked of those souls who need Your saving grace to change their lives. I ask this in the precious name of Jesus. Amen.

## CREDITS AND/OR INSPIRATION

Motorcycle ministry experience and Acts 9.

# Rock Bottom

**CONCEPTS**

Jesus is the cornerstone of our faith and hope. He is the Rock on which we stand.

**PURPOSE**

This Spur provides an opportunity to preach or teach the gospel on a subject people are familiar with and can identify with philosophically and spiritually. People want to know they have a firm foundation. Only Jesus Christ can provide that faith and ultimate eternal reward.

**SCRIPTURE BASE**

1 Corinthians 3:8–15, Mathew 7:24–27

**BACKGROUND**

The verses in 1 Corinthians outlined in this Spur have convicted many pastors, writers, and theologians. Yet we are all subject to Paul's words as His laboring few. We all need to be conscious that only God supplies and sustains us in everything and that it is His foundation in Jesus we build upon. Anything else is sinking sand.

**SPUR**

In 1 Corinthians 3:8–9, we read, *Now he that planteth and he that watereth are one: but each shall receive his own reward according to his own labor. For we are God's fellow-workers: ye are God's husbandry, God's building.*

To paraphrase, while reading further, the essence is that since Jesus Christ dwells in us, we are God's building, and He is our foundation. Our lives are like buildings, and our foundation is vital to the strength of our structure. Reading further in the passage, we see that building upon what God has given us is up to us, and we must be careful what we do. Whatever we do, make, or say that is attributed to us will eventually be tested to stand compared to the truth and righteousness of God's foundation in Jesus. If what we do is wrong or unworthy, it will fail and fall short of His will.

Mathew 7:24–27

> *Every one therefore that heareth these words of mine, and doeth them, shall be likened unto a wise man, who built his house upon the rock: and the rain descended, and the floods came, and the winds blew, and beat upon that house; and it fell not: for it was founded upon the rock. And every one that heareth these words of mine, and doeth them not, shall be likened unto a foolish man, who built his house upon the sand: and the rain descended, and the floods came, and the winds blew, and smote upon that house; and it fell: and great was the fall thereof.*

In this story, Jesus tells us of two men who built houses. One man built his house on stone, and after a storm came, one of the houses still stood firm. Why? Because it was built on a foundation of rock. The second man built his house on the sand, and when a storm came, his house fell. Why? Because although the house may have been strong in structure, it fell because the sandy foundation eroded.

The two Scripture passages have similarities concerning foundations but are different in context. Though they are different in context, they relate to the same thing. The strength of our roots in Christ is vital in times of life's storms. Take time to look at your foundation. Is it as strong as it should be? Ask God for the wisdom to strengthen your foundation through faith in Christ Jesus. Whatever you do, whatever you build upon, if your foundation is Jesus, you will know it is the rock of Jesus you stand on when you are tested or hit rock bottom. He is the rock and will support you; you will see a difference in your life!

Ask, what are you standing on?

## PRAYER

Lord God, give us wisdom and understanding. Lead us and inspire us to do Your will. We know if You are not behind us supporting us with Your divine approval, we have nothing, make nothing, and do nothing worthy. We ask You, Lord, to bless our endeavors as we want only to glorify You. Amen.

## CREDITS AND/OR INSPIRATION

It is usually when you hit the bottom that you become thankful that the Rock of salvation is as far as you'll go. From there everything is up. I feel as though I have been standing only on the Rock several times in my life. Praise God, He is faithful.

# Don't Fool Yourself

**CONCEPTS**

Our constant mental battle is waged between what we fool ourselves into thinking is right and what God says is right in His Word. Compromise and rationalizations are satan's tools.

**PURPOSE**

The Spur reminds Christians of the existing spiritual battle and how to overcome satan's whispers in our ears.

**BACKGROUND**

To be called a fool is one of the worst insults a Hebrew can launch upon another. Do not be insulted; do not allow anyone to call you a fool, but better than that, don't be one. Live in Christ and allow His Spirit to live in you. The foolish life will fade away.

**SCRIPTURE BASE**

Ephesians 5:17, Proverbs 12:15, Proverbs 19:20, Proverbs 3:5–6

**SPUR**

Ephesians 5:1–20 is one of Paul's teachings on living as a Christian—holy, set apart—Kingdom living as best we can on earth. He begins by saying that we need to try to live in God's image because we are children of God. We are to be like Christ, loving and giving our lives in service as Jesus did.

Paul continues with what we shouldn't be or do because we are Christians. The list is long and undistinguished as immoral and decadent. Instead, we should always be thankful to God, for we are assured that we will have no share in God's Kingdom if we live a deceitful and evil life.

We must guard ourselves against those who confuse or deceive us with foolish talk. Instead, we should focus on the light of Jesus and remove ourselves from the darkness of the world around us. We are to shine separated from the dark because we have the light of God within us.

Paul admonishes us to be careful how we live—to be wise and not ignorant, making good use of our opportunities to shine, for these are evil days.

When I read these words of Paul, I sometimes become amazed at how well his words fit our condition today. So, all of this is relevant for that place and time for the Ephesians and us in our place and time. That is why it is so important to listen and understand what he is saying in the context of then and now.

For me, the kicker verse of all that Paul wrote climaxes with verse 17:

*Wherefore be ye not foolish, but understand what the will of the Lord is.*

I remember old cartoons where the character had a little devil on his left shoulder and an angel on his right. Satan would whisper something evil in one ear and the angel something righteous in the other. Way back then, as now, it speaks to the issue in this Spur and how close to reality that battle rages on in our heads.

Proverbs 12:15

*The way of a fool is right in his own eyes; But he that is wise hearkeneth unto counsel.*

We often rationalize our sins by fooling ourselves instead of listening to God's Word. As Christians with the Spirit within us, we know what is wrong but tend to talk ourselves out with rationalization or compromise.

Ephesians 5:17 is Paul's wake-up verse. These words are commanding, as he uses the foulest thing to call someone who might be acting like a fool.

I could write of a thousand ways we try to fool ourselves when faced with issues we either know are undesirable or might hurt us or our loved ones for a season. Health and humility are two that you might be able to identify. Have you ever put off a decision regarding doing something about your health because you wanted to avoid the pain, discomfort, or forced humility to do what you know must be done? Use those stories to invoke the jest of this Spur. Funny (or not), we often put off these choices until it is the only choice we have left. Then, we knock ourselves in the head for doing what we should have done much earlier. That's being a fool.

It is painful and can even become worse when we think we didn't make a decision that we should have made. But the truth is, we did make a decision—we decided not to decide, which is always the wrong decision.

Proverbs 19:20

*Hear counsel, and receive instruction, That thou mayest be wise in thy latter end.*

Think of this wrong decision. That decision you talk yourself out of when the Spirit of God is tugging on your heart to accept Jesus. The decision you talk yourself out of when called to come forward and give your life to Him. The words you say to yourself that you will put this off until later and that you don't have to do it now—you have plenty of time. Maybe you think you're too bad to be saved, and you need to clean up before you accept Jesus; what will your wife think, or your friends, your family, your kids? These are all the things that little devil whispers in your ear.

Proverbs 3:5–6

> *Trust in Jehovah with all thy heart, And lean not upon thine own understanding: In all thy ways acknowledge him, And he will direct thy paths.*

## PRAYER

Lord, God and Father in heaven, I pray before You today to show me my foolishness. I ask You to test me on the decisions I've made in the past that affect my future. Give me wisdom, Lord. Show me where, when, and how I need to repent, turn myself around, and choose a better way: Your way, within Your will. I ask these things in Jesus' holy and mighty name. Amen.

## CREDITS AND/OR INSPIRATION

Andy Stanley. *Better Decisions, Fewer Regrets: 5 Questions to Help You Determine Your Next Move.* Audible Audiobook. Zondervan Reflective. 2020.

# Integrity

**CONCEPTS**

The concept introduced is a comparison between two words, *integrity* and *holy*. To be holy is beyond our human ability to obtain. On the other hand, we can attain integrity, and though it is difficult, we should never give up and stop trying. Undoubtedly, some people do not know Jesus but have a high degree of integrity.

**PURPOSE**

As Christians, we should never stop seeking integrity in our pursuit of holiness. This Spur reminds us of why we can not stop trying.

**SCRIPTURE BASE**

1 Kings 9:4, Psalm 25:21, Psalm 26:1, Psalm 26:11, Psalm 78:72, Proverbs 2:7, Proverbs 11:3, Proverbs 20:7, Proverbs 28:6

**BACKGROUND**

This Spur might be as hard for you to read or speak from as it was for me to write. The level of integrity God calls us to is hard to achieve. Only Jesus met the ultimate criteria for holiness; the rest of us might only get close, but as humans, we will never make it to holiness until we walk the streets of gold in heaven. God calls us to be holy, so we must try to achieve that goal. Having integrity is the path to becoming holy.

## SPUR

One definition of integrity is the steadfast adherence to a strict moral or ethical code (Merriam-Webster.com).

We all consist of three people living three different lives. We have a public life that everyone can see. We have a private life that only our closest friends and family see. and a secret life that only God sees. Having integrity is when the three lives are the same. Being holy has similar attributes. God is holy in Three Persons: Father, Son, and Spirit. All three are inseparably the same. If we strive for integrity, we also become holier, as God is holy. I am convinced that God wants us to be holy, set apart to glorify Him. He said so: *"Be ye holy, for I am holy"* (Leviticus 11:44). Easier said than done. Having the integrity to match our three lives is also easier said than done. We can work on it and aim to lead a life of integrity, but most of us fail, if not daily, too often. We can also become holy—but those paths are different. We need God for us to become holy.

However, the word *integrity* is used to describe the condition of the human heart. Job has several references about how he had a heart of integrity, he was a good man, and his integrity pleased God, but he was not referenced as holy.

The books of Genesis, 1 Kings, Psalms, and Proverbs all refer to the integrity of men and the worth being found in integrity over fame or riches. A man with integrity is upright, trusted, and wise. To be known as a man of integrity is akin to being on the level with a good judge. Indeed, if a judge is without integrity, he is worthless and corrupt.

Read the list of verses in Scripture Base. Each is different, yet each points to a life worthy unto God. Only one life was worthy of

God, and that is Jesus. To know people who have these attributes and do not accept Jesus as Lord perplexes me. They are so close and yet so far. You may have people in your congregation who think that if they are upright and live a life of integrity, they will make it into heaven on those traits alone. It is sad for them, as they will never see those golden streets.

## PRAY

God and Father, I praise You for Your holiness. Point me in Your ways that I might live a life of integrity. I will never be worthy without You. Thank You for Jesus, who, through His sacrifice, made me holy and worthy of being called a priest, a saint, and a child of God. Lord, help me not to offend You when I slip from living righteously. May I always keep my integrity in serving and loving You. Amen.

## CREDITS AND/OR INSPIRATION

In a movie called *Meet Joe Black,* the main character, a rich and powerful man a man full of integrety, asks Death (Joe Black) at the end of the movie, knowing he just died, if he has anything to worry about. Death tells him that a guy like him has nothing to worry about, implying that he'll go to heaven as a good man. What a terrible lie.

Marvin Brest, dir. *Meet Joe Black.* Universal Pictures. 1998.

# Works

## CONCEPTS

There are two main points to emphasize. One is works do not get anyone into heaven. Two, our faith is dead without works.

## PURPOSE

This Stem is to incite believers into action.

## SCRIPTURE BASE

The following listed Scripture verses supports the Stem. Use any or all of them.

James 5:16, 1 John 1:9, 1 Peter 4:8, James 2:17, James 2:26, 1 Corinthians 15:58, 1 Corinthians 3:7–9, Matthew 9:37–38, Luke 10:2, Colossians 1:10, 1 Corinthians 16:14, 2 Corinthians 1:3–4, John 9:4

## BACKGROUND

This Spur combines well with the Stem titled "Compelling Devotion."

## SPUR

Let's get this works issue out of the way. You can't get into heaven by being good, if you don't know. You can't get there by doing good. You can't get there through good works. You cannot buy your way to heaven. Nothing you can perform for the good of yourself or others will earn your way to God. If you have not confessed with your mouth and believed in Jesus as the one and only

Savior, if you don't know that He is the only way, truth, and life; if you have not accepted that gift of grace, then no work or anything else will get you into heaven. That's not what this Spur is about.

I'm not talking to the lost here. I'm talking to those who have accepted Jesus—those who are saved. Guess what? We still sin. We still offend our God. We still need to wash off our feet when walking around in this world. Our flesh still trips us up, and we sometimes do what we don't want to do. We are to continue confessing and repenting from that sin even though Jesus has already forgiven us.

James 5:16 and 1 John 1:9 both speak of our confessions. James 5:16 says to confess to one another and pray for one another that we will be healed. 1 John 1:9 says that if we confess our sins to God, He will keep His promise and do what is right; He will forgive our sins and purify us from all our wrongdoings.

God wants us to live a Kingdom life, seek His face, and love one another. Yes, love covers a multitude of sins, as stated in 1 Peter 4:8. How are we to show our love for one another? How do we show our gratitude for the gift God has given us? How do we show that we have faith in God and praise the name of Jesus? How do we shine our light to let others see our obedience, devotion, and witness that Jesus lives within us? How do we obtain the joy of our salvation? Go to church on Sunday? Go to Sunday school and all the meetings? Is that all that He expects? James 2:17 and 26 say faith without works or actions is dead.

You have the gift of eternal life. What are you going to do with it while you are still here? God is looking for a few good men and women. He needs us to be His army. He wants us to do battle against satan for Him. He needs reapers for His harvest. He has given us the Great Commission. Do you think that you can do any of that without effort? Without sweat? Without toil? Without blood?

Without sacrifice? Without work? Sorry. The laborers are few: 1 Corinthians 15:58, 3:7–9, Matthew 9:37–38, Luke 10:2, Colossians 1:10. So, we can't work our way into heaven. But we can work to get others into heaven, which is the work we are called to do with our salvation. Do all your work in love (1 Corinthians 16:14).

Paul explains with perfect logic that God gives us the preparation we need to help others in their troubles because He has helped us in ours. Therefore, there is no better model of service or faith than to use the comfort God gave us to give to others.

> 2 Corinthians 1:3–4, says, *Blessed be the God and Father of our Lord Jesus Christ, the Father of mercies and God of all comfort; who comforteth us in all our affliction, that we may be able to comfort them that are in any affliction, through the comfort wherewith we ourselves are comforted of God.*

I'm just saying. You didn't hear it from me; God's Holy Word says we must get to work. Not for our own glory. Not for us to brag about our conquests, efforts, the count of converts or success, or to secure our pathway to heaven. Cast your crowns before the altar in heaven. Praise God on earth and give Him the glory because it's ALL about Him. If not for Him, there is no "us" from the beginning to the end. My obedient response to Him is to work. I pray it is yours also. I want to work for His glory and His honor. And I pray my blessings come from serving my God.

John 9:4 says we need to get to work for another good reason. Jesus sent us to get all the work done that we can for a night is coming when no one can do any more work.

## PRAYER

God and Father, I praise Your Holy Name. Your Word tells us that the harvest is large, but the laborers are few. Forgive us for failing to be better workers. Give us strength, inspiration, and more faith to be better workers and do more to build Your Kingdom for Your glory. Amen.

## CREDITS AND/OR INSPIRATION

I have received countless blessings from my Lord and Savior during service hours to Him. I have continuously prayed for more people to join in the efforts.

# Compelling Devotion

## CONCEPTS

We are called to be courageous Christians. Yes, meekness and humility are traits we should aspire to, but forthrightness, faithfulness, righteousness, and bravery as soldiers for Christ are also attributes Christians should manifest in the face of evil. When Christians evangelize and preach the Word to the lost, we fight against the unseen forces of evil, and if we are weak in Spirit or faith, we will lose and be ineffectual. We can never forget that we are the children of God and heirs to the throne with the power of the Holy Spirit so strong as to raise the dead. We must call upon that power to defeat satan and put on the full armor of God as described in Ephesians 6.

## PURPOSE

This Spur is written to call Christians to action. We are to fear for the lost and fight for their salvation.

## SCRIPTURE BASE

Exodus 1:13–14 (NASB 2000), Matthew 27:32, Luke 14:16–23 (NKJV), 2 Corinthians 5:14–15 (NKJV)

## BACKGROUND

My wife and I were asked to chaperone a home missionary trip to the Outer Banks of NC with a youth group from our church. The purpose of the trip was to minister and spread the gospel to vacationers and inhabitants of the area. I was disappointed that the expedition leaders were only interested in going to the beach and prayer-walking through neighborhoods. No one was introduced to the Lord, and the youth group received very little discipleship training in witnessing or evangelizing. I wrote this devotional treatise for the breakfast morning devotion of the last day there. The devotional made the point that we had not done our job.

## SPUR

I like words, and often I like to play with their meanings by finding and using double entendres, or words with double meanings. It helps to build a good vocabulary. I like words, especially God's words.

*Compel* is one of those words you can say about ten times in a row, and it becomes a sound instead of a word. Depending on the version, the Bible uses the word *compel* in only a few places, and the word possibly provides an alternate meaning than our English language emphasizes.

Exodus 1:13 says,

> *The Egyptians used violence to compel the sons of Israel to labor; and they made their lives bitter with hard labor in mortar and bricks and at all kinds of labor in the field, all their labors which they violently had them perform as slaves.* (NASB 2000)

It is kind of funny to hear that—a rather compelling understatement to use the word *compel* to enforce slavery. I do not think it was too funny to the slaves of the Egyptians.

So, what does it mean to compel someone? Let us try it. What would I have to do to compel you to go to church on Sunday? Toned down from what the Egyptians did to make Israelis work, but more urging than just asking someone, don't you think? Let us look at another example.

Matthew 27:32

> *And as they came out, they found a man of Cyrene, Simon by name: him they compelled to go with them, that he might bear his cross.*

Most Christians who grew up in Sunday school know that Simon was not asked nicely to help bear Jesus' crucifixion cross. The centurions did not say, "Golly, mister, do you mind taking this criminal's cross and carrying it up to Golgotha for him?"

Let us look at Luke 14:16–23:

> *Then He said to him, "A certain man gave a great supper and invited many, and sent his servant at supper time to say to those who were invited, "Come, for all things are now ready." But they all with one accord began to make excuses. The first said to him, "I have bought a piece of ground, and I must go and see it. I ask you to have me excused." And another said, "I have bought five yoke of oxen, and I am going to test them. I ask you to have me excused." Still another said, "I have married a wife, and therefore I cannot come." So that servant came and reported these things to his master. Then the master of the house, angry, said to his servant, "Go out quickly into the streets and lanes of the city, and bring in here the poor and the maimed and the lame and the blind." And the servant said, "Master, it is done as you commanded, and still there is room." Then the master said to the servant, "Go out into the highways and hedges, and compel them to come in, that my house may be filled." (NKJV)*

Compare the uses in the Bible and tell me what Jesus has asked us to do.

The parable is Jesus speaking about the intensity with which He wants to bring people into His house, salvation, and peace. This story was quoted in His words. I am talking bold red letters here. His use of the word *compel* is entirely different from the same word we use. How do we compel others? Where do we go to compel them? Do we go out to the highways and byways? Does that mean knocking on doors in friendly neighborhoods? Or is conducting a prayer walk enough? Or does it mean getting out of your comfort zone to witness to strangers boldly? Does it mean going out on the street, grabbing people by the arm, and telling them they must attend church? Whatever it means, I do not think it is the meek and mild Christian way, but neither do I think it is by threat of a whip. It is something else.

Try this one.

2 Corinthians 5:14–15

> *For the love of Christ compels us, because we judge thus: that if One died for all, then all died; and He died for all, that those who live should live no longer for themselves, but for Him who died for them and rose again.* (NKJV)

Does Christ's love compel you to live for Him?

We must think about what compel means and then compel others to meet Christ. Be BOLD for God. Tell others about Jesus. Make it your purpose to find lost and fallen souls and bring them closer to Jesus. Then, lead, follow, or get out of the way to accomplish God's calling.

## PRAYER

Lord, God and Father, my prayer for this Spur is to spur our church to be bolder in our testimony. I pray we hear what You say in approaching the Great Commission You gave us to spread the gospel worldwide. Give us more faith and strength to step up with Your power within us to reach the lost of this world. Amen.

## CREDITS AND/OR INSPIRATION

See the background on this Spur.

# Immortal Combat

## CONCEPTS

As Christians living in this evil world (where we don't belong), our lives are continually in immortal combat with the ruler of this world. We tend to forget that and therefore disarm ourselves. Keeping perpetually vigilant is daunting; we drop our guard and allow satan to attack. Then, we fail to understand that we are under attack, and we need to look to the power of our Savior to overcome.

## PURPOSE

This Spur is written to remind us to stay vigilant, especially when doing good works serving our Lord. Satan hates our success against him, and during those times, when we shine our lights the brightest, he attacks. If we are sedentary and not doing what we were called to do for Jesus, satan will leave us alone because we are no problem for him. In fact, we are right where he wants us. We should be blessed when attacked and thankful that satan works so hard against us. We should take that to mean we are doing what God has called us to do as servants to Him.

## SCRIPTURE BASE

Job 1:10, Ephesians 6:10–18, 1 Peter 5:8–9, Isaiah 65:23

## BACKGROUND

Throughout my life in service to my Lord, Jesus, I realized that it was beyond coincidence that troubles, accidents, and failures occurred in the middle of a Christian gathering or other event glorifying God. After I realized there were no coincidences, I began to give sound warnings to my fellow servants while planning for an event. I fervently asked them to bathe these times in prayer for God's hedge of protection and be ready for war with the unseen spirits that were bound to defeat us or diminish our efforts. Knowing up front that we were going into battle, immortal combat, our successes increased with less counterinsurgency from evil to defeat us. If you are not thinking or praying in advance when planning an event to evangelize or bring glory to God, I suggest you begin now. We are always in immortal combat against the adversary, and he can defeat us when we fail to prepare or forego bathing our plans in prayer.

## SPUR

In the verses above, the stated concept, purpose, and background of this Spur is the Spur. We are in a constant battle against evil, set out to destroy everything we try to accomplish for our Lord. It may sound like a play on the movie title *Mortal Kombat,* but be assured that there is no playing around here. The Spur title of "Immortal Combat" is a fact because whether satan wins or we belong to Jesus, our immortal souls will continue either in hell or heaven.

Get prepared for battle. Pray that God provides a hedge of protection around your works and blesses your efforts.

Job 1:10

*Hast not thou made a hedge about him, and about his house, and about all that he hath, on every side? [T]hou hast blessed the work of his hands, and his substance is increased in the land.*

If you take your concordance and search for the word *hedge*, you will find many verses that use the word to protect or keep the enemy out or keep what needs to be protected. Use it in your prayers to spiritually shield your work serving God.

Preparing is essential before the event, but preparing for battle is also important. If you have not read Ephesians 6:10–18 lately, you might want to consider how to get armed to fight as individuals before going into battle.

Watch for and remove distractions. Calamity is one of the worst things that can happen to you. God uses calamity-like wrath throughout the Old Testament to destroy enemies, punish the wicked, and disrupt the efforts of the unrighteous. But He is not the ruler of calamity; satan is. You can plan, prepare, finance, and gather dozens of friends to help, but if you are working against God's will, He allows satan and calamity to knock you flat. However, if you are working to glorify God, He will protect you from calamity and give you success.

1 Peter 5:8–9

>*Be sober, be watchful: your adversary the devil, as a roaring lion, walketh about, seeking whom he may devour: whom withstand steadfast in your faith, knowing that the same sufferings are accomplished in your brethren who are in the world.*

Isaiah 65:23

>*They shall not labor in vain, nor bring forth for calamity; for they are the seed of the blessed of Jehovah, and their offspring with them.*

Conversely, if you want satan to leave you alone in peace, do nothing. He will leave you alone because you are no longer his problem. You have lost your salt. Go and find some.

## PRAY

Lord, God and Father, I ask for Your favor and countenance upon all I do to glorify You. I know, Lord, if You are not in it, I can do nothing to make it successful. I ask to know and do Your will and receive Your blessing. I'm not asking You to join me; I pray that I join You in what you want that glorifies You. Lord, I ask before I begin that You are in it, alongside me, and I'm not alone. Protect me, Lord. Protect those around us in this work, grant us success, and expand our territories. In Jesus' holy and precious name, I pray. Amen.

## CREDITS AND/OR INSPIRATION

Motorcycle ministries are very prone to satan's attacks. My experience has shown me time after time that satan did not want Jesus to take and save some of the most sinful men and women in America out of the satan's grip had them in. He has many outlaws deep in drug addiction, human trafficking, debauchery, theft, strong-arm coercion, and murder. We would see a blessing when Jesus wiped their sin away and the Spirit changed lives.

# Be the Light

## CONCEPTS

Many people do not have the vision to see the power of God in themselves. They lack confidence in themselves and faith in God who lives within them.

## PURPOSE

Building faith in people begins with showing them the untapped power of God. His Word is a lamp to our feet and the light to our path. Shine on.

## SCRIPTURE BASE

Matthew 5:14, Matthew 5:16, 1 John 1:5–6, Philippians 4:13, Romans 8:28

Read Ephesians 1:18–23. These verses are crucial to understanding the power within each of us to shine His light in this world.

## BACKGROUND

We make our plans, and God's will changes everything about us. I planned to serve Western North Carolina when I was first called to minister at BikerDownLiftedUp.org. I thought God had called me to cover Mission Hospital in Asheville, NC, and the surrounding area of twisty roads and the mass of people from all over the country who ride motorcycles. Our organization was about a year old, and I had given out many business cards. Heaven's Saints Motorcycle Ministry had begun to endorse and talk about us wherever they went.

One night, I got a phone call. This guy was distraught. He asked me if we were the prayer supporters for downed bikers. I said we were, and he said he had a friend who had an accident and needed prayer.

I occasionally get these calls, but this was the first time the caller said he was in Southern California but only visiting there on business. His home was in Florida, and he had received a business card and got our hotline number from the card. So, we were the first support organization he had called.

He said a friend had been riding his motorcycle and run off the road, crashing into a ditch and face-planting into a dirt embankment. The accident had crushed his chest, and he had many internal injuries. He said it happened in Billings, Montana, and his friend was at the Deaconess Hospital. He asked if I could get someone to visit, as his friend was alone and needed prayer and someone to care for him. Unfortunately, he didn't know where to turn because neither he nor his friend had friends who lived there.

With confidence and no hesitation, I said, "Yes." I got his friend's name and said I'd have someone check in on him that night. He thanked me.

I broke down in tears right then. I knew God was telling me that Western North Carolina was not my only turf. My turf was whatever God put on my plate to pick up. You see, God wanted His light to shine.

When this guy called me, he didn't know I was in Western North Carolina. He didn't realize how odd it was that he was from Florida and called me from Southern California to serve his friend in Billings, Montana. He had no idea I was born in the very hospital his friend was in and that I was raised in Billings, Montana.

I called my sister, who still lives there, and asked her to go and meet this man, pray over him, and let him know others were praying for him. She didn't hesitate. That was a God thing, and from then on, I knew God's plans for this ministry were bigger than mine. God confirmed my calling into this ministry again. The light that God had given us to shine was much bigger than my small expectations. I had my light on low beam. But God always has His on the high and heavenly beam.

But what a friend that guy had. His friend couldn't go to Montana himself, but he grabbed a straw—anyone who could go to see his friend and pray over him while he was in the hospital. He had trust and faith. God answered that call, not me.

Friends, isn't it great when you know you have a faithful friend?

## SPUR

Matthew 5:14 says, *Ye are the light of the world. A city set on a hill cannot be hid.* This verse should be written in red ink. It is a quotation of Jesus, saying that we are the world's light. As Christians, we must shine with God's love to glorify Him. If we hide our light under a bushel, God's glory is not seen as He wants it to be seen.

Light is extraordinary energy. Scripture uses light imagery to describe the characteristics of God, Christ, and the Holy Spirit. You can find light references throughout the Bible, and I could give you verse after verse to prove it.

Darkness cannot extinguish the light. More darkness is nothing and cannot stop illumination. Multiple lights provide more illumination and shine even brighter. Darkness cannot multiply like light.

Matthew 5:16 says,

*Even so let your light shine before men; that they may see your good works, and glorify your Father who is in heaven.*

God is glorified when He shines His light through us. The more we gather as Christians, the more God is glorified. Darkness cannot extinguish His power; therefore, we are called to show His light wherever darkness prevails. This analogy is another way the Word of God shows us that God is holy (pure light) and is more significant than any sin (darkness) in this world. His holiness cannot be hidden.

And yet we often hide because of fear to stand out in the darkness. Isn't that denying the power of God? How do we let our light shine if we do not go out into the darkness? How do we extinguish the evil darkness of the world around us if we do not show the glory of God in works that we can and should do?

The German atheist philosopher Nietzsche once said, "I was in darkness, but I took three steps and found myself in paradise. The first step was a good thought, the second, a good word; and the third, a good deed" (AZQuotes). From the lips of an atheist, I couldn't have said it better.

Can we be credible Christians if we do not perform as well as an atheist? But, on the other hand, if we did as well, would we glorify our Lord in the name of God? I think that the answer is yes.

How great is our God? Without question, He is greater than we can imagine. Can you put a limit on what He can do? What are our limits to shine for Him?

These verses are the carrot God gives us in His Word.

Philippians 4:13

*I can do all things in him that strengtheneth me.*

Romans 8:28

> *And we know that to them that love God all things work together for good, even to them that are called according to his purpose.*

These verses are the stick.

1 John 1:5–6

> *And this is the message which we have heard from him and announce unto you, that God is light, and in him is no darkness at all. If we say that we have fellowship with him and walk in the darkness, we lie, and do not the truth.*

It's hard to say much more about that. God's Word speaks quite well and needs no help from me.

## PRAYER

God and Father, Light of the World, I ask You to shine Your light through me today. Let me see through Your eyes where the darkness and shadows lie and where You want to shine through. Let me be not only Your light but also Your hands and feet to work Your will in the lives of others so that they may also see Your light in their paths. Amen.

## CREDITS AND/OR INSPIRATION

AZQuotes. "Friedrich Nietzche Quotes." Accessed March 10, 2022. https://www.azquotes.com/author/10823-Friedrich_Nietzsche.

Felicia Buckner, Lifetime Member of BikerDown-LiftedUp.org.

# Change of Address

## CONCEPTS

Men of the present age have two problems within our churches. Men interpret the messages of meekness and humility as weakness, or they are already too weak to become adequate church and family leaders. God inspires men to be men.

## PURPOSE

This message considers the docile and vulnerable paradigm and shows what God expects of men when they have humility and meekness while standing boldly for Christ in their lives, families, and church. To be under powerful self-control.

## SCRIPTURE BASE

Psalm 56:10–13, 2 Timothy 1:7, Deuteronomy 31:6, Luke 12:4–5, Psalm 34:11, 2 Corinthians 10:1, 2 Corinthians 5:8

## BACKGROUND

"Someday you will read or hear that Billy Graham is dead. Don't you believe a word of it. I shall be more alive than I am now. I will just have changed my address. I will have gone into the presence of God." (Graham qtd. in Lindgren)

## SPUR

Much of present-day Christian rhetoric has evolved around the Beatitudes and the teachings of Jesus about humility, meekness, peacemaking, love, peace, and forgiveness. We know these are good, and our attitudes of thankfulness and gratefulness require us to soften our demeanor and treat others as we want others to treat us. There is nothing wrong with these gentle, peaceful actions and thoughts.

Recently, an article discussed how this constant dialogue and message is not good for the church, especially men, because it denies their desire to lead, be a force of nature, and be known as men of God. The constant communication to become meek and mild falls deafly on male leaders. They specifically do not want to hear it consistently as what a Christian should be. The consequence in many churches is the tuning out of men from sermons and church altogether. Another consequence is the creation of men without salt, conviction, leadership spirits, and vigor to lead Christian lives as ambassadors and witnesses for the glory of God.

Men want to be men. God wants men to be men, Christian men. So, how can you be masculine and manly while being asked to be a Christian wimp?

Look at this verse and the use of words to see what we should be.

2 Timothy 1:7

*For God gave us not a spirit of fearfulness; but of power and love and discipline.*

No fear! Joshua is one of my favorite Old Testament heroes. Here, God tells Joshua what He wants from the very beginning in 1:9:

*Have not I commanded thee? Be strong and of good courage; be not affrighted, neither be thou dismayed: for Jehovah thy God is with thee whithersoever thou goest.*

175

There is a balance, and it is a balance that requires wisdom to manage effectively as a Christian—strength under control. In 2 Corinthians 10:1 Paul says to his church:

> *Now I Paul myself entreat you by the meekness and gentleness of Christ, I who in your presence am lowly among you, but being absent am of good courage toward you.*

The passage sounds like Paul might be living two different lives. When I am with you, I am a nice guy, but I am tough when I am away from you.

Why? Do you ever hear of anyone as bold or as tough as Paul? Yeah, Jesus. Think of all the trials Paul went through to stand as a Christian. Do you need a model tough guy? Paul fits that description. It is Paul who essentially says, "What can mortals do to me? They can only change my address. Because if I am not here in the body, I am with Christ my Lord in heaven."

2 Corinthians 5:8

> *We are of good courage, I say, and are willing rather to be absent from the body, and to be at home with the Lord.*

Jesus tells us who to fear and the only one we need to fear. In Luke 12:4–5, Jesus says:

> *And I say unto you, my friends, Be not afraid of them that kill the body, and after that have no more that they can do. But I will warn you whom ye shall fear: Fear him, who after he hath killed hath power to cast into hell; yea, I say unto you, Fear him.*

What a dichotomy! Fear the one who gives you the courage to fear no one. Trust in Him and understand that the One you fear ensures you need not fear others. He is great and mighty and will not forsake you. Though you might die in this world, you will live with Him forever.

Does it sound like I am recruiting suicide bombers? I am saying, men, be bold and hear God's Word. I am not the one saying it. It is His Word that says this:

Psalm 56:10–13

> *In God (I will praise his word), In Jehovah (I will praise his word), In God have I put my trust, I will not be afraid; What can man do unto me? Thy vows are upon me, O God: I will render thank-offerings unto thee. For thou hast delivered my soul from death: Hast thou not delivered my feet from falling, That I may walk before God In the light of the living?*

That is not a suicide bomber. That is a sound Christian who is walking before God in the light of life. Kingdom living.

So, are you tough? Do you want to be a tough guy? Try being a Christian in this world.

Many of you may not know Alice Cooper. He was a theater rocker in the seventies and considered the godfather of shock rock. He was radical. He wrote and performed many controversial and rebellious songs that the youth of that era admired. Alice Cooper said, "Drinking beer is easy. Trashing your hotel is easy. But being a Christian, that's *a tough call*. That's real rebellion" (QuotesGram). He turned his life and his addictions around with the power of the Holy Spirit and Christ. Do you think it might have been tough for him to stand up and be counted and held accountable as a Christian? Can you?

Not tough enough? What have you got to lose? What have you to gain? Weigh it. Get tough. Fear nothing. Trust God.

## PRAYER

Lord and Father, I pray that this message instills that You alone are to be feared. Our meekness and humility pour out before a mighty God who holds sway over our lives. You ask us to boldly approach Your throne of grace with our petitions and go out into the world to witness and spread the Good News of the same grace that saved us. Men need to lead our families and church through Your Word, instruction, discipline, and wisdom without fear in the face of a world and powers that would like the opposite. Teach us, Lord, how to courageously become mighty men of God. Amen.

## CREDITS AND/OR INSPIRATION

Life as a Christian biker.

Calebe Lindgren. "Someday You Will Read or Hear That Billy Graham Didn't Really Say That." ChristianityToday. February 21, 2018. https://www.christianitytoday.com/ct/2018/february-web-only/billy-graham-viral-quote-on-death-not-his-d-l-moody.html.

QuotesGram. "Alice Cooper Christian Quotes." Accessed April 30, 2025. https://quotesgram.com/img/alice-cooper-christian-quotes/10003262/.

# Control Yourself

## CONCEPTS

The hymn lyrics of "Blessed Assurance, Jesus Is Mine" sound conceptually lovely, but the fact is, many people don't feel it, don't know it, and don't use the power God gave them through His Spirit. That power allows us to lean on Jesus and His Word to overcome temptation as He did.

## PURPOSE

Much of this Spur is written in first person; use the parts you relate to concerning our salvation and the power within us to defeat satan's wiles and fiery darts. We give up too quickly, and we allow satan too much sway. We must remember that the final battle has been won, and Jesus is our Victor. Live it, preach it.

## SCRIPTURE BASE

Romans 8:38–39, Matthew 5:28, Matthew 13:3–9, Philippians 4:13

## BACKGROUND

Like Paul, I have battled with doing what I don't want and not doing what I want to do. I don't think I'm the only one, but I have, through the grace of God, fought toe-to-toe with satan over my sin, and not that I have won every time, but I have won enough to know when to start fighting. I start in my head when those evil thoughts begin to form. God's Word and the Spirit are my weapons, suitable for us all.

# SPUR

Many Sundays after the altar call, we have seen that everyone there must be saved. If that is true, that's good. We are in good company. Let's assume for a moment that we are all saved. If we don't know everyone, we have eternity to compensate for it. When does our eternity start? Our lives with Jesus are eternal right now. Have you ever thought about that?

Why don't we always act like we are saved by Christ? Christ saves us from sin by His grace, cleansed by His blood, right? We should be living a Kingdom life. I mean, you can't kill a Christian— did you know that? We will never die! This earthly body will go to a grave, to dust, but I will live eternally. So, all you can do to me on this earth is change my address.

What do I have to fear being a Christian? I don't have to be tough enough. I have Christ; he's tough enough. I'm His heir, and He's my Father. Whom shall I fear? I wasn't saved to be silent. But I know a few things not everyone is going to tell you.

First off, I'm possessed. Romans 8:38–39 says so:

> *For I am persuaded, that neither death, nor life, nor angels, nor principalities, nor things present, nor things to come, nor powers, nor height, nor depth, nor any other creature, shall be able to separate us from the love of God, which is in Christ Jesus our Lord.*

Many places in the Bible assure me of my salvation, but that's my favorite. The Holy Spirit has me, and nothing can separate me from His love and His hold on me. NOTHING. NOTHING. Not even me.

Secondly, even though I'm saved and possessed by God, I still sin. I do! I admit it. Like Paul, I hate it when I do that, but it still happens when I'm weak, and I ask God to forgive me and help me not to sin anymore. I found a way to help me not sin. And it works.

As Jesus spoke in Galilee:

Matthew 5:28

> *But I say unto you, that every one that looketh on a woman to lust after her hath committed adultery with her already in his heart.*

I firmly believe that if you think about doing sin, like adultery, the Lord knows your heart, and He can see what you're thinking, and you have already sinned. My reaction to hearing that the first time was, "That is not fair! I just thought about it. I didn't do it. I just had a little fantasy, and hey, no harm, no foul, I didn't do nothing." So, follow me down this rabbit trail for a minute.

It's all in your head. If you've been a Christian for a while, you've heard the parable of Jesus when He talked about scattering seeds on fertile ground. Preachers, teachers, and evangelists all love that parable. So read it from Matthew 13:3–9:

> *And he spake to them many things in parables, saying, Behold, the sower went forth to sow; and as he sowed, some seeds fell by the way side, and the birds came and devoured them: and others fell upon the rocky places, where they had not much earth: and straightway they sprang up, because they had no deepness of earth: and when the sun was risen, they were scorched; and because they had no root, they withered away. And others fell upon the thorns; and the thorns grew up and choked them: and others fell upon the good*

*ground, and yielded fruit, some a hundredfold, some sixty, some thirty. He that hath ears, let him hear.*

Consider how the devil works just like that too.

Please note that this is written to make a point and not to be heretical. Allow me to rewrite those verses about satan:

Satan's 13:3–9: Behold, satan went forth to sow seeds of evil; and as he sowed, some seeds fell by the wayside, and the Lord's angels came and devoured them: and others fell upon places, where Jesus was the Rock and Foundation: and straightway they dissipated when the Son arose, and they were scorched because they had no root, they withered away. And others fell upon the church, and God's righteous Word grew up and choked them: and others fell upon the wicked, fertile soil in thoughtless minds, and yielded fruit, some a hundred-fold, some sixty, some thirty. He that hath ears let him hear.

If you give thought to evil and sin in that dark, dirty place you call your mind, that's where satan finds fertile soil to provide action in making you sin. That's right. Who do you think sows those seeds? Satan sows his seed through dirty movies, hate, revenge, murder, TV, porn, the internet, and some advertising all come through your eyes and ears! So be careful, little eyes, what you see.

There you are alone in your head, and you're thinking something sinful like you must do this, you hate that, somebody wronged you, and you want revenge, she's hot and needs me, I must have this or that, I'm addicted and need that. The list continues. Since satan has tempted people for thousands of years, he's pretty good at it. He doesn't have the power to put those thoughts in your head. He only ensures you are exposed to those things so you can think about them. What grows from there is on you.

182

That's where you must fight, right there in your head. Nothing has happened yet. Think. Pray to God right then. Ask Him to get those junky thoughts out of your head. "Help me, Lord, I don't want to think like that anymore."

Stop it! Be a quitter! Ask for help. Don't let those thoughts make you do it. Wash them out with the power Jesus gave you over sin.

Nip them in the bud right in your head. Read some Scripture. Think good thoughts. Good things. If no one ever knows what you thought because you never let it get out of your head and didn't act on it, the sin stays between you and Jesus. He already knows what you're thinking anyway; just don't let those thoughts control you and your actions, because actions of sin lead to consequences and lies.

I'm not saying it is easy. You can't do it alone. I can't do it by myself either. But with God, we can!

Philippians 4:13

*I can do all things in him that strengtheneth me.*

This application is an excellent way to use this verse. Remember it. Try it. The Spirit of God will remind you while you're thinking about it, you get in the habit of praying about it, and God will be faithful to help you through it. Try. Get closer to God, and He will get closer to you.

He can only do that if He's in you and possesses you. Is He in you? Have you allowed or asked the Spirit of God to possess you? Only you can know that. If you are not sure, He's there to help. Let somebody show you how you can be confident and know that you know God's Spirit is there for you. Have no doubt. And you will have "blessed assurance, Jesus is mine."

I once had a friend who partnered with me at work. We spent years working together, teaching teachers about technology. At first, she didn't know much about technology, but I did. I knew some about teachers, but she knew more. Sometimes, we didn't agree on how to proceed on one subject or another. We were both very stubborn, but I learned something about her that cut our conversations short. I would look at her and ask, "Do you know what you know?" Or, in the middle of the discussion, she'd cut us both short and say, "I know what I know." When she said that, I learned she knew and was sure of her position without a doubt. She was never wrong when she said that. Somewhere in her mind, she KNEW the truth. Have you ever felt that strongly about something? I do. I learned from her that you know the truth when you know a fact. You can't be wrong. You can stand up and get in the face of satan. That's the strength of faith, knowing God's Word.

It has its assurance. Peace comes over you, knowing that you know. You have no doubt. Do you know where you are going after you die? You're going somewhere. The Bible says there are only two places where you will spend eternity. Let me give you a clue as to what I'm writing: It's hell without Jesus! If you don't know what you know, don't know the truth, or don't have God's peace and assurance, you better get right with Him today. Know that you know.

## PRAYER

Jesus, Lord, and God of all, thank You for Your Spirit that dwells within me. Thank You for pecking at my heart when I think sinful thoughts. Thank You for being so powerful in helping me overcome my weaknesses. Most of all, God, thank You for Your saving grace and forgiveness when I fail and offend You. You are my hope and assurance that pulls me out of my pits of failure. Thank You, Lord, for being my God and for loving me. Amen.

## CREDITS AND/OR INSPIRATION

Knowing what I know. No doubts. "No doubt" was a biker church slogan that prevailed to become an inspiration to an entire community of believers and their ultimate revival.

# Discipline

## CONCEPTS

Scripture can be challenging to read yet easy to understand—especially the discipline the Lord gives His people. The formula is simple. If we expect heavenly rewards after we leave this old world, we need to expect discipline as a consequence of our actions while we are here. Without accepting the sacrifice of Jesus for our sins, it will be hell as retribution.

## PURPOSE

God is a disciplinarian. There is no denying it. He hasn't changed, and He never will. He is demanding, fair, and, best of all, He loves us. He is the perfect Father. His discipline is perfect.

## SCRIPTURE BASE

Hebrews 12:8, Matthew 10:28

## BACKGROUND

People I witness to and talk with have a problem understanding how God can be so severe in the Old Testament and so loving in the New Testament. Understanding that He is the same God and hasn't changed is difficult for nonbelievers and the faithful. Reading God's Word tells it all. The Spirit leads believers to have faith and understand what it means to fear God and love God. He's the best Father I have ever had, and I know what He has done for me. His discipline guides us to righteousness.

## SPUR

To paraphrase Hebrews 12:8, if you are not disciplined, like everyone else, you are illegitimate children and not sons. These are harsh words to consider, but the essence is there. God wants you to expect to be chastised if you call yourself His heir.

I have said before how much I enjoy studying the meaning of words. Of course, I enjoy researching God's Word specifically, but I appreciate other words too. Words often carry such meaning for me that the research becomes fascinating—learning the mystery behind the meanings, how they might have developed, and how they are used now. The study of words is called etymology.

Etymology sounds like the study of bugs or something else, but it comes from the Greek stem, which means "true sense." *Ology* is an extension, meaning "the study of," so, in short, the word *etymology* means "the study of the true sense," or finding the real meanings of the words we use.

Discipline is a word like that for me. You can take almost any word and dissect its parts to find the truth of where the word came from, which interests me.

The word we are getting into today is essential to our vocabulary and has been around for a long time. In all that time, till now, the term was modified, repurposed, and misused, and in some cases, it was given an entirely different meaning.

Think about it for a second. How many uses can you think of for the word *discipline*? Let me try.

- I am a student, and my discipline of study is education.

- I took that child of mine and gave him some discipline on his bottom.
- If you can't discipline yourself, return to your desk.
- The teacher maintained strict discipline in using grammar.
- He disciplined his body every day, enabling him to run faster.

The word can is used as a verb for action or a noun as something. The original use was quite severe. To discipline meant to punish as a means of instruction. People would discipline themselves when they sinned to punish themselves for being weak and succumbing to temptation or evil. The word was always used to educate, teach, or give knowledge.

Discipline often comes in the form of pain. No pain, no gain. Face it; the truth is that pain is a great instructor. How long did it take you before you knew what *hot* meant or what hot did to your fingers? Some people take a long time to learn what causes pain and how to avoid it. Some people enjoy the pain and never quite understand what burns their fingers repeatedly. Of course, I'm speaking allegorically. Some people never learn what is hurting them.

Discipline has been diminished in our society over the past four decades because child psychologists think discipline is linked to punishment, and using punishment is not how we want to instruct our children in the 21st century. But I'm afraid I can't agree wholeheartedly, and the concept is anti-biblical.

God made us; He knows us better than we know ourselves. The wisdom of God far outweighs the fantasies of those who think you can raise a child to respect their parents and, ultimately, the authority of God without the knowledge of punishment and the results of one's actions. Regardless, if parents and teachers do not teach using a form of consequence or punishment, it is most certainly taught by life. If you do such and such, it is going to hurt. Taking discipline and punishment out of our schools has not improved our education system. Instead, it has weakened our society with wanton disrespect and willful anarchy.

Talk to anyone about how they achieved greatness or talk to people who have worked or been in several jobs during their career, where many people participated in accomplishing the goals of an organization. A trucking company or a military unit would fit that criterion. There isn't enough time to discuss why discipline works; it does. If you have ever worked in an organization described above, you know that when the boss was strict and fair, he may not have been well-liked. Still, people liked the job and enjoyed working in an environment where they knew what was expected and everyone did what they were supposed to do. Morale is high, and teamwork is expected and essential. This workplace is nourishing and happy.

Take the same working environment and change the boss to one who plays favorites, imparts no discipline and standards, expects very little, and cuts every corner to get through the day. The workers in that place become unmotivated, unhappy, challenging to work with, indifferent, and lacking in morale. That workplace becomes a caustic working environment.

What if our God asked for no respect or fear? What if there were no consequences for our sinful lives? What if there was no heaven or hell, no punishment of death for sin? We wouldn't need Jesus or God. There would be no law, rules, or justice, only anarchy. There would be nothing that separates us from animals.

God demands discipline, requires consequences, and is not wishy-washy about it. He gave the law to Moses verbatim. God punished His chosen people and disciplined them for forty years until they became the people He wanted. He was tough, but He was also fair. He gave His Son, who died on the cross, to pay for the entire world's sins because of His love for us.

Consequently, somebody must pay. We will all be judged for our actions on earth. Thank God, right now, for giving us a Savior who took the punishment for our sins. We are paid in full.

Matthew 10:28

*And be not afraid of them that kill the body, but are not able to kill the soul: but rather fear him who can destroy both soul and body in hell.*

If you don't know the world's Savior and fear you will be punished for your sins, I can tell you what you must do today: Get right with God, and call upon the Lord Jesus.

## PRAYER

Dear Lord, God and Father, what a mighty God You are. Thank You for choosing me to be Your heir; thank You for Your discipline that reminds me of Your love for me. Thank You for Jesus, who paid it all on Calvary as atonement for me and all the world. Remind those who hear Your Word in Hebrews 12:8 how You show Your love to us as heirs and children of God. Amen.

## CREDITS AND/OR INSPIRATION

Admittedly, few people enjoy being reprimanded for their digressions from God's law. If it were not for those reprimands from God, then when we find ourselves as low as our consequences take us, there is no repentance and no desire to seek Him. I need God, and you need God.

# Friends

## CONCEPTS

The friendship Jesus offers those who believe in Him is often overlooked as something special. Today's friendships are minimized as trivial and non-permanent.

## PURPOSE

Our friend Jesus is not trivial. His friendship is paramount; people need to hear what a real friend means.

## SCRIPTURE BASE

Isaiah 41:8, 2 Chronicles 20:7, James 2:23, Genesis 2:18, John 15:13, John 15:14, Proverbs 18:24, Hebrews 13:5

## BACKGROUND

Social media and personal friendships are often meaningless or easily discarded and wasted. Jesus' friendship is not that way, and our Bible tells us His friendship is much greater than many know or, for some, remember.

## SPUR

Friends, isn't it great knowing you have a faithful friend? If you are fortunate, you have known someone you knew was a friend.

Do you realize the next generation of youth is taking over? They are the next working generation about to become America's significant wage earners. The new leaders. They are Generation Y, born between 1981 and 1996. (I have two children born in this era.)

I am happy they do not fit this description of their generation, but the statistics about this group are disturbing (Study.com).

Though not all people who fall into this identified group are the same in all respects, many have enough similar traits to be identifiable. For example, Gen Y people have been identified as being independent but capable of working and enjoying teamwork. Most are technically literate and use media technology fluently.

A significant minority of Gen Y people are lonely and lost. While they have the most "friends" of any generation, they also have an increasing sense of loneliness. How can that be? Social theorists think social media has much to do with it by redefining a friend. You can read too much about this, but it is vital to our lives and future.

I use Facebook. I used to use it a lot. I had many so-called Friends, but I can tell you that I have never met many of them. However, I have often run into some of them at events at churches I visit or at events I attend, and when I recognize the name of someone, I say, "Wow, I know you from Facebook. Nice to meet you." Or people come up to me and say, "Are you that guy on Facebook with BikerDown?"

How many people did you call friends that you had never met before social media? Maybe a pen pal. Oh! A pen pal—does anyone remember those? There is no substitute for authentic face-to-face friends.

I can cast off a Facebook friend and Unfriend somebody in a heartbeat. That does not bother me in the least bit. I do not know them, and I will probably never meet them. Just tick me off, say something bad, or disagree sharply about something I feel strongly about, and that Friend gets Unfollowed or Snoozed, at least for thirty days. I sometimes ask people to Unfriend me. I do not compromise on many things; most Facebook trolls are unnecessary.

But you do not do that to an actual face-to-face friend. I have had many sleepless nights when I have broken up with a real friend for one reason or another. Sometimes, I search for old friends I have lost contact with. I have searched online with those Search programs for high school and military buddies I long to see or talk to again. It is always a good day to renew an old friendship or talk to or meet up with a friend you have not seen in years.

Real friends are treasures—jewels you cannot throw away with such disregard as the one you might kick to the curb on Facebook.

Friends are partners. Partners are people you work with, struggle with, walk the same path with, and believe in the same mission with.

God had someone He called a friend. Look up and read Isaiah 41:8, 2 Chronicles 20:7, and James 2:23. God called Abraham a friend, and the partners they became make up much of the world today. Like Himself, God has always intended for us to have friends. Genesis 2:18 says,

> *And Jehovah God said, It is not good that the man should be alone; I will make him a helpmate for him.*

So, the first friendship other than Adam and God was between Adam and Eve.

The Bible gives us numerous examples of friends and partners. Let me name a few in history.

- Moses and Aaron. Brothers, yet partners who changed the world and, with God, created a nation that has affected human history, current history, and the future to come.

- In 1 Samuel, David and Jonathan became friends. Jonathan, the king's son, loved David so much that he saved his life despite the orders of Saul, his father, the king.

- In Matthew 10, Jesus sent His disciples out into the world in twos for a reason. You need a partner; you need a friend. The Bible even gives us a splendid example of friends who sharply disagreed, broke up, chose new partners, and later became friends again because of their love and example—Paul and Barnabas.

- In Acts 8, we read about Peter and John. They performed remarkable miracles. Later in Acts, we read about Paul and Barnabas, Barnabas and Silas, Judas and Silas, Barnabas and Mark, Paul and Silas, Paul and Timothy, and more.

- Partnerships. Jesus' endorsement of marriage is an example of collaboration and friendship. Your spouse should be your second-most crucial partner and friend. Unhappy is the married couple who are not friends.

Anyone here without a friend? Sometimes, we feel that way when we get depressed or when nothing seems to be going right.

Friendships are essential in our lives. God gave His Son so we could have a friendship, love, and relationship with Him. God created us to be friends with Him. From the Garden of Eden, when Adam and Eve walked and talked with God throughout history, God made His people, shaped them, and molded them to be His. He wanted their worship, and in return, He blessed their land and people.

We are to love our God. And when we love, we love with our human ability to love. God loves us but loves us with His godly love that we cannot match. What a friend we have in Jesus. He loves us. Let me remind you of His love for us lest we forget:

John 15:13

> *Greater love hath no man than this, that a man lay down his life for his friends. Ye are my friends, if ye do the things which I command you.*

Proverbs 18:24

> *He that maketh many friends doeth it to his own destruction; But there is a friend that sticketh closer than a brother.*

Who do you suppose that is? What kind of friend sticks closer than a brother? What kind of friend would die for you? What kind of friend would never leave you or forsake you? With a kind of love only God could give, within a power that only God has. Jesus is love.

Hebrews 13:5

> *Be ye free from the love of money; content with such things as ye have: for himself hath said, I will in no wise fail thee, neither will I in any wise forsake thee.*

Do you have a good friend? Do you have a friend so close that you would give your life for them? Do you have a friend so close they would give their life for you? It is hard to say what you will do once you must run into a house on fire or a car ready to explode to save the life of a friend.

I have a friend who has already died for me. And He has died for you. Not only did He give us His life that we might become His friends, but He endured torture no other person has ever endured. I am not talking about His beating. I am not talking about the fact that He was hung on a cross and nailed through His hands and feet. Others throughout history may have been tortured to death harder than that.

But I am talking about the fact that Jesus bore and endured the sins of all humanity. And it killed Him. Yes, Jesus endured all your sins and the sins of all humanity to be your friend. Could you ask for a better friend than that? All the rotten things you and I have done? He has paid for them all.

Then, miraculously, He did something more. He raised Himself from the dead. He defeated death to show us He is God. After He was crucified and died, laid in a tomb, sealed with a stone, He showed himself alive to His friends. And He promised His Spirit to save us and that He will return to take us with Him so one day we can be with Him, His friend for eternity.

Do you know Jesus as your personal friend? Do you know Him as your God, Father, Friend, or do you Friend Him on Sundays and Unfriend or Snooze Him the rest of the week?

If you don't know Him and need a friend, ask Him to Friend you today. Ask Him to touch your heart, move your feet, and accept His friendship today. Ask Him to forgive you the sins He paid for. He holds your debt, and as a friend, He will toss that debt away, and all He wants from you is to be His friend.

You see, once He Friends you, it is eternal, permanent friendship. He will never leave you or forsake you. That's His godly promise. You might fail to be His friend daily, but He will never Unfriend you. For He is good, and He loves with a love only God can love with, for God is love. He is all the love and friendship you will ever need.

## PRAYER

Lord Jesus, Father and friend, thank You for Your love for me. Thank You for asking me to be Your personal friend, closer than a brother. Thank You for not being a wishy-washy kind of friend who will leave me when I misbehave, but one that forgives me when I'm wrong. Thank You, Lord, for Your promises and Word that tell me how deeply You love me and that You will never leave me. Lord, draw me nearer each day into a deeper relationship with my best friend. Amen.

## CREDITS AND/OR INSPIRATION.

After singing "What a Friend We Have in Jesus" in church one Sunday, I began thinking about my so-called Friends on Facebook and thanking God for the remarkable differences.

Scriven, Joseph M. "What a Friend We Have in Jesus." Hymnal.net. Accessed April 30, 2025. https://www.hymnal.net/en/hymn/h/789.

Study.com. "Generation Y: Definitions and Characteristics." Accessed April 30, 2025. https://study.com/learn/lesson/generation-y-characteristics-personality.html.

# What's an Hour?

**CONCEPTS**

A good Bible concordance has several references to the word *hour* in Scripture. We need to notice what an hour is and how it is used in God's Word.

**PURPOSE**

Relativity is how a word, a meaning, or a message affects us or someone else in a meaningful way. It has little meaning or impact on our lives if it is not relative. Applying the relationships between the relative significance and our lives helps us understand the importance of the word or message. The word *hour* in Scripture has intense and relative meaning to us, and that relativity is the message.

**SCRIPTURE BASE**

Mark 14:27, Mark 14:41, John 12:27, John 12:23, John 17:1, Matthew 27:45–46, 1 Corinthians 15:30, Matthew 6:27, Matthew 25:13, Matthew 24:44, 1 John 2:18, Luke 12:11–12, Revelation 3:10

**BACKGROUND**

There are twenty-four hours each day, many of which sift through our hands like sand with no meaning or memorable impact. Then there are those hours of importance that make our memories and change our lives. We all have hours we wish we had never spent or hours we want to have back to live again. The Bible shows us hours that changed the world and more to come.

# SPUR

Can you talk for an hour? Can you stand for an hour? How long is an hour?

Ever spend a long hour? Let me list a few long hours: an hour in a dentist's chair, an hour in an emergency room while you are overcome with pain or fear, an hour waiting for word about someone you love after an accident, an hour driving in traffic, an hour waiting in an airport terminal, an hour in an MRI examination, an hour in hard labor delivering a child. How about an hour-long prayer meeting? The sleepless hour before sunrise. The hour you can't decide.

Compare those with a short hour: an hour watching your favorite sport, an hour visiting with a loved one you miss, an hour on social media, an hour taking a nap, an hour out to eat, an hour touring on your motorcycle. How about that hour before you go to work or school or have lunch? The hour you must decide.

Time is relative, and few people understand what that means. An hour is not any longer or shorter than sixty minutes, but in relation to specific events, those minutes and that hour seem long or short; therefore, time is relative to what is happening in our lives during that notable hour.

I once watched an action-packed show supposedly recorded in real-time for one hour weekly. It was called *24*. It was intense to share the same time with someone going through such traumatic and dramatic events. Every second was recorded as the show star was pulled from pillar to post for an entire hour. It was a fast hour-long show that kept everyone on the edge of their seat, often challenging them to keep their eyes open, yet they didn't dare miss a minute. Honestly, it wore me out.

Jesus took three disciples—Peter, James, and John—to the Mount of Olives. There, Jesus asked His disciples to pray while He went to pray by Himself. But they couldn't stay awake.

Mark 14:27

*And he cometh, and findeth them sleeping, and saith unto Peter, Simon, sleepest thou? couldest thou not watch one hour?*

Mark 14:41

*And he cometh the third time, and saith unto them, Sleep on now, and take your rest: it is enough; the hour is come; behold, the Son of man is betrayed into the hands of sinners.*

Why didn't they know the urgency of that hour? Jesus told them what was about to happen more than once, yet they couldn't pray with Him for an hour. So it was a long hour for them and a short hour for Jesus.

John 12:27

*Now is my soul troubled; and what shall I say? Father, save me from this hour. But for this cause came I unto this hour.*

John 12:23

*And Jesus answereth them, saying, The hour is come, that the Son of man should be glorified.*

John 17:1

*These things spake Jesus; and lifting his eyes to heaven, he said, Father, the hour is come; glorify thy Son, that the Son may glorify thee.*

Matthew 27:45–46

*Now from the sixth hour there was darkness over all the land until the ninth hour. And about the ninth hour Jesus cried with a loud voice, saying, Eli, Eli, lama sabachthani? that is, My God, my God, why hast thou forsaken me?*

Jesus had many hours that our Bible describes as both beautiful and horrendous. Hours of happiness and hours of stress, sorrow, and pain. Jesus also told us of hours we needed to look forward to that are yet to come. They may not seem relevant to us right now, but they will likely be the most critical hours in our lives.

1 Corinthians 15:30

*Why do we also stand in jeopardy every hour?*

Matthew 6:27

*And which of you by being anxious can add one cubit unto the measure of his life?*

Speaking of our lives, I'm sure everyone knows no one is leaving this place alive. But, of course, I'm talking about this vehicle that turns around the sun called Earth. If the Rapture doesn't take us and transform us on the way home, we will all experience the next level.

Matthew 25:13

*Watch therefore, for ye know not the day nor the hour.*

Matthew 24:44

> *Therefore be ye also ready; for in an hour that ye think not the Son of man cometh.*

Concerning the Rapture, Jesus tells us there is an hour in which He is coming, but we won't know when it is. He also tells us that we might be tested for an hour before the Rapture.

1 John 2:18

> *Little children, it is the last hour: and as ye heard that antichrist cometh, even now have there arisen many anti-christs; whereby we know that it is the last hour.*

Luke 12:11–12

> *And when they bring you before the synagogues, and the rulers, and the authorities, be not anxious how or what ye shall answer, or what ye shall say: for the Holy Spirit shall teach you in that very hour what ye ought to say.*

Revelation 3:10

> *Because thou didst keep the word of my patience, I also will keep thee from the hour of trial, which is to come upon the whole world, to try them that dwell upon the earth. He will save us from our last hour.*

What are your life's most important, significant, and relative hours? The hour of your death? The hour of your hardest tribulation? How about the hour you decided to accept Jesus as your Savior?

You don't know when those other hours will come, but you can control this. You can choose to make this hour the most critical one in your life and make it relative to the rest of your life and all eternity. So, pick this hour and decide your eternity. Choose Jesus this hour.

## PRAYER

Lord God, thank You for choosing me in the hour of my need to confess, repent, and accept Your grace. You, Lord, are our only hope, our only salvation, when You will be faithful to defend us in our hour of judgment. You have already spent Your hour for us. Thank You for Your immutable sacrifice for my sins. I praise You, Lord, for saving me. I ask that this message be used to bring glory to Your name as others in this hour of choice accept Your grace and make You relative as Lord and Savior in their lives. Amen.

## CREDITS AND/OR INSPIRATION

Too many long hours thinking it could be worse. I wouldn't trade my long hours of suffering with His.

# Have You Overcome Sin?

## CONCEPTS

Sanctification is a lifelong process. God accepts us as we are, generally, while we are rooted in sin. When we accept Jesus as our Savior, He dwells in us with the Spirit. The Spirit begins to clean our soulful house in our walk to become holy. The Spirit supplies us with gifts for His glory in service to Him and His church.

## PURPOSE

We must remember that we are called to be holy for His purpose and to glorify Him.

## SCRIPTURE BASE

Romans 7:15, Ephesians 2:10

## BACKGROUND

What if the only reason God made us was to save us? If that were true, He would have no other purpose for us and would take us home to heaven. Mission accomplished. No. He fills us with the Spirit to glorify Him with our lives.

## SPUR

Have you ever been convicted about a particular sin and repented? If you have, praise God. If you struggle with sin and are not comfortable committing that sin, you should feel blessed. Keep fighting until the power of Christ and the Spirit of God help you to overcome and win. "Sin will cost you more than you want to pay" (Goodreads). Just do not think you are unusual.

Paul writes in Romans 7:15 (GNTD)

*I do not understand what I do; for I don't do what I would like to do, but instead I do what I hate.*

In short, Paul struggled with sin too. Read the rest of that chapter, and you will get it.

Please, do not think the Spirit did not give the grace to save you because all your sinful bad habits did not disappear overnight. Some will. For some converts, bad habits and their sinful nature disappear entirely. If you have faithfully given your life to Christ, much of the old life will not feel comfortable anymore. Christ is better, and the old ways do not fit your commitment to Him. No cookie-cutter formulas or potions dissolve a life of sin in an instant. The Spirit promises never to leave you, and He is there to help you. God will forgive—already has forgiven—us our sins because of what Jesus did for each of us on the cross. He has set us free from sin and its power over us. He is there to convict us to change and then provides His power within us to do it. Sometimes we do not even know we are sinning. We can ask God to show us our sins and give us the strength to overcome them.

A parishioner asked a wise old preacher, "How do you know you are saved?" He said, "Are you comfortable sinning?" If you are comfortable in your sin, you might need to reexamine yourself and ask, "Is the Spirit of God within you?" That comfort level of sinning willfully, wantonly, or longingly should ring fire sirens in your head if the Spirit is within you.

So, what is next? Why did God save me? Did He save me so He could forgive me of my sins? Did He save me so I could live eternally with Him in heaven? Did He save me because He has chosen me to do something for Him? The answer is, absolutely, yes!

Ephesians 2:10

*For we are his workmanship, created in Christ Jesus for good works, which God afore prepared that we should walk in them.*

I am not one of those Christians who believe I am above another sinner. I try my best not to judge another because they sin differently than I do. My Savior has promised me eternal life, which began when I was saved. I should live a life that shows I am a citizen of heaven. I happen to live in a sinful world, and He understands. Sin has no power over me, for the power within me is greater than the power in this world. God has a purpose for me. He gave me the talent to use for His glory, and if I begin to do just that alone, I am blessed that I am doing His will in me and for Him.

**PRAYER**

God, I ask You today to show me Your way. Be a lamp unto my feet and a light unto my path. Lead me not into temptation, but deliver me from evil. I ask in the mighty name of Jesus for temptation and sin to flee from my thoughts and the weakness of my flesh. Give me inspiration, faith, love, compassion, forgiveness, and whatever I need to do the works You have prepared for me. Finally, allow me to serve You with devotion, love, and gratitude for what You have done for me. Amen.

**CREDITS AND/OR INSPIRATION**

As humans, we all struggle with our desires and sin. Paul did. Reading God's Word inspires me to write about my critical thinking. God gets the glory.

# Hens and Chicks

**CONCEPTS**

We are Jerusalem. We are the children of God—His bride, the church.

**PURPOSE**

People need to be reminded how simple God's love is for us. He wants to protect and love us; all we need to do is accept His shelter and go to Him.

**SCRIPTURE BASE**

Matthew 23:37–39, Isaiah 41:10, Romans 8:31

**BACKGROUND**

I am a father of two children who are now adults. They have given me four grandchildren. I have memories of the times my children were injured or became ill. I know how I felt when I could comfort them and soothe their hearts. God loves us more. He loves with a love only God can give. Only He can heal the sin-sick heart. May we never forget God's love for us and His ability to comfort and save us when we let Him.

**SPUR**

Jesus laments in Matthew 23:37–39 as He looks upon Jerusalem. He knows the time He has left is precious. Jesus has only a few days left to walk this earth as a man. He is gazing from the Mount of Olives, which has a beautiful view across the narrow Valley of Jehoshaphat. He says,

> *O Jerusalem, Jerusalem, that killeth the prophets, and stoneth them that are sent unto her! how often would I have gathered thy children together, even as a hen gathereth her chickens under her wings, and ye would not! Behold, your house is left unto you desolate. For I say unto you, Ye shall not see me henceforth, till ye shall say, Blessed is he that cometh in the name of the Lord.*

Look at this example or definition of the love God has for us. He wants to protect and raise us with a love independent of whether we want it or not. In the face of torturous death, He only wants to love us with the care of a mother for her children. What mother would not give her life to protect her children?

You ask, "Protect us from what?" The answer is sin and eternal death. Without Him, Jesus knows where we are going better than we know. In a simplistic but accurate statement, it's going to be hell for you without Jesus.

We may not have had a loving mother or father as children, but you understand the concept. God loves us whether we want it or not. I remember that kind of love from a mother. She protected me even when I wanted the opposite. Ever been there?

I miss her dearly. But I have a love of another that is even better. His name is Jesus. I only had to look for Him and find Him standing there with open arms to love me like no other can. A love that died for me on the cross. Let Him love you. Jerusalem has yet to accept His love. Do not reject Jesus as Jerusalem did. Do not stone Him or kill Him in your heart. Crawl on your knees and let Him cover you with His wings in loving care, and you will be the one who comes in the name of the Lord. Call upon His name.

For those of you that are parents, have you ever comforted your child after falling and cutting their knee, elbow, or chin? Did you embrace them? Hug and kiss them and tell them not to cry? Did you get your bandages out, patch them up, or take them to the hospital for the best care you could provide? How did you feel when comforting their crying and tears? How did you feel when you held them in your arms and had them quiet down in the security and love you provided?

You know God does the same thing and more because His love for you is greater. Why would you want to deny Him the opportunity to comfort you? Go to Him with your pain and suffering. Go to Him with your confession of sin. Go to Him when you are hurt. Let Him embrace you and cover you with His comfort and peace. There is no other love better than the love of our God.

Protecting our family is a built-in sense of responsibility. How much more is God's protection for us?

Isaiah 41:10

> *Fear thou not, for I am with thee; be not dismayed, for I am thy God; I will strengthen thee; yea, I will help thee; yea, I will uphold thee with the right hand of my righteousness.*

What do we have to fear if God is for us?

Romans 8:31

> *What then shall we say to these things? If God is for us, who is against us?*

Come to Him in the name of Jesus, our Lord.

**PRAYER**

God, thank You for Your love. God, I know You are love. Your love is as inconceivable to us as Your power, majesty, holiness, and being. Everything good we receive comes from You because of Your love for us. Thank You, Lord. May we never forget the unfathomable depth of Your love. Amen.

**CREDITS AND/OR INSPIRATION**

I have been to Israel and viewed Jerusalem from the Mount of Olives. Our guide spoke to our group and referenced the verse about hens and chicks in Matthew 23. Knowing that Jesus knew how close He was to the end of His ministry on earth, His heart was breaking, knowing that He would be rejected and killed by the place He loved so much. We never want to break His heart. Do not reject Jesus, His Spirit, or His Father.

# I'm Not Responsible

**CONCEPTS**

To be called to preach God's Word is a tremendous responsibility. It is also a demanding vocation and a heart-wrenching life to live. Blessings abound here, living in this place and time, but nothing like the time to come when we all go home.

Romans 10:14–15

*How then shall they call on him in whom they have not believed? And how shall they believe in him whom they have not heard? and how shall they hear without a preacher? and how shall they preach, except they be sent? even as it is written, How beautiful are the feet of them that bring glad tidings of good things!*

**PURPOSE**

The verses and the story below are written to inspire all who read them. More people need to hear a sermon like the following example.

**SCRIPTURE BASE**

Romans 10:14–15, John 3:17–18, Matthew 10:7, 2 Timothy 4:2

**BACKGROUND**

This is from a sermon I heard from a bi-vocational biker preacher on a Biker Sunday.

## SPUR

*The minister is not responsible for his success. How-*
*ever, he is responsible for what he preaches. He is account-*
*able for his life and actions, but he is not responsible for the*
*actions of other people. If I preach God's word, and there*
*was never a soul saved, the King would say, "Well done,*
*good and faithful servant!" If I should give my message and*
*no one listens to it, he would say, "You have fought the good*
*fight, here is your crown." Paul said about preachers of the*
*gospel, "We are the aroma of Christ to God among those*
*who are being saved and among those who are perishing."*
(AZQuotes)

One of the best gospel sermons I've ever heard about the saving grace from Jesus ended with no one accepting the gift. It was
disappointing to see a good sermon like the one I heard preached
have no effect. Maybe everyone there was already saved. Perhaps,
but I doubted it then, and I doubt it today. I felt dismayed for the
preacher too. You could see he poured out his spirit, and the Spirit
of God was thick in the atmosphere of the congregation.

His closing remarks hit me at a level I had not heard before,
and they are the basis of this Spur. He said, "Hey, I did what I was
supposed to do. Even Jesus didn't win everyone who heard Him
speak. I'm glad you haven't tried to stone me or throw me off a cliff.
The bottom line is, I can't save you. I can't make you accept Christ,
but I know that you know that you have heard the gospel. You know
you're a sinner, and without Christ, you will go to hell. Did I not
make that clear? When I read the Bible, did you not hear that you
need Christ? Maybe you were falling asleep; perhaps you were distracted and didn't listen.

"You heard the truth, and now you must decide. You can never say you didn't know. You can't claim to be ignorant by leaving a precious gift lying on this altar. On your judgment day, you can't say to Christ, 'I didn't know!' He knows you have been offered His salvation, and you turned it down. By the way, what you are doing by walking away is the only unforgivable sin. You can't reject the Holy Spirit of God and expect you will ever see heaven. Everyone recognizes or knows the verse in John 3:16; do you know verses 17 and 18?

> *For God sent not the Son into the world to judge the world; but that the world should be saved through him. He that believeth on him is not judged: he that believeth not hath been judged already, because he hath not believed on the name of the only begotten Son of God.*

"So, that's on you and not on me. I pray that the Spirit gives you another chance to accept Him. He may never call on your heart again, and then you will go to hell only to see the truth too late. Do not deny Christ today; step forward and accept His gift while you can."

That's some tough love. Nothing wrong with what he said, but that delivery might be too harsh for today's church-going people. It's too bad for some because those who want entertainment and have their ears tickled need to hear and fear the truth. It's hell without Jesus.

Matthew 10:7

*And as ye go, preach, saying, The kingdom of heaven is at hand.*

Charles Spurgeon once said, "No Christ in your sermon, sir? Then go home, and never preach again until you have something worth preaching" (Goodreads).

2 Timothy 4:2

*Preach the word; be urgent in season, out of season; reprove, rebuke, exhort, with all longsuffering and teaching.*

Many of my ideas for sermon content come from reading other authors. They mention a topic going in one direction, and when I read it, I end up on a rabbit trail in my mind going in another direction, applying the experiences of my life. All these roads lead to some content based upon living a more holy life. I lose sight of my purpose when I look at my own life, consider how evil I have been, and consider those things that have taken me out or urged me to repent. But because I am in Christ, I face no condemnation. Satan, get thee behind me. I cannot help but think that these experiences might help another with sin or a bad habit. My purpose is that all sermons should always point to Christ. God's grace, His Spirit, and the sacrifice of Jesus on the cross are the subjects that have made an actual difference in my life. Daily reading His Word cements that foundation. The good news in God's revelation about anything that saves me from eternal death gives me the faith to know what I know. I'm saved. Praise God.

A famous football coach liked to tell his team to "Just do your job." Speak God's Word. Preach His gospel. Choose the worthy subjects of Christ's redemptive power, eternal forgiveness, infinite grace, and sacrificial love of Christ. Let God. When you can't do that anymore, go home.

## PRAYER

My Lord, God and Father, thank You for who You are and everything You have done for me. Your blessings are beyond my ability to express, and I want only to praise Your Holy Name before all the world. Only You are good; thank You for Your love and sovereignty over me and the world around me. I pray this Spur inspires others to speak Your gospel story boldly as long as they live. Amen.

## CREDITS AND/OR INSPIRATION.

Charles Haddon Spurgeon and Pastor W. Scott Creasy, International Chaplain, Heaven's Saints Motorcycle Ministry.

Goodreads. "Charles Haddon Spurgeon Quotes." Accessed April 30, 2025. https://www.goodreads.com/quotes/10747543-a-sermon-without-christ-in-it-is-like-a-loaf.

# FOMO (Fear Of Missing Out )

**CONCEPTS**

Truly, there is a fear among this generation called FOMO. Rightfully so. FOMO comes in the sinful form of those who delay accepting and living for Christ because they want to have fun and live the experience of a sinful life promoted by our media and the current morals of this country. They need to realize that they are missing out on the blessings from all the good things of God and His most precious gift of life, eternity with Him.

**PURPOSE**

The battle is real, and it goes to the depths of fighting the evil principalities of this world for the souls of our youth and others. Using the Word of God to guide us, our responsibility is to walk with the Spirit and lead these souls to the grace of Jesus. The standard approaches—using a carrot or stick, or even fear tactics— might work to scare or cajole people to Christ. But there is a better way.

**SCRIPTURE BASE**

Romans 4:1–16

**BACKGROUND**

While teaching Sunday school to a small class of middle-school-aged boys and girls, I noticed a certain lack of interest in a pair of brothers about a year apart. They happened to be the sons of one of the church's deacons. I asked them point-blank why they weren't interested in the week's lesson. They told me as boldly that they studied the lesson and the Scripture passage but didn't think it was meant for them. The lesson resource was asking them to live for

Christ. They didn't want to commit to being "good" because if they did, they wouldn't be able to have the fun they saw others having—drinking, dating, carousing, and generally being disobedient to their parents and the Christian lifestyle being pushed on them. They both said they would become good Christians after high school and college when it was time for them to settle down. They were both "saved" and baptized at a very young age. The boys were convinced their delay tactics were right for them. They had each other and most of their peers to lean on for their thought processes. Their folks and this Sunday school teacher were not making a dent in their decisions. I don't feel I did a very good job convincing them otherwise. The real issue is that there are many lost souls out there with the same philosophy. They are not just youth but all ages.

**SPUR**

Have you ever seen any of the Scared Straight documentaries on TV? Some programs still exist that use hardcore prisoners to scare troubled youth about prison life. The local sheriffs take the boys and girls into real prisons to see and talk with murderers and rapists about the harsh realities of life in prison and what they can expect if they stay on their path of crime and misbehavior. The documentary-type programs say it works on a percentage of those who go through the day-long verbal and mental abuse from actual prisoners inside. The self-proclaimed tough ones learn there are consequences for disobeying the law. Someone is waiting for them, which is always more brutal, and fear is real. The truth about these programs is that they don't always work (P.U.R.E.). Fear of the outcome lasts for only so long. Does the prospect of hell scare people to Jesus? Yes, for a few who have been there. Jesus talked of hell more than He spoke of heaven. How about the other fear tactic standard, "You aren't promised tomorrow; you could get killed on the way home." Does anything *always* work?

Our plans are not God's plans. Even Jesus did not convince every person He met to believe in Him. We do what we can to plant the seeds of obedience and faith and then pray for the Spirit to do the rest. That's what we are called to do. We are the fishermen; the Spirit is the soul catcher. Our battle is against the principalities of a world and satan pulling down people with sin. And he has been doing that for much longer than we have been trying to lead a good church program. He has powerful tools and is well-equipped with a game plan that is tested and proven.

But ... our God is stronger! He has defeated satan from the beginning to the end. We are on the winning team. Amen? Amen!

If people have the FOMO, how about we change that to a FOMO on the blessings of heaven? Satan has been bombarding our society with the destruction of the family and belonging, not just with one another but the entire church family. The church should be a family with genuine relationships, including worship and devotion to a real God and life everlasting. People are looking for unity—a place to belong.

Few churches excel at discipleship education and experiences. We must teach the expectations of being faithful and loving to those around us. I'm not talking about a school atmosphere but a family atmosphere built on love and trust. In that whole-church concept, we must develop the talents and gifts given to our family with opportunities to use them and share them with the entire church. Think of Acts when people met in homes instead of segregated rooms. Our churches should create an environment where everyone is worshipping together instead of segregated youth, college-aged, professionals, young married, retired, and elderly groups.

Want to learn a culture and how to speak a foreign language? The church is unfamiliar and alien to many not raised there from birth. Immerse them in the culture and assimilate their time and energy into church activities and relationships with other Christians. Create a community of people with the unity of the Holy Spirit.

I know this is not a unique concept of what a perfect church might look like, but we fail to do our best if we are not trying to create this environment of unity, love, and respect for our fellow Christians. We ask God to join us much too often. We need to join Him using the plan He developed. Jesus is the root vine; God is the tender of His vineyard. We are the shoots to make fruit.

## PRAYER

Lord, God and Father, we praise Your name. Remind us each day how You are the perfector of unity. Even the Persons of the Trinity are a constant reminder of unity in One. Jesus, You have asked everyone to come to You, to be united in one Spirit and one family, in one faith. Show us how to gather into one church without division or separation. Bring us together as Your church, a family of Christians living for You. Amen.

## CREDITS AND/OR INSPIRATION

Reading Romans to understand what Paul and the Spirit of God want from each of us personally is a definitive study of Scripture. The book of Romans calls us to make a servitude effort (slave-like) to do as God has given us the talent.

Romans 4:1

*I therefore, the prisoner in the Lord, beseech you to walk worthily of the calling wherewith ye were called.*

P.U.R.E. (Parents Universal Resource Experts). "Family Consultants: Sue Scheff." Accessed May 13, 2025. https://helpyourteens.com/family-consultants/.

# It Might Be the Devil

**CONCEPTS**

Everyone answers to someone—everyone. As simple as it may seem, whoever one serves and obeys is the one that controls and binds them. We may not like to admit it, but we may have even more than one we serve. Can we choose them or deny them? We can't always, but God can. *Slavery* and *slaves* are insensitive words in our society, as they should be. I don't take using these words lightly. We have all been slaves to sin before we met Jesus.

**PURPOSE**

Many people never even realize they are enslaved people and bound in chains of sin. They are not free. Jesus is the chain breaker and sets us free. This Spur points to His power, mercy, and grace.

**SCRIPTURE BASE**

Romans 6:16, Romans 14:11, Galatians 4:3, Exodus 9:1, Galatians 4:3, Galatians 4:8, Galatians 5:1, John 8:36

**BACKGROUND**

I had a friend who was caught up in a power struggle with two supervisors placed at equal levels above him. Each was in charge of different aspects of the overall project. My friend also had two mid-level supervisors in his chain of command. The problem was that my friend, the project manager, was responsible for the job. He was constantly torn between all the other bosses he had to answer to as they all wanted to do things their way. He couldn't please them all and was always in trouble for trying. His situation made me consider how our lives become entangled in sin when we try to please ourselves and everyone around us. We become slaves to many masters when there is only One we need.

## SPUR

Bob Dylan sings in one of his songs from the album *Slow Train Coming*, "It might be the devil, or it might be the Lord, but you gotta serve somebody" (Dylan).

You, too, are going to serve someone.

Romans 6:16

> *Know ye not, that to whom ye present yourselves as servants unto obedience, his servants ye are whom ye obey; whether of sin unto death, or of obedience unto righteousness?*

Who's your master? There are many possibilities, if I may make a small nonexclusive list: boss(es), spouse or ex(s), kid(s), friends, habits, hobbies, money debt, an exhaustive group of mediums we get sucked into. If any of these come before your Lord and Savior, you might need to reexamine your life with a first-things-first priority assessment.

The entire Bible, both the New and Old Testaments, talks about slavery in one form or another. From Abraham through Moses, Habakkuk to Revelation, slavery is a common theme. In Greek and Hebrew, the word *salvation* is interchangeable with freedom. The word *freedom* is derived directly from slavery. As we were once slaves of sin, redemption from sin, the purchase from sin is salvation from sin and death. Old Testament stories of peoples' bondage, especially Hebrews, relate to slavery and salvation.

In a speech at Prager University, Candace Owens stated that slavery might be the oldest occupation (if that is the correct word for it). It has been part of the human condition since humans (FrontPage.Mag). Sorry to say, it is still with us in the 21st century. But it makes sense because satan is the ultimate slaver, and Jesus is the ultimate redeemer.

Romans 14:11

*For it is written, As I live, saith the Lord, to me every knee shall bow, And every tongue shall confess to God.*

Moses is credited as the first of God's faithful to free enslaved people when he called on the pharaoh of Egypt to release His people, the Israelites. It is important to note that the references used in Exodus explain to the pharaoh why God wanted His people, the Israelites, to be free. The reason was so they could serve and worship Him.

Exodus 9:1

*Then Jehovah said unto Moses, Go in unto Pharaoh, and tell him, Thus saith Jehovah, the God of the Hebrews, Let my people go, that they may serve me.*

Paul explains that before we knew Christ, we were all slaves in bondage to something, but it was Jesus who freed us from our chains.

Galatians 4:3

*So we also, when we were children, were held in bondage under the rudiments of the world.*

Galatians 4:8

*Howbeit at that time, not knowing God, ye were in bondage to them that by nature are no gods.*

Galatians 5:1

*For freedom did Christ set us free: stand fast therefore, and be not entangled again in a yoke of bondage.*

Jesus was put in bondage for a time too. Matthew chapters 26 and 27 vividly describe how Jesus was captured, bound, beaten, and imprisoned on His way to Calvary for us.

The parallels throughout the Bible and the miracles performed by Jesus point to our worldly relationship and the power of sin over us. The complete set of stories relates directly and indirectly to how we are all slaves to something and need to be free. Then the story changes. The New Testament shows explicitly who it is and how we can be freed.

John 8:36

*If therefore the Son shall make you free, ye shall be free indeed.*

## PRAYER

God and Father, You are a mighty God to save us and break every chain. Help us, Lord, put our faith deeper into who You are and what Your saving grace means to us. Please give us more faith to believe You can free us from our shackles and break the chains that bind us. Show us Your peace, protection, mercy, and grace. Amen.

## CREDITS AND/OR INSPIRATION

We rarely think about the fact that we might be slaves to something. Choosing whom we will serve is a fundamental human right. Choose wisely.

Bob Dylan. "Gotta Serve Somebody." Bobdylan. Accessed April 30, 2025. https://www.bobdylan.com/songs/gotta-serve-somebody/.

FrontPageMag. "Prager U Video: A Short History of Slavery Video." August 27, 2021. https://www.frontpagemag.com/prager-u-video-short-history-slavery-prager-u/.

# Move Your Feet

## CONCEPTS

Many people hear the call from Jesus and never answer. To deny the Spirit is without excuse and is unforgivable.

## PURPOSE

This is a "Come to Jesus" Spur. It is straightforward. This Stem is written to impact those out there in the pews who want to accept the call of Christ but fear it for whatever reason. They must know they have to make the second move. Christ made the first, and He may never tug on their hearts again.

## SCRIPTURE BASE

Luke 14:15–24, Matthew 10:33, Luke 12:9, Matthew 12:32, Mark 3:29, Luke 12:10

## BACKGROUND

People say they believe in Jesus. They say they know Him and talk to Him occasionally. They say, "Me and the Man Upstairs are OK." I don't know about that. Those words and attitudes do not sit right with me, and from what I read in God's Word, I don't think it sets right with Him either. I think of when Jesus said there will be people who will cry to Him, "Lord, Lord!" and He will say, "I never knew you." That brings me to tears for the Lost when I think of that. Everyone should know for sure, without a doubt, that Jesus knows their name.

## SPUR

There are time-honored sayings or proverbs that many people say and still know pretty well. Some of you will have heard these before; this might be the first time for others. For instance:

"Time heals all wounds."

"Move your feet and lose your seat."

"If it ain't broke, don't fix it."

"Put the pedal to the metal."

"What you see is what you get."

"When the going gets tough, the tough get going."

Do any of those sound familiar? Depending on the last comedy you've seen, you may have heard a few of these sayings have different or funnier versions. Comedians change the words around and make them punny. The best ones redone for fun are "Time wounds all heels" or "When the going gets tough, repent."

Have you ever heard of this modification? "Move your feet or lose your seat."

Let's talk about that one for a minute. Jesus spoke a famous parable written in Luke 14:15–24. You might have heard a sermon or two preached about this parable, and I want to focus on the gist of the conversation a bit differently.

> *And when one of them that sat at meat with him heard these things, he said unto him, Blessed is he that shall eat bread in the kingdom of God But he said unto him, A certain man made a great supper; and he bade many and he sent*

*forth his servant at supper time to say to them that were bidden, Come; for all things are now ready.*

Yes, everything is ready. The place has been prepared.

*And they all, with one consent, began to make excuses. The first said unto him, I have bought a field, and I must needs go out and see it; I pray thee have me excused.*

Really? I bet that piece of land will be there tomorrow, maybe even next week.

*And another said, I have bought five yoke of oxen, and I go to prove them; I pray thee have me excused.*

Oh, that's a good one. So, those oxen will be just fine tomorrow. So, you'd give up a banquet of a King's feast for five yokes of oxen?

*And another said, I have married a wife, and therefore I cannot come.*

What? Have you ever heard of "plus one"? Bring her along!

I hate hearing excuses. It comes from my military background. I assure you that when you make excuses, the forthcoming punishment will be more brutal.

"I'm sorry. I'm not going or can't make it." When pressed by the person inviting you, and if you get annoyed, tell them you must mow the lawn. That excuse is just as good as the ones given in this passage in Luke.

I apologize for providing a mixed message here. You are probably asking yourself, "Does he want me to make an excuse or not?" I want you to show up, so you don't have to make an excuse.

*And the servant came, and told his lord these things. Then the master of the house being angry said to his servant, Go out quickly into the streets and lanes of the city, and bring in hither the poor and maimed and blind and lame. And the servant said, Lord, what thou didst command is done, and yet there is room. And the lord said unto the servant, Go out into the highways and hedges, and constrain them to come in, that my house may be filled. For I say unto you, that none of those men that were bidden shall taste of my supper.*

When discussing an invitation from the Master, you need to show up.

The moral of the story. "Move your feet or lose your seat."

You get it. The story relates to our Father in heaven. His calling invites us to sit at His table and sup with Him. He has prepared a feast for us. And the invitation is to come and join Him for eternity.

So, what's your excuse if you haven't accepted the invitation?

Is your excuse that you don't want to show others you have accepted Jesus as Lord? The Master does not tolerate rejection well. So, His Word says:

Matthew 10:33

*But whosoever shall deny me before men, him will I also deny before my Father who is in heaven.*

Jesus even said it twice:

Luke 12:9

*But he that denieth me in the presence of men shall be denied in the presence of the angels of God.*

There is only one unforgivable sin I know:

Matthew 12:32

> *And whosoever shall speak a word against the Son of man, it shall be forgiven him; but whosoever shall speak against the Holy Spirit, it shall not be forgiven him, neither in this world, nor in that which is to come.*

And again, Jesus says:

Mark 3:29

> *But whosoever shall blaspheme against the Holy Spirit hath never forgiveness, but is guilty of an eternal sin.*

You might think it's critical to read it for the third time written in God's Word:

Luke 12:10

> *And every one who shall speak a word against the Son of man, it shall be forgiven him: but unto him that blasphemeth against the Holy Spirit it shall not be forgiven.*

Some people think this is about cussing or making fun of God and His Holy Spirit; well, that's not a good thing either. What this is talking about is your denying faith in Jesus. It's about your lack of belief that He died for your sins. It's about you denying the tug on your heart telling you that you are a sinner in need of a forgiven Savior. It's about ignoring the Spirit knocking on your heart to accept Him. When you don't receive Him, when you deny Him before men, you blaspheme and reject the Holy Spirit. There is no forgiveness for that—none.

Too often, we see people sitting or standing next to their pews or seats, head bowed, eyes closed, and too afraid to step forward as the heart in their chest calls them to acknowledge Christ and accept the invitation. They are denying Christ and do not understand the consequences of quenching the Spirit Whose calling. They should be too afraid not to run down that aisle and drop to their knees confessing Jesus as their Lord.

## PRAYER

Lord, God and heavenly Father, I pray these words and this Stem break the hearts of those who hear Your Word. I pray they receive Your gracious gift and come forward to accept Your love and salvation through Jesus. Lord, may none refuse, reject, or deny Your Holy Spirit calling them. In Jesus' name, I pray. Amen.

## CREDITS AND/OR INSPIRATION

We have all likely heard that great sermon by a preacher that didn't bring forth one to be saved. It is painful to everyone who has no doubt they are saved and are confident there are those in the crowd who need Jesus. Pray for them that God will give them time and another invitation. May they not deny the Spirit again.

# Nothing to Prove

## CONCEPTS

This is a relatively short Spur, but one I couldn't leave out. It clarifies with solid references who Jesus is and our relationship to Him as Christians.

## PURPOSE

I find these verses motivational. It is hard to emphasize how much Christ is in us through a few written words. His fullness in us enables us to tap His power with His blessing and will. It reminds me of the times Jesus chastised those closest to Him with words of frustration when He saw their lack of faith. We need more faith, and often, that fire needs tending. This Spur is a short exclamation to kick those coals around and get the fire for Jesus going.

## SCRIPTURE BASE

John in 1:1, Colossians 2:8–10, Romans 6:5, 1 John 3:2

## BACKGROUND

This world can get you down sometimes. I get weak in Spirit, and my faith falters to a point I'm ashamed to be called a Christian. When I read something or hear an inspiring discourse, my batteries get charged, and I know it was God speaking to me. Many subjects and verses can do that for me. This set of verses is my go-to.

## SPUR

I like putting first things first. It is a good habit and one you should never forget. Christ first. Others might want to beat around the bush about this, but I want to run right over the bush when preaching specific topics.

Often, as preachers, we fear the hardline approach to Christianity. Many preachers like to slide in the side, catch people off guard, sneak attack them through an impromptu feeling, or segue into a valid point of circumstance. A preacher I admired, Pastor Jarvis Brock, was better at that than anyone I ever met. He had the gift or knack of catching you laughing at the beginning of his sentence and crying by the time he got to the end. He preached the hard stuff, too, but he was a gentleman in his approach.

I'm not saying that the ambush preaching styles are ineffective means of evangelizing because we have all done it, including Jesus, Paul, and Peter. But unfortunately, this subject doesn't quite meet those criteria.

This subject is essential to get correct from the beginning, and as John wrote in 1:1, he said,

*In the beginning was the Word, and the Word was with God, and the Word was God.*

I'm not going to insult your intelligence, but I, too, wish to be precise. John was speaking of Jesus Christ. From the beginning, with added clarity for the Trinity, Jesus is in part and fully the Godhead. Let's step through the points in Colossians 2:8–10:

*Take heed lest there shall be any one that maketh spoil of you through his philosophy and vain deceit, after the tradition of men, after the rudiments of the world, and not after Christ:*

Don't be fooled by anyone or any writing, philosopher, or other fool or spiritual teaching from false religion. Jesus is the Christ—the Son of God.

*for in him dwelleth all the fulness of the Godhead bodily,*

Speaking of Jesus, He is God in the flesh, fully human and fully God. No one can make it plainer than that. Jesus is God in the flesh.

*and in him ye are made full, who is the head of all principality and power.*

Here comes a big jump of faith for many of us. This verse says that in Christ, we are complete—full. As Jesus was described as fully God (verse 9), we are also His, and He is ours. He is within us, and the power that raised Him from the grave is the same power that lives in us. Not a watered-down version of Spirit but the same Spirit.

Sidenote: Please don't assume I think we are as good as Jesus or we are like Him. We are not—at least not now—but someday we will be.

Romans 6:5

*For if we have become united with him in the likeness of his death, we shall be also in the likeness of his resurrection.*

1 John 3:2

*Beloved, now are we children of God, and it is not yet made manifest what we shall be. We know that, if he shall be manifested, we shall be like him; for we shall see him even as he is.*

Feeling insecure about who you are? If you are good enough? Do you have the right stuff? If Colossians 2:9 is true, then 2:10 must also be true. Do you believe verse 2:9 is true? (Furtick).

These statements are powerful when presented to believers who lack faith. It may seem nonsense to nonbelievers because they don't have the Spirit within them to hear or understand what this all means. But these words fire me up. I feel like I have just put on my cape, broken out of the phone booth, and need to preach the gospel.

Ever heard the saying, "Name it and claim it?" That saying is not well-accepted in many circles, but I get the concept when associated with these verses. Know where you stand on the Word of God, for He is our foundation.

## PRAYER

Lord, God and Father, thank You for the gifts of fullness You give us through our faith. What a mighty God and Savior You are! Forgive us when we offend You with our lack of faith. Lord, continue to remind us how great and mighty You are and that Your Spirit is within us, always. Amen.

## CREDITS AND/OR INSPIRATION

Steven Furtick. *(Un)Qualified: How God Uses Broken People to Do Big Things.* Multnomah, 2016.

# Weakness

## CONCEPTS

Pride is a sneaky sin that creeps into people's lives without their being conscious of it. It is likely one of those sins we consider a sin of omission. The question we need to ask ourselves is, "Is there sinful pride in me?"

## PURPOSE

These verses lead us to consider our weakness as strength and how our pride hinders our worship and prayer life.

## SCRIPTURE BASE

James 4:13–14, Proverbs 16:9, 2 Philippians 4:11–12, Corinthians 12:10, Proverbs 11:2, Proverbs 16:18

## BACKGROUND

Pride is my most personal and challenging sin to repent of. My pride and lack of humility are constantly at odds with my personal growth and relationship with God. I would be closer to righteousness and holiness if I had less pride and more humility. I pray that God shows me daily how to come closer to Jesus as the model I need to aspire to, not the world around me.

## SPUR

How can weakness be a strength? Every day we talk about what we are going to do. Maybe tomorrow. Maybe next week. Maybe next year. The Bible tells us we shouldn't talk like that.

James 4:13–14 says, Now listen up, those of you who speak like this—

> *Today we will go to this or that city, spend a year there, carry on business and make money*  —is wrong.

Why?

> *Because you don't even know what will happen tomorrow. Your life is a vapor. You are a mist that appears for a little while and then vanishes.*

Proverbs 16:9

*A man's heart deviseth his way; But Jehovah directeth his steps.*

So, what are we without God? Consider Jesus in the garden of Gethsemane as He prayed before His capture and crucifixion. Who on earth had more power than Jesus Christ? And yet He made Himself weak to be sacrificed unto death. How much more powerful did He become revealing that weakness? How about the first example of humility in Jesus? He came from heaven as king to a lowly manger as a servant.

Our society does not embrace weakness, especially in men. Women also fall into the trap of not showing weakness. It is drilled into us from childhood and is part of our competitive society. Society says, "Don't ever let them see your fear," and "Meekness is a sign of weakness."

Pride is the foundation of all these thoughts, and it is one of satan's favorite lies he uses to forge the fires of those lies within us. Bosses bombard us, and commercials, spouses, and friends tell us not to be content with who we are, what we have, and how important we should be. In truth, those are all lies. Listen to Paul again:

Philippians 4:11–12

> *Not that I speak in respect of want: for I have learned, in whatsoever state I am, therein to be content. I know how to be abased, and I know also how to abound: in everything and in all things have I learned the secret both to be filled and to be hungry, both to abound and to be in want.*

Paul makes an example of the process we need to consider. He could brag. Paul had it all, and he had it all taken from him. After he meets Jesus, he states how happy he is in whatever condition he's in because that is what God has given him.

Having the faith that God will provide for every need and promises to bless us (make us happy) beyond our expectations is not easy to embrace. That's humility, and in error, we often believe the opposite. The world says, "I made me who I am. What has God done for me? To whom do I give credit? How much of what I have done did I earn and deserve, and how much did God do? I didn't ask for this; I earned it. Because I'm so good, I got what I have."

Paul says in 2 Corinthians 12:10,

> *Wherefore I take pleasure in weaknesses, in injuries, in necessities, in persecutions, in distresses, for Christ's sake: for when I am weak, then am I strong.*

Let's break this down into a comparison to what the world tells us.

Never show your weaknesses. If you're injured, walk it off. Don't tell others you're sick or need prayer for your ailments—that's weak.

I don't need anything or anyone because I can get my own. I'm innovative and powerful and don't need anyone or any prayers.

Watch what you say to me; I'll get you back for every word. I'm self-made or come from good stock and education; you can't put me down. So, watch me fire back in kind.

Distress? Are you kidding me? I'm strong; I can overcome; I'll show those guys.

Proud, stubborn, rich, self-righteous, independent people don't need God.

Strong in what? Why does God want us weak? Why do you suppose God delights in our weakness? When we finally realize that we can't do it ourselves and need someone else, we will depend more on Him if we become wise.

Proverbs 11:2

*When pride cometh, then cometh shame; But with the lowly is wisdom.*

Proverbs 16:18

*Pride goeth before destruction, and a haughty spirit before a fall.*

We are nothing without Him. Thank Him for allowing you to take your previous breath, and praise Him that you are still breathing. Ask Him for your next. That's humility. That's needy. That's where God wants to meet us, so we know we exist for Him. We are to praise His Holy name and depend on Him for everything. To give ourselves up totally to His care. When you are there, look to God for your salvation, humble yourself, and He will draw near to you.

## PRAYER

God and Father, I come to You each day and ask not that You make me humble but that You show me how to be humble. I ask You to remove my pride and soften my heart to be more like Yours, gracious and forgiving. Thank You, Lord, for Your Spirit that shows me my sin and encourages me to repent. Keep me in Your love each day. Amen.

## CREDITS AND/OR INSPIRATION

I am inspired to write this and remind myself to take second place. Jesus is first. More of Him and less of me, every day.

# Put Me In, Coach

## CONCEPTS

Few people listen to the call of their Savior. Many hear it, and they ignore it. Others stop up their ears and misconstrue any call by God that would send them off to some jungle as a missionary. No one should fear what God plans out of His love for them.

## PURPOSE

God has a service and calling for each of His children. He gives each of us a gift and/or talent to be used for His glory, but many refuse to listen or fail to hear His whisper. Our desire for people around us to do what we want is unnecessary. What is important is what God calls us to do beyond our expectations. The men Jesus called dropped what they were doing and followed Him. Do you suppose those who watched them walk off the job were pleased?

## SCRIPTURE BASE

Mark 1:16–20, Jeremiah 10:23, Psalm 139:16, Proverbs 20:24, Ephesians 2:10, Romans 11:29, Isaiah 41:9–10, Matthew 6:33, Proverbs 3:5–6, 2 Thessalonians 1:11–12, Romans 8:28

## BACKGROUND

People are called by God where they are to go, what He has prepared and supplied to accomplish His plans. The hundreds of ministers I have met who were called to do what they were doing knew why they were there. Many have testified that God called them, and they answered, being surprised their life was where it was and not what they expected. Paul said he was always content in what he endured and where he was. That peace only comes from God. I'm at peace—are you?

## SPUR

Have you ever attended a job fair, job exploratory, or taken an employment survey? Many schools and every branch of the military use skills assessment evaluations. Schools, through counselors, use these to help students find their interests or skills. The military uses these evaluations to place recruits in career positions best suited for them. Colleges use similar tests to help students decide on majors and fields of study to obtain the most fulfilling careers.

Ever wonder how Jesus chose His twelve apostles? We have read the story in Luke in Sunday school but seldom discuss how Jesus knew who to call as His disciples. Read Mark 1:16–20.

Many formal studies and theological students have authored essays, theses, and dissertations on the personalities and the leadership styles of Jesus and His twelve apostles. We are not going that far. However, it is awe-inspiring to outline how Jesus chose His group. Mark states the selection in a matter-of-fact way that was entirely of God. Of course it was, but it seemed divine in that Jesus didn't need to convince anyone. There were no interviews or tests, and it seemed Jesus knew that the men He casually met would become the most impactful group of pastors, missionaries, healers, and authors the world has ever known. Consider how one man/God with a handful of untrained, uninitiated ordinary men became world changers.

The business of commercial fishing, then and now is a difficult job. The name tells it all. They don't call the job catchermen. That's not even a word. But as fishermen, it means sometimes you don't catch what you need to eat, and other times you catch enough for a week's pay. But notice what Jesus says to these men. *"Come, follow me, and I will make you fishers of men."* What a career change! What else could He have said? "Hey guys, I see you're fishing. Drop those nets and follow Me, and we'll go out and heal the sick and feed thousands." Jesus called to them, and within His divine power, He chose the men He would mold and make into the greatest evangelistic soldiers ever assembled.

Think about it for just a second. Jesus didn't just grab a couple of guys out of the crowd. He knew every one of them—before they were born, before time began. Jesus even knew His traitor and still chose him to be close to Him for three years. He didn't pick any of them haphazardly. Not even Judas. Instead, He chose them in order to fulfill His destiny—to the cross and for the rest of eternity. That's impactful beyond imagination.

Jeremiah 10:23

*O Jehovah, I know that the way of man is not in himself; it is not in man that walketh to direct his steps.*

Consider that God chooses us in the same way. Each of us is God's creation. He knows everything about us. He is our potter, and we are His clay. Even if we choose our surroundings, everything that made us and who we are was preordained for us. Nothing in our lives isn't a part of who we are. God knows how to call us. We have only to listen and obey.

Psalm 139:16

*Thine eyes did see mine unformed substance; And in thy book they were all written, Even the days that were ordained for me, When as yet there was none of them.*

Proverbs 20:24

*A man's goings are of Jehovah; how can man understand his way?*

These men didn't say to Jesus, "Hey, take me!" He chose them because He knew who they were. He knew the end long before the start began. Each one served God in the way God wanted them to serve. It is that way with us as well.

Ephesians 2:10

*For we are his workmanship, created in Christ Jesus for good works, which God afore prepared that we should walk in them.*

Have you ever been called by God to serve Him? Have you been called to use your talents, gifts, life experiences, education, training, wealth, and skills? Did you drop your nets and straightaway answer His calling as they did?

Romans 11:29

*For the gifts and the calling of God are not repented of.*

This verse might mean more when you strip back and understand what Paul is saying unveiled. He says that God does not take back His gifts or calling. It means you can't ignore God like Jonah tried to do. It didn't work for Jonah, and it will not turn out well for anyone who denies God when He calls you.

Isaiah 41:9–10

*Thou whom I have taken hold of from the ends of the earth, and called from the corners thereof, and said unto thee, Thou art my servant, I have chosen thee and not cast thee away; fear thou not, for I am with thee; be not dismayed, for I am thy God; I will strengthen thee; yea, I will help thee; yea, I will uphold thee with the right hand of my righteousness.*

What do you think Jesus wants from you? He says He only wants your love and praise. Jesus wants you to put Him first in your life. Does that mean He wants you to preach? To be a deacon? To be a missionary? To witness to all your family and friends? To go to church on Sunday and give Him your money? To stop being bad? To stop sinning? I mean, what? What's the cost of His love? What do I have to do? Do I have to stop having fun? So many questions, but they are all easily answered. He wants you right where you are. Drop your nets and follow Him. Accept His invitation and love. When His spirit enters you because of your faith in Him, the other answers will come to you. I don't have those answers. He does.

Matthew 6:33

*But seek ye first his kingdom, and his righteousness; and all these things shall be added unto you.*

But first, you must have faith to accept Him as your Lord. Surrender everything and say, "Lord, I don't know what to do or what You want, but I give You my life to do with me as You wish. I trust You, Lord, to do better with my life with You in control than with me. Take my offering of who You have made me be and use me to do Your will."

Proverbs 3:5–6

*Trust in Jehovah with all thy heart, And lean not upon thine own understanding: In all thy ways acknowledge him, And he will direct thy paths.*

It is hard to give it up as quickly as that. You might not be able to trust that easily. You've been hurt by trusting someone or some program that disappointed you. Jesus will never leave you or forsake you. What you will get in return for your surrender far outweighs what you give because you can't outgive what God has in store for you. Trust Him.

2 Thessalonians 1:11–12

*To which end we also pray always for you, that our God may count you worthy of your calling, and fulfil every desire of goodness and every work of faith, with power; that the name of our Lord Jesus may be glorified in you, and ye in him, according to the grace of our God and the Lord Jesus Christ.*

Whatever your calling is.

Romans 8:28

*And we know that to them that love God all things work together for good, even to them that are called according to his purpose.*

## PRAYER

Lord, God and heavenly Father, deal with those who hear Your words. Increase their faith to listen and be brave enough to answer Your calling in their lives. Open their ears to accept what You have in store for them according to Your purpose, Your glory. Amen.

## CREDITS AND/OR INSPIRATION

Hearing and answering God's call to serve is an awesome responsibility and privilege. To refuse it or ignore it can lead to a catastrophic life. Read Jonah.

# Seasons

## CONCEPTS

Ecclesiastes 3:1 says that everything has a season and a time for every purpose. Every means every, and when it comes to our lives, the seasons come and go, fast and short, good and bad, long and everlasting. So, make today a season of decision.

## PURPOSE

This Spur reflects on the seasons of our lives and how we need to react and obey as the season of decision might be upon us.

## SCRIPTURE BASE

Ecclesiastes 3:1, Hebrews 4:7, Hebrews 4:12

## BACKGROUND

I have always been fascinated by the Earth's seasons and our lives. We start with the season of our youth, and if we are blessed to live a full life, we experience all the other seasons until death. God created the seasons we share in weather; He also makes the seasons to reveal the purposes in our lives.

## SPUR

The God-given wisdom of Solomon shines forth in chapter 3. King Solomon writes about seasons, and from the first time I read it until now, it has fascinated me. I had tried to think of something Solomon might have missed when he wrote in verse one:

*For everything there is a season, and a time for every purpose under heaven.*

He then proceeds to try to name everything and every purpose. If we think of something he forgot, he's fully covered with the word *every* because I'm sure we can take that to mean exactly what it says.

I know I have gone through many seasons of not just weather but also joy, tribulation, sickness, love, and sorrow. Maybe you can relate some of your seasons and how, looking upon them historically, you can articulate precisely how God prepared you for them, walked you through them, and grew your faith and love for Him as He did. That's the critical part. In everything, we must remember to look for God's sovereignty. God is good all the time, and all the time, God is good.

As Job showed us, even in the most challenging seasons of our lives, it is okay to ask why, but we should never fail to praise God while waiting for the season to end. It will end. We will only have seasons while we live, for I am confident heaven has no seasons. Ever think about that? God never changes, and when we reach heaven, we will be eternally in His light. I'm not expecting much change, and I pray I'm right. I don't expect to be bored because I look forward to meeting many friends, family, historical characters, and you. We will have eternity to get to know one another.

Never judge someone based on a season. Author Steven Furtick makes the following observation:

• One season, David was a murderous adulterer; the following season, he was a broken, humbled man.
• One season, Rahab was a prostitute; the following season, she was married and was a matriarch to Jesus.
• One season, Peter was a coward; the following season, he was the most courageous voice for Christ.

• One season, Paul was a Christian killer; the following season, he was being beaten, imprisoned, and dying for Christ.

We serve a God who transplants new hearts into weak and lost men and women. Don't give up on people. Watch from a distance if you must, but don't give up. Keep praying for them.

There is one season a majority of us will have before we die. That is the season of decision. As God rested on the seventh day of creation from all His works, Hebrews 4 refers to the "rest" promised us. He promised that if we believed, we would enter His rest, but if we did not hear His Word and did not unite with Him in faith, we would fall short and not enter. The sub-climax of the chapter is in verse 7:

*Today if ye shall hear his voice, harden not your hearts.*

The rest of the chapter describes how the season of deciding will determine whether you enter into His rest or not. The main point of the chapter is one of the most essential verses we all should remember.

Hebrews 4:12

> *For the word of God is living, and active, and sharper than any two-edged sword, and piercing even to the dividing of soul and spirit, of both joints and marrow, and quick to discern the thoughts and intents of the heart.*

Have you heard the gospel of Jesus Christ? Have you decided to accept His rest? If not, today is your day and season to decide. What does your heart say?

Hebrews 4:16

*Let us therefore draw near with boldness unto the throne of grace, that we may receive mercy, and may find grace to help us in time of need.*

## PRAYER

Father in heaven and Lord of all, I pray as I approach the throne of grace, my heart is open to You and Your Word. As You, Lord, discern my thoughts and intents, I pray that You are blessed with what You see in me. Lord, soften my heart with Your love as I anticipate Your promised rest from all labor. In Jesus' name, I pray. Amen.

## CREDITS AND/OR INSPIRATION

God inspired the wisdom of Solomon, and I looked into the past seasons of my life and times.

Steven Furtick. *(Un)Qualified: How God Uses Broken People to Do Big Things.* Multnomah, 2016.

# The New Covenant

## CONCEPTS

This devotion came from a desire to prepare for a more informed witnessing capability. Many people have doubts. They doubt God and the saving grace of Jesus. The covenants made by God are in the blood because life is in the blood. Sacrifices made in the Old Testament were blood-based from the very beginning. Life for a life, sin was death; only blood (life) could wash away the penalty of sin—death.

## PURPOSE

Confusion is a lie that satan uses to blur the minds of those unequipped with the Word of God. Satan uses confusion and doubt to destroy the faith of believers. His target is those with weak knowledge, like those whom Jesus spoke to in the parable of The Man Who Went Out to Sow Grain, in Mark 4. The parable is about the seed that fell on rocky ground or grew among thornbushes to be choked out. The verses and information here are to cultivate and water the seeds planted. This information provides wisdom to enrich the soil and help the roots go deeper where the plant can repel the wiles of satan and lies. This presentation might be best used on a Sunday night church Bible study or in a similar venue.

## SCRIPTURE BASE

Exodus 24:8, Luke 22:20, and many other Scripture verses are quoted below.

## BACKGROUND

I met a man who played in a renowned orchestra. The orchestra specialized in classical Christian music, and he had played in hundreds of churches and venues where pastors preached their versions of God's Word. He endured hundreds of sermons from various denominations and fringe churches that grew large enough to bring in the orchestra. In a shallow discussion, I offhandedly spouted off a saying I aspire to as "Once saved, always saved." Immediately, he became serious. I knew him to be a Christian, but his following few questions took me off guard. He asked, "How do you know that? How are you sure you are always saved and can't lose your salvation?" At the moment, without my Bible, I was unprepared to show him what I knew as the truth from God's Word. Consequently, I searched for all the references to prove God's love is eternal. The following is a collection of those verses.

## SPUR

What is a covenant? As stated in Merriam-Webster's online dictionary:

> 1: a usually formal, solemn, and binding agreement: compact "…international law, which depends upon the sanctity of covenants between rulers." (George H. Sabine)

> 2a: a written agreement or promise, usually under seal, between two or more parties, especially for the performance of some action

> 2b: the common-law action to recover damages for breach of such a contract.

252

Synonyms for *covenant* include *contract, agreement, under-taking, commitment, guarantee, warrant, pledge, promise, war-rant, indenture.*

The Old Covenant, initiated by God, who cannot lie or deceive, was with Abraham's family. He enforced that covenant with the performance of a blood sacrifice through the act of faith with Isaac in Genesis 22. God further confirmed and sealed this covenant with Moses and the twelve tribes of Israel with sacrificial blood in Exodus 24:8.

Exodus 24:8

> *And Moses took the blood, and sprinkled it on the people, and said, Behold the blood of the covenant, which Jehovah hath made with you concerning all these words.*

Each of these covenants required performance from both sides. With Abraham, it was circumcision. Moses and the twelve tribes of Israel adhered to the Ten Commandments and circumcision when they went into the promised land.

The New Covenant (or New Testament) is the promise God makes with humanity that He will forgive sin and restore fellowship with those whose hearts are turned toward Him. Jesus Christ is the mediator of the New Covenant, and His death on the cross is the basis of the promise.

Luke 22:20

> *And the cup in like manner after supper, saying, This cup is the new covenant in my blood, even that which is poured out for you.*

The performance to seal this deal is to accept the gift of grace and believe in the name of Jesus as Lord.

The following are verses that confirm this covenant:

John 6:37–40, Jesus speaking:

*All that which the Father giveth me shall come unto me; and him that cometh to me I will in no wise cast out. For I am come down from heaven, not to do mine own will, but the will of him that sent me. And this is the will of him that sent me, that of all that which he hath given me I should lose nothing, but should raise it up at the last day. For this is the will of my Father, that every one that beholdeth the Son, and believeth on him, should have eternal life; and I will raise him up at the last day.*

John 10:25–30, Jesus speaking:

*Jesus answered them, I told you, and ye believe not: the works that I do in my Father's name, these bear witness of me. But ye believe not, because ye are not of my sheep. My sheep hear my voice, and I know them, and they follow me: and I give unto them eternal life; and they shall never perish, and no one shall snatch them out of my hand. My Father, who hath given them unto me, is greater than all; and no one is able to snatch them out of the Father's hand. I and the Father are one.*

Romans 8:35:

*Who shall separate us from the love of Christ? shall tribulation, or anguish, or persecution, or famine, or nakedness, or peril, or sword?*

Verses 38–39 say:

*For I am persuaded, that neither death, nor life, nor angels, nor principalities, nor things present, nor things to come, nor powers, nor height, nor depth, nor any other creature, shall be able to separate us from the love of God, which is in Christ Jesus our Lord.*

And what is the love of God?

John 3:16, Jesus speaking:

*For God so loved the world, that he gave his only begotten Son, that whosoever believeth on him should not perish, but have eternal life.*

1 Corinthians 6:19–20:

*Or know ye not that your body is a temple of the Holy Spirit which is in you, which ye have from God? and ye are not your own; for ye were bought with a price: glorify God therefore in your body.*

Is God faithful?

1 Corinthians 1:7–9:

*So that ye come behind in no gift; waiting for the revelation of our Lord Jesus Christ; who shall also confirm you unto the end, that ye be unreproveable in the day of our Lord Jesus Christ. God is faithful, through whom ye were called into the fellowship of his Son Jesus Christ our Lord.*

What is a guarantee, a seal, a promise, an heir, or an inheritance?

2 Corinthians 1:21–22:

> *Now he that establisheth us with you in Christ, and anointed us, is God; who also sealed us, and gave us the earnest of the Spirit in our hearts.*

Read all 2 Corinthians 4:16–5:8 but written here is 5:5–8:

> *Now he that wrought us for this very thing is God, who gave unto us the earnest of the Spirit. Being therefore always of good courage, and knowing that, whilst we are at home in the body, we are absent from the Lord (for we walk by faith, not by sight); we are of good courage, I say, and are willing rather to be absent from the body, and to be at home with the Lord.*

Galatians 3:26–29:

> *For ye are all sons of God, through faith, in Christ Jesus. For as many of you as were baptized into Christ did put on Christ. There can be neither Jew nor Greek, there can be neither bond nor free, there can be no male and female; for ye all are one man in Christ Jesus. And if ye are Christ's, then are ye Abraham's seed, heirs according to promise.*

Galatians 4:6–7:

> *And because ye are sons, God sent forth the Spirit of his Son into our hearts, crying, Abba, Father. So that thou art no longer a bondservant, but a son; and if a son, then an heir through God.*

Ephesians 1:13–14:

*In whom ye also, having heard the word of the truth, the gospel of your salvation, —in whom, having also believed, ye were sealed with the Holy Spirit of promise, which is an earnest of our inheritance, unto the redemption of God's own possession, unto the praise of his glory.*

Ephesians 4:30:

*And grieve not the Holy Spirit of God, in whom ye were sealed unto the day of redemption.*

1 Peter 1:3–5:

*Blessed be the God and Father of our Lord Jesus Christ, who according to his great mercy begat us again unto a living hope by the resurrection of Jesus Christ from the dead, unto an inheritance incorruptible, and undefiled, and that fadeth not away, reserved in heaven for you, who by the power of God are guarded through faith unto a salvation ready to be revealed in the last time.*

Titus 1:2–3:

*In hope of eternal life, which God, who cannot lie, promised before times eternal; but in his own seasons manifested his word in the message, wherewith I was entrusted according to the commandment of God our Saviour.*

Read all of Hebrews 6:9–20, but here are verses 17–19:

*Wherein God, being minded to show more abundantly unto the heirs of the promise the immutability of his counsel, interposed with an oath; that by two immutable things, in which it is impossible for God to lie, we may have a strong encouragement, who have fled for refuge to lay hold of the hope set before us: which we have as an anchor of the soul, a hope both sure and stedfast and entering into that which is within the veil;*

Hebrews 7:24–25:

*But he, because he abideth for ever, hath his priest-hood unchangeable. Wherefore also he is able to save to the uttermost them that draw near unto God through him, seeing he ever liveth to make intercession for them.*

John 4:14–15:

*But whosoever drinketh of the water that I shall give him shall never thirst; but the water that I shall give him shall become in him a well of water springing up unto eternal life. The woman saith unto him, Sir, give me this water, that I thirst not, neither come all the way hither to draw.*

Read all 1 John 4:12–19, but here is 4:14–15:

*And we have beheld and bear witness that the Father hath sent the Son to be the Saviour of the world. Whosoever shall confess that Jesus is the Son of God, God abideth in him, and he in God.*

1 John 5:11–13:

*And the witness is this, that God gave unto us eternal life, and this life is in his Son. He that hath the Son hath the life; he that hath not the Son of God hath not the life. These things have I written unto you, that ye may know that ye have eternal life, even unto you that believe on the name of the Son of God.*

Philippians 1:6:

*Being confident of this very thing, that he who began a good work in you will perfect it until the day of Jesus Christ:*

Hebrews 6:4–6:

*For as touching those who were once enlightened and tasted of the heavenly gift, and were made partakers of the Holy Spirit, and tasted the good word of God, and the powers of the age to come, and then fell away, it is impossible to renew them again unto repentance; seeing they crucify to themselves the Son of God afresh, and put him to an open shame.*

2 Peter 1:3–4:

*Seeing that his divine power hath granted unto us all things that pertain unto life and godliness, through the knowledge of him that called us by his own glory and virtue; whereby he hath granted unto us his precious and exceeding great promises; that through these ye may become partakers of the divine nature, having escaped from the corruption that is in the world by lust.*

## PRAYER

Dear Lord, God and Father, thank You for Your life-giving Word, for Your promises that give hope and peace to our troubled hearts. Your Word builds, strengthens, and encourages my faith. It gives me confidence and assurance in my salvation and relationship with You. Thank You. I have NO doubt. Amen.

## CREDITS AND/OR INSPIRATION

See Background. I never want to be without an answer again.

Merriam-Webster.com. "Covenant." Accessed April 30, 2025. https://www.merriam-webster.com/dictionary/covenant.

# Division

## CONCEPTS

Division within the Christian community can be devastating. Though pruning is a form of eventual growth, division for the wrong reasons is a means by which the unseen evil powers of satan seek to destroy and tear down spiritual growth and progress. Satan's use of division quenches the Spirit of God, and within our American society, the divisions between people are growing dangerously deeper.

## PURPOSE

As with many of the Spurs within this writing, the intent is to remind us how God's Word and gospel show the way of salvation for all tribulation.

## SCRIPTURE BASE

Ephesians 4:3–5, Genisis 1:26, 1 Corinthians 1:10, Matthew 5:9, Luke 22:24–26, 1 Corinthians 3:3

## BACKGROUND

Division in America is, in my opinion, at an all-time peak since the Civil War. I don't believe that is an exaggeration. Politics, mainstream media, race, sex, age, social status, foreign powers, and worldly influence are all divided. Christianity has a unique time in history to be united and espouse unity in our testimony by showing our love for God and one another. God's answer is love, for He is love.

## SPUR

Divisions occur daily among families, businesses, partners, friends, siblings, and churches. Some people seek to divide or cause disunity without even thinking of the mischief they create. These troublemakers forge headlong into controversy, considering themselves righteous to point out a wrong.

How is this done? It can be done through gossip, false accusations, or people thrusting themselves where they have no business and then twisting the information they get, causing a division. When we see folks like that in the South, we wish they would "stay in their lane." Other tools satan uses to divide are misaligned jealousy, self-righteousness, pride, power, and money.

Our Bible has enough stories and examples about division and conflict to fill another book. But there are some distinct places we can look to and find God's will about unity, for it is His nature, and He wants it to be ours. If He were divisive, there would be no Trinity. It sounds basic, but God's example for unity is in Himself.

Ephesians 4:3–5

*Giving diligence to keep the unity of the Spirit in the bond of peace. There is one body, and one Spirit, even as also ye were called in one hope of your calling; one Lord, one faith, one baptism.*

I'm confident you've considered this before, but as it relates to His example of unity, what better description can we see in God's Word? First, God united us in harmony with the heavenly host while united in heaven. Then He separated His human creations by giving us dominion over the other living things on earth: evident unity and specific division in one verse:

Genesis 1:26

*And God said, Let us make man in our image, after our likeness: and let them have dominion over the fish of the sea, and over the birds of the heavens, and over the cattle, and over all the earth, and over every creeping thing that creepeth upon the earth.*

When we see division, we should immediately become peacemakers. Do not allow division between brethren to fester and become cancerous. Jesus and Paul give us examples, and God's Word instructs us:

Matthew 5:9

*Blessed are the peacemakers: for they shall be called sons of God.*

Luke 22:24 shows the twelve disciples arguing among themselves about who is greater. The jealousy and pursuit of power here become a spirit of division. Jealousy and desire for more power are satan's tools to cause division among people and groups.

In chapter 22 of Luke, this passage starts with verse 24, showing the disciples in argument, and then Jesus instructs them immediately:

*And there arose also a contention among them, which of them was accounted to be greatest.*

The discussion sounds like your typical argument between two children, so you can imagine what it sounded like between twelve adults. Jesus answered them:

Luke 22:25–26

*And he said unto them, The kings of the Gentiles have lordship over them; and they that have authority over them are called Benefactors. But ye shall not be so: but he that is the greater among you, let him become as the younger; and he that is chief, as he that doth serve.*

What is said here is that the greatest person we can be is the one who has a servant's heart. By the way, relating to peacemaking, Jesus is the peacemaker here. He is also God, and as God, He is the greatest peacemaker.

Paul not only had to deal with divisions identified in the churches he started, but he also had to contend with fellow disciples who didn't work well together. Paul's approaches to these issues are straightforward and bold:

1 Corinthians 3:3

*For ye are yet carnal: for whereas there is among you jealousy and strife, are ye not carnal, and do ye not walk after the manner of men?*

Paul, writing to the people of Corinth, was telling them they were not walking in the Spirit but in the flesh, according to the world's standards instead of God's. We see this happening today where people want to keep up with the Joneses and desire everything instantly. They don't consider God's wants because they focus so much on worldly things. This train of thought can bring forth satan's ability to work his way into a situation, causing envy and strife and thus ultimately creating a division among people.

So, you see, satan uses different tools to break or divide groups, and he doesn't care what kind of group it is. Therefore, we must be constantly vigilant to fight his schemes as he tries to destroy the creation of God at any cost. To fight is to pray and call upon the name of Jesus. For when we do, satan must flee.

## PRAYER

Father, Lord my God, my prayer before Your throne of grace today is to help us become peacemakers. Enable us to fight the unseen powers of darkness when they attack to destroy and devour Your servants and their desires to honor and glorify You. Help us hear Your Word and boldly react to stomp out division wherever we see it in our lives and the lives of our brothers and sisters in You. We ask You in Jesus' mighty name to make satan flee. Amen.

## CREDITS AND/OR INSPIRATION

Divisions within our churches hurt people in so many ways. Families are broken, friends are forsaken, and Christianity suffers when the Spirit is grieved and quenched. May it not be so. We can fight division if we identify where the roots grow. This Spur might help a church in trouble, but only God can heal and cure.

# Reserved Seating

**CONCEPTS**

Kingdom living begins when you accept Christ as your Savior. Eternity with Christ starts right then, not when you die. People forget about that. They allow satan to steal their joy. Many people think that heavenly bliss comes after they are dead. But Christians often miss the many blessings God intends for us in this life on earth. The concept is unfamiliar to many.

**PURPOSE**

This Spur was written to change the train of thought for some Christians who lack faith. To think of something in a completely different way is called a paradigm shift. Looking toward heaven as a secured reservation gives people peace, hope, and faith. God means for us to live life abundantly.

**SCRIPTURE BASE**

John 10:10; Ephesians 2:1–10, 19–20; John 14: 2–6

**BACKGROUND**

While teaching Sunday school to an adult group of men and women (average ages forties and fifties), a discussion ensued, leading to earnest research on Kingdom living. This Spur is the result of that research and discussion.

## SPUR

Have you ever made reservations at a fancy restaurant? You give your name, and they do the rest. After you have that reservation, do you worry you might not get in? You know you have a seat at a table and will not have to wait. You'll be greeted by the maître d' and seated as soon as you give them your name at the door. You pass right by all those folks waiting in the lobby. You are special because you know that you've got reservations even before you get in the car to leave for the restaurant. You have reserved seating.

How about seating at a basketball game or music concert? You can walk into a crowded arena or theater and have reserved seats. Just walk in, give your tickets to the usher, and let them seat you—what a great feeling. No worries, no hurry, my place is reserved. Knowing your place is reserved for the big event makes you feel less anxious, almost peaceful, that you have nothing to worry about. The seat is already paid for; it's yours. They were expecting you and reserved a place just for you. How cool is that?

Ephesians 2:1–10, 19–20

*And you did he make alive, when ye were dead through your trespasses and sins, wherein ye once walked according to the course of this world, according to the prince of the powers of the air, of the spirit that now worketh in the sons of disobedience; among whom we also all once lived in the lusts of our flesh, doing the desires of the flesh and of the mind, and were by nature children of wrath, even as the rest:—but God, being rich in mercy, for his great love wherewith he loved us, even when we were dead through our trespasses, made us alive together with Christ (by grace have ye been saved), and raised us up with him, and made us to sit with him in the heavenly places, in Christ Jesus: that in the ages to come he might show the exceeding riches of his grace in kindness toward us in Christ Jesus: for by grace have ye been saved through faith; and that not of yourselves, it is the gift of God; not of works, that no man should glory. For we are his workmanship, created in Christ Jesus for good works, which God afore prepared that we should walk in them.*

*So then ye are no more strangers and sojourners, but ye are fellow-citizens with the saints, and of the household of God, being built upon the foundation of the apostles and prophets, Christ Jesus himself being the chief corner stone.*

Jesus says in John 14: 2–6,

*In my Father's house are many mansions; if it were not so, I would have told you; for I go to prepare a place for you. And if I go and prepare a place for you, I come again, and will receive you unto myself; that where I am, there ye may be also. And whither I go, ye know the way. Thomas saith unto him, Lord, we know not whither thou goest; how know we the way? Jesus saith unto him, I am the way, and the truth, and the life: no one cometh unto the Father, but by me.*

So, you call yourself a Christian. Are you? Do you have a reservation in heaven? Did you make that reservation through Jesus? He's the only one that has the book of reservations.

Ok, for those who know the truth—act like it! Be bold. No one can take your seat! It's reserved! What do you have to fear? Do you know what they call it when Christians live a Kingdom life? Do you know? Kingdom living? Holy? Joyful? Full of Christ? Sold out for Jesus? They call that faith. Do you have more or less faith in your reservation in heaven than you do for that seat at the restaurant? Live it!

For those who want that reservation or are unsure you have a place reserved for you in heaven, this is your time to have Jesus write your name in the Book of Life! And get that reserved seating at the table as a family member of God and join the banquet. He's waiting for you to call. The invitation is open right now. Declare that you want a seat beside our Lord Jesus. He's the one who gave His life and shed His blood so you could get that invitation for free. He paid for it already. He paid it all for you.

## PRAYER

Lord, God and Father, thank You for Your provisions here and in heaven. Thank You for Your Word to encourage and teach us how much You love us and what You have in store for us; we can only imagine. Lord, remind each of us that we are Your children and that our home is with You for eternity. Teach us how to live like we are in Your presence. Amen.

## CREDITS AND/OR INSPIRATION

It is difficult to say this, but I meet far too many professed Christians who forget the benefits and blessings God intended for us when we were saved. This world sucks us down. God lifts us up.

# Repent, for the Kingdom Is at Hand

## CONCEPTS

We need to remain aware that Christ's return is unknown. His calling of our lives to Him is also unknown. We are to plan, but we are also to keep our eyes on the eastern sky for His return.

## PURPOSE

John the Baptist and Jesus preached over two thousand years ago for all to repent, for the Kingdom of Heaven is at hand. These truths are found in Matthew's Scripture references below. Has anything changed since then? If not, why are we not preaching the same?

## SCRIPTURE BASE

Matthew 3:1–3, Matthew 3:6–12, Matthew 4:17, John 10:10, John 3:3–9, Ephesians 4:7

## BACKGROUND

During a county-wide fall festival in a nearby town, my friends and I walked the streets, enjoying the merchants and artists selling their wares and foods. At each end of the long main street where most of the crowds entered or exited the fair, two young men, one at each end of the street, stood on the proverbial and literal soapbox with banners that read, "Repent for the Kingdom of Heaven Is Near." They each had electronic megaphones and were preaching to the crowd a theme on repentance and God's saving grace —before it's too late. They received a great deal of verbal persecution and heckling. Consider this was in the Bible Belt South. I prayed for them and praised God for their boldness to preach God's Word. I'll never forget what the hecklers said to them, thinking how bold those two young men were to stand so bravely for the Lord.

## SPUR

Movies often show some made-out crazy guy on the streets waving a sign that reads, "Repent for the Kingdom of Heaven Is Near." The secular world loves to point to these scriptural verses and ridicule the religious nuts who espouse this far-out, right-wing religious prophecy. The secular world looks at these verses, the street prophets and preachers, and rails at them, laughing at the fact that they predict the End of the World, the Day of the Lord, the Apocalypse.

Satan uses this blasphemy to persecute and make people doubt or think disparagingly about Christians. Even some religious leaders who walk the middle of the road theologically, shy away from sidewalk prophets who make this call to the world. You may have heard some say we need Christians, not religious nuts. Please, don't call my Jesus and John the Baptist religious nuts. Shame on them and shame on us if we think the same.

John the prophet and Jesus the Christ are not wrong, even if what they said was spoken over two thousand years ago. The Kingdom of Heaven is near for each of us, and we must repent to be saved.

I'm much older than John the Baptist or Jesus when they walked this earth. The Kingdom of Heaven is closer to me now than yesterday. When is the Kingdom of Heaven coming for you?

Kingdom living is a state of mind and devotion that we can live in each day. God intended for us to live our lives with His Spirit within us to give us peace, joy, and fullness of life each day.

John 10:10

> *The thief comes only to steal and kill and destroy; I have come that they may have life, and have it to the full.*

We are assured we will be with Jesus when we pass from this world. We will be like Him with Him.

John 3:3–9

> *Or are ye ignorant that all we who were baptized into Christ Jesus were baptized into his death? We were buried therefore with him through baptism into death: that like as Christ was raised from the dead through the glory of the Father, so we also might walk in newness of life. For if we have become united with him in the likeness of his death, we shall be also in the likeness of his resurrection; knowing this, that our old man was crucified with him, that the body of sin might be done away, that so we should no longer be in bondage to sin; for he that hath died is justified from sin. But if we died with Christ, we believe that we shall also live with him; knowing that Christ being raised from the dead dieth no more; death no more hath dominion over him.*

If that is not the Kingdom of Heaven, describe to me what is. To have that thin veil so close for us to pass through, we must have repented and accepted His grace and believed in Jesus as Lord.

Like the Pharisees in Jesus' day, we want to make getting to heaven something to earn, something deserved, something we must work toward. But unfortunately, they didn't understand grace, and many of us also want to forget what grace is. Grace is not given in measures but in full.

Ephesians 4:7

*But unto each one of us was the grace given according to the measure of the gift of Christ.*

Repent, for the Kingdom of Heaven is at hand! It is nearer than you think for every one of us. Is it time for you to repent and begin living a Kingdom life? What does that mean to you?

## PRAYER

Lord, God and Father, I praise Your Holy Name. You are mighty to save, Lord, and I owe everything to You. Whether You come for me today or rapture us all tomorrow makes no difference in my love for You. Lord, help me live for You each day, for I know how near You are to me. Make me bold to tell others of Your amazing grace. Amen.

## CREDIT AND/OR INSPIRATION

All credit and glory goes to God in the Highest. The inspiration goes to two young men so bold to preach His Word on the street despite a heckling crowd.

# Smell That Smell?

**CONCEPTS**

We live in a society that has become comfortable with the sins of this society. Many of those sins are the same that have been around since the fall. We must wake up, recognize, and repent from our sin and the sin we allow around us. At this time, many believers and non-believers have become "nose blind."

**PURPOSE**

God calls us to be holy because He is holy. Being comfortable in our sin is not being holy.

**SCRIPTURE BASE**

Psalm 115:6, Matthew 23:27–29, Philippians 4:13, 1 Peter 1:16, Acts 3:19, Ephesians 6:11

**BACKGROUND**

I recently watched a few news programs on which people calmly discussed how various mainstream religious denominations have split or rewritten charters to accept sin expressly identified as sin in the Old and New Testaments. It sickens me to see organizations that embrace sin along with the sinner who continues to live in sin. They have cherry-picked what they want to hear from God's Word. That is beyond being nose blind. They have accepted the smell of corruption.

# SPUR

A group of Southern rock and roll musicians named Lynard Skynard published a song in 1977 called *That Smell*. If you are familiar with it, you know it is about the smell of death and the dangerous effects of the use of alcohol and drugs (Vitagliano).

Our New Testament and Old Testament do not have many smell-related verses. God smells the aroma of prayers lifted to Him, written in Revelation 5:8 and Psalm 141:2.

Psalm 115:6

*They have ears, but they hear not; Noses have they, but they smell not.*

We often see more references to "Open your eyes to see and open your ears to hear" having the same connotation. But the sense of smell is not a sense that Jesus or the other writers and prophets spoke of. Our sense of smell can be offended or blessed quite easily. Bad smells repel us. Bad smells can protect us, warning us to get away from danger. Pleasant aromas bring feelings of joy and peace and experiences we have enjoyed. On the other hand, manufactured smells are used to change our moods, excite us, or make us hungry.

Have you ever heard of nose blindness? It is a real thing, and it may be a sense that God has given us to protect us from the unpleasantness of smells that are repelling and putrid. Have you ever known anyone who lived in a "Paper Town" or near an oil refinery? Have you ever known anyone who worked in a rubber factory, butcher house, or local dump yard or drove a live animal transfer truck? There are hundreds of other places people work and live that smell horrendous. At least they smell horrible if we do not live or work there.

Those who spend whole days or several hours daily in those environments, maybe near a pig farm or chicken processing plant, do not smell it over time; if they do, it does not bother them. They are comfortable with it. Sometimes they go away for a while and return to the area; at first they may notice the smell but soon they forget or do not seem to detect that nasty smell that might make anyone else vomit. It is funny how that works. They live, work, and were raised there, and it doesn't smell very good, and they do not seem to mind. When others ask how they can stand the smell of that pork meat manufacturing plant, they will look at you and say something like, "Smells like money to me." That is about the fact that where they work is their livelihood. It puts food on the table, clothes on their backs, roofs over their head, and Christmas presents under the tree. You can not fault anyone for that. Besides, I like my bacon and forget how it got to me. I do not care to think about it. Besides, the smell of bacon cooking on the stove removes all those other thoughts.

But you know it works the same way with sin. Here is the comparison. Sin might bring you all those things I just listed. Think of all the jobs and activities that make the money that provides the food, clothes, housing, cars, jewelry, and Christmas presents. That sin does not seem wrong to those sinners. They do not smell the sin that wreaks havoc in their lives. The rest of us who still have a sense of moral values see it, point at them, and judge them for it like we are better than they are. Our problem is that we are nose blind to our sin. We judge them because they sin differently than we do, but sin is sin, and it all stinks to God. You might not like to hear that any more than the Pharisees did when Jesus pointed it out to them.

Matthew 23:27–29

> *Woe unto you, scribes and Pharisees, hypocrites! for ye are like unto whited sepulchres, which outwardly appear beautiful, but inwardly are full of dead men's bones, and of*

*all uncleanness. Even so ye also outwardly appear righteous unto men, but inwardly ye are full of hypocrisy and iniquity.*

I'm pretty sure Jesus told them they stunk of sin.

There is another kind of nose blindness that our society is very guilty of. We see and hear it, but we no longer smell it. Our acceptance of sin is the very downfall of our society. Our biggest problem stems from the fact that some of that sin has been legalized even though our Bible points it out as sin. We must accept it in our media, schools, workplaces, and homes. Many denominations have accepted the practice of some sin in our churches and preached acceptance from the pulpit. It smells, and many Christians cannot smell it because we have become comfortable with it in our modern life. Read God's Word and believe it for what it says. God has not changed—He can still smell it and call it what it is because He is holy.

How do we get out of it? How do we unclog our noses and smell our own stink? It may sound simplistic, but it is not always easy.

Philippians 4:13

*I can do all things in him that strengtheneth me.*

One way is to get away from it for a while. If we stop and do something more worthwhile, we could see the sin and situation that is so wrong. Sometimes, our sense of smell and blindness to sin is so bad that we can not identify what stinks. That is when we need to ask God to show us our sins. Ask God to reveal what it is that offends Him. Ask God to help you smell the stink in your life and then clean the house, computer, phone, and sin out of your life. You can do that, and He will show you. Then, when you see it, smell it, identify it, get rid of it. Unload that sin, turn away from it, drop it, and run from it. That is repentance.

1 Peter 1:16

*Because it is written, Ye shall be holy; for I am holy.*

Acts 3:19

> *Repent ye therefore, and turn again, that your sins may be blotted out, that so there may come seasons of refreshing from the presence of the Lord.*

Could it be possible that the refreshing here might be some clean air to breathe?

Another active approach is to reject sin from infiltrating our lives. We cannot always fight city hall, but we can make our influence and that of the Word of God known whenever possible. We will be reviled for it. We will be judged, and we may even suffer for it. We should expect this because it is precisely what Jesus said would happen if we follow Him and obey His Word. So, put on the full armor of God and stand up for what is in God's Word.

Ephesians 6:11

> *Put on the whole armor of God, that ye may be able to stand against the wiles of the devil.*

I suggest you reread chapter six of Ephesians to get that warrior spirit.

**PRAYER**

Lord, God and Father, You have called us to be holy men and women. Please help us to be all You have called us to be. Please give us more faith and wisdom to see our sin and repent from it. Help us see the sin around us where the principalities of evil have temporarily prevailed over us. Lord, help us stand up and call upon

Your name to defeat satan and all he has claimed on this earth. Please give us the power to reclaim what is Yours. In Jesus' precious and mighty name, amen.

## CREDITS AND/OR INSPIRATION.

The inspiration came from watching the news and seeing our society fall deeper into accepting sin as progressiveness. So many people accept it and do not see it or rail against it. If a righteous man fails to act, sin will prevail.

Joe Vitagliano. "Behind the Song Lyrics: 'That Smell,' Lynyrd Skynyrd." American Songwriter. December 21, 2021. https://americansongwriter.com/that-smell-lynyrd-skynyrd-behind-song-lyrics-meaning/.

# The Proper Response

## CONCEPTS

This is how a Christian should glorify God despite the tribulation we endure.

## PURPOSE

Because we all have periods of tribulation in life, our careers, and society.

## SCRIPTURE BASE

Ephesians 6:19–20, Habbakuk—all chapters (1, 2, and 3)

## BACKGROUND

At the time of this writing, the United States was in turbulent times unseen in decades. This division is perpetuated by mainstream media, professional and personal media platforms, political parties, economic pressures, Hollywood elites, professional sports personas, big pharma monetary influence and false science, and dozens of minion organizations on both liberal and conservative sides. Players formed to split our nation along race, sex, wealth, health, foreign policy, education, constitutional rights, and religion, whether unintentional or by design, the result is the same. It is sometimes hard to see the best in the worst of times. Brother against brother, father against son, a war of social unrest constantly brewed and spilled into the streets. The time was the new roaring 2020s

.

## SPUR

Habakkuk is a timeless lesson in Christian maturity; we need reminding. If only we would consider his example today, what a blessing we would receive.

Do you know the story of Habakkuk? Have you heard a sermon or a Sunday school lesson about Habakkuk? If you haven't, here is a treat for you. Listen well. Habakkuk's story is that of a model Christian, except that he lived in the days of the Old Testament.

Let us begin with getting his name right. How do you pronounce Habakkuk? Say, Have a cup? Have a cup. Now adjust Hab a kuk? Hab uh kuk. Habakkuk. Some will surely disagree with that pronunciation.

Habakkuk was a prophet in a horrible time in Hebrew history when he was the prophet of awful news. The shocking news God instructed him to write was news about an irreversible decision He had made. Israel was about to be destroyed. Not just taken over by their enemies but also their cities annihilated, their people slaughtered, their women and children taken as captives, becoming enslaved people for the conquerors. Habakkuk was amid the war and the tribulation like other prophets who wrote during this period, like Ezekiel did.

*Tribulation* is an unusual word study. What is tribulation? Christians consider The Tribulation the "Big One"—the End. John wrote about the Big One in Revelation. But tribulation in the Bible means much more. Tribulation can be a season of suffering or circumstances in an individual or people.

Habakkuk has three chapters and is broken down into three realities of life in tribulation.

Chapter One. Habakkuk is mourning. His life is nearly unbearable, and he asks the Lord, as we would ask, "Why me? Why don't You hear me? You have not helped me. I need You, and You are not there for me."

The Lord answers him. "Sorry, H, but I am destroying Israel and using the worst enemies I have found to do it to you."

Habakkuk is shocked! He asks what we might ask, "Are You, my God? Why will You allow these enemies to hurt us?"

Chapter Two. Habakkuk tells God that he is watching and waiting for an answer his pleading.

The Lord answers him, "Yes, write the vision I have given you about what will happen. Wait for My answer. Let the people know I, the Lord, will punish all the wicked for their sins." Then God tells him how Israel has been living and that justice is coming to those without remorse for their sin. Then God reminds him not to forget that He is in His temple.

Chapter Three. Habakkuk gets it. He realizes and sees the wrath of God amid the tribulation and tells God that he will not stop praising and glorifying God regardless of how bad it gets. The list he provides, which could happen, is the very sustaining lifeblood of the country. He imagines all of it could be gone.

Compare what happened in Israel and Judah to what could happen in our country. Like those in other countries, life in this country could be horrible. Look at what happened to Argentina. Once a robust economy and government, the country suffers high inflation, lack of food, poor energy production, poor transportation, and no relief. The United States is not so rich that it could not fall.

Habakkuk asks for mercy but understands God's perfect will and sovereignty over all He created.

There is a lesson here. How often do we see tribulation in our lives and ask God, "Why me? Are You there? What is the purpose of all this trouble? Have mercy." The story of Habakkuk gives us this example and teaches us how to work through our tribulations.

Do we take that next step? Do we wait for His answer? Do we recognize His ultimate control in our lives? Do we pour out our hearts to Him, give Him our burdens, and ask for His mercy? Do any of us have that much faith? Do you realize He is God and will answer us, now or later? Are we willing to wait on Him when we are caught in the crossfire?

Our example is this: Habakkuk tells God he will not stop praising and glorifying God regardless of how bad it gets.

**PRAYER**

God, Your will is perfect. You grant all authority on earth as it is in heaven. Who can we complain to when You alone are the author of our tribulations and remedies? We ask for Your mercy, Lord. We ask for Your forgiveness. We lean into Your promises of protection. For we know all good things come from You, Lord, and we know You have only good things for those who love You and obey Your commands. Amen.

**CREDITS AND/OR INSPIRATION**

The book of Habakkuk.

# Test Yourself

## CONCEPTS

People should not choose and parse the Word of God as to what they believe and that which they do not. God's Word must be entirely accepted as truth, or there is no truth. Therefore, if the hearer of God's Word does not believe in faith or what is taught, they are lost, and the Spirit is not in them.

## PURPOSE

People who call themselves Christians and do not have the Spirit of God within them to reveal the truth of God's Word need a wake-up call. This Spur is not intended to separate people from their church membership, but to draw them into a deeper faith. If preached as this is written, the result might become a revival or the shedding of the unfaithful. Either way, it will be a "Come to Jesus" meeting. The verses below are not exclusive or inclusive but gathered to use at your discretion, however God speaks to you.

## SCRIPTURE BASE

Proverbs 30:5—*Every word of God is tried: He is a shield unto them that take refuge in him.*

Isaiah 40:8—*The grass withereth, the flower fadeth; but the word of our God shall stand forever.*

Mark 7:13—*Making void the word of God by your tradition, which ye have delivered: and many such like things ye do.*

Luke 1:37—*For no word from God shall be void of power.*

1 Corinthians 1:18—*For the word of the cross is to them that perish foolishness; but unto us who are saved it is the power of God.*

Hebrews 4:12—*For the word of God is living, and active, and sharper than any two-edged sword, and piercing even to the dividing of soul and spirit, of both joints and marrow, and quick to discern the thoughts and intents of the heart.*

Revelation 22:18—*I testify unto every man that heareth the words of the prophecy of this book, If any man shall add unto them, God shall add unto him the plagues which are written in this book.*

Revelation 22:19—*And if any man shall take away from the words of the book of this prophecy, God shall take away his part from the tree of life, and out of the holy city, which are written in this book.*

Proverbs 21:2—*Every way of a man is right in his own eyes; But Jehovah weigheth the hearts.*

2 Timothy 3:7–9, 13–17—*Ever learning, and never able to come to the knowledge of the truth. And even as Jannes and Jambres withstood Moses, so do these also withstand the truth; men corrupted in mind, reprobate concerning the faith. But they shall proceed no further: for their folly shall be evident unto all men, as theirs also came to be.*

*But evil men and impostors shall wax worse and worse, deceiving and being deceived. But abide thou in the things which thou hast learned and hast been assured of, knowing of whom thou hast learned them; and that from a babe thou hast known the sacred writings which are able to make thee wise unto salvation through faith which is in Christ Jesus. Every scripture inspired of God is also profitable for teaching, for reproof, for correction, for instruction which is in righteousness: that the man of God may be complete, furnished completely unto every good work.*

2 Corinthians 13:5—*Try your own selves, whether ye are in the faith; prove your own selves. Or know ye not as to your own selves, that Jesus Christ is in you? unless indeed ye be reprobate.*

John 16:13—*Howbeit when he, the Spirit of truth, is come, he shall guide you into all the truth: for he shall not speak from himself; but what things soever he shall hear, these shall he speak: and he shall declare unto you the things that are to come.*

Revelation 3:14–16—*And to the angel of the church in Laodicea write: These things saith the Amen, the faithful and true witness, the beginning of the creation of God: I know thy works, that thou art neither cold nor hot: I would thou wert cold or hot. So because thou art lukewarm, and neither hot nor cold, I will spew thee out of my mouth.*

## BACKGROUND

God's Word says it. I believe it. I may not understand it entirely, but I cannot cast it aside in disbelief. God's Word is the Truth. There is no other—all in or all out.

## SPUR

I have many questions for those reading today. Consider it a test for yourself. Think about each one.

Do you believe in God? Do you believe in His Word? Reference the Spur "Unbelievable."

Did God create the heavens and the earth in six days? Really? Consider all the stuff that was made. Think of all the science we've seen on TV and in school. Consider all we think we know of the universe and all we can see with our telescopes and deep space devices. Think of all the earth and billions of planets and stars like our solar system, if not trillions.

Do you think God made humanity through Adam and Eve? What about all those fossils and discoveries of manlike bones and tools, images drawn on cave walls? Can you explain that in relation to Adam and Eve?

And what about Noah? Did God cause the flood that covered the WHOLE earth and save His animal kingdom and humankind through Noah?

Did you ever question the stories in Exodus and how God performed the miracles for Moses? Like all the plagues of Egypt, the parting of the Red Sea. How about manna, shoes that never wore out, water spouting from rocks, and pillars of fire and smoke that led over a million people in the harshest desert for forty years? Really?

Did God stop the earth for nearly a whole day at the request of Joshua so he could defeat his enemies in battle?

Did God destroy Sodom and Gomorrah?

Did God make a donkey talk?

Do you really believe all those stories and many not listed, just because they were written on paper that has survived thousands of years?

Maybe you pick and choose what you believe. As in, I might believe that one, but I'm not too sure about this other one. Have you created your own religion based on what is written in the Bible? That is not a wrong question. There are whole religions based on accepting parts and discounting other parts of God's written Word.

Test yourself.

If you doubt these, how can you believe in the virgin birth of Christ?

How can you believe a holy man, God in the flesh, walked on earth for thirty years and performed miracles like raising the dead, healing the sick, and making the blind see?

So, you might believe He was crucified, but how can you believe He rose from the grave? Did angels take care of Him?

How can you believe that after His supposed death and resurrection, He walked this earth for many to see, and after many saw Him over many days, He ascended to heaven?

How do you know He can save you from hell and that He has reserved a place for you in heaven beyond all doubt? Can you trust that?

Do you even believe there is a heaven or hell?

These are all points of religious contention. Are you religious, or are you a Christian? Nearly all these questions require faith. Test yourself—do you believe some stories and not others? You failed the test. Logically, practically, spiritually, if you doubt one aspect of the Word of God, then likely none of it might be the truth, and we are wasting our time hanging out here today.

I may have just talked you out of being a Christian, or maybe you'd instead go to some other church that doesn't preach the Word of God. Have you passed or failed the test? Now, you have two choices.

We need to have a moment of "Come to Jesus." Are you all in or just a mediocre Christian? God does not care for a lukewarm Christian. Today is the day to commit and surrender to what the Word of God says and try to live the way God has instructed us to live with all your might. We might fall and sometimes fail, but He says He is faithful to forgive those who believe.

Do you need proof that the Spirit of God is real and lives within you and me? He lives in me—I know. But does He live in you? Do you want to believe and have the peace and assurance only God and the Spirit of God can give you?

## PRAYER

Dear Lord, God and heavenly Father, forgive me when I doubt. Give me more faith every day to believe in Your Word. Thank You, Lord, for the Spirit within me and the assurance of my salvation. In the precious name of Jesus, I pray. Amen.

## CREDITS AND/OR INSPIRATION

Forgive me if this Spur seems repetitive in driving the same point about what we read in God's Word. I can't seem to help myself, for you see, the Word of God is life, and if we do not believe it, we have no foundation for our life now or hereafter.

# Tough Choice

## CONCEPTS

This Spur reminds us of our priorities and how we sometimes get them mixed up. Putting the first things first is what each of us needs to do.

## PURPOSE

Reminding us to put God first in our lives, our relationships, our families, our homes, our church, our school, and our jobs.

## SCRIPTURE BASE

Philippians 3:14, Exodus 33:1–23, Romans 10:13, James 4:8

## BACKGROUND

I am speaking only for myself, but you may be able to identify with my story. I have gone off the track in my life. I acted as though I were a dog off the chain. I left what I knew to be honest and genuine for my life and went on to do what I thought was different, exciting, and possibly better. I had my priorities messed up, and I put not one, two, or three but several things I unconsciously considered more important than God. That was a mistake, and I thank God that He remained in the driver's seat every day and showed me, like a prodigal son, the way home and back to Him.

## SPUR

Think of all the pursuits we have in life. Every one of us has them. We all wanted to do something, accomplish something, finish something, acquire something, or pursue a goal from the time we were small. We want! We have structured our whole lives around the quest for something. Maybe it is to be happy. Perhaps it is to leave a legacy or accomplish a feat no one has ever done. Maybe we want to pay off the car early. We can all name at least one and a few more if we think a bit. Do not get me wrong; these are not all bad; we prioritize them when things get messed up.

In Philippians 3:14, Paul writes,

> *I press on toward the goal unto the prize of the high calling of God in Christ Jesus.*

Sometimes, we must give up one pursuit because of priorities to press toward another quest. Those dilemmas require thought and planning; if we have wisdom, we pray about them.

Personal story—you have one, I am sure. I bought my first brand-new, off-the-showroom-floor automobile. My wife and I had only been married for a few years. We had no kids, and we wanted to have fun while we were young and not tied down too much. We purchased a convertible sports car, and it was a beauty. We already had more than one car because we both worked, but we really wanted this brand-new sports car and could afford it—if we bought it on time. So, we got it, and we were doing fantastic for a few years until we decided on another goal—kids and a family. Kids and sports cars with no back seats do not work too well. A decision was required, and the priority was family, not the sports cars. We couldn't afford another vehicle, and we were sure that if we were to have a family, we needed something that could haul us all and the stuff you must carry when you're parents of a small child or two. So, we had to sell the sports car, which broke our hearts. After the kids arrived, though, we forgot about the sports car. This story is a typical dilemma; many will utterly identify with the circumstances.

Check out the priorities Moses set for his life. In Exodus 33, God talks to Moses in verses 1–4, and He says concisely, "I am keeping my promise to My people and their fathers before them. I want you to go into the promised land and take it. I will send an angel before you, and you will not have any problems with the people who live there. The land is yours as promised, but I am not going with you." In fact, in the following few verses, God says, "If I went with you, I might just kill you all because you people make Me angry for all your sinfulness."

Moses and the people were sad about this announcement. They were about to go into the promised land. It had been their goal and struggle for forty years, and when they were about to have it all, God said, "Go on, take it, but I am not going with you."

Moses cannot bear to hear it. To paraphrase verses 15–16, Moses says to God, "If You do not go with us, do not take us there, because if You are not with us, how will Your people or I know we have Your grace and favor?"

Moses got his priorities straight. Do you think that was a hard choice? He told God he would rather have Him and His grace than all the good life of milk and honey over the Jordan in the promised land. God was impressed by that choice. Paraphrasing verse 17, the Lord says to Moses, "I will do what you ask because you have My grace, and I know you by name."

Wow, that is what I want. I want God to give me His grace and tell me He knows my name. Priorities. Answer the question: What is more important—this life in a land we are just passing through or eternity with God? The same question is in front of each of us. Is it the world we want, or is it the grace of Jesus and life eternal? Tough choices?

Not so hard when you think about it, and you can make that choice today. You can draw near to God just like Moses did. It was easy to change God's mind to give Moses grace. All Moses had to do was choose the most significant thing in this life and the next: God. God even gave us a straightforward way to do that. Ask! Call upon the One who is the way, the truth, and the life, Jesus.

Romans 10:13 says,

> *Whosoever shall call upon the name of the Lord shall be saved.*

James 4:8 says,

> *Draw nigh to God, and he will draw nigh to you. Cleanse your hands, ye sinners; and purify your hearts, ye doubleminded.*

Today might be the day for you to decide what your priorities are. What is your goal in life? What is your destination for eternal life?

## PRAYER

God, Father and Lord, I thank You for being faithful to me when I was unfaithful to You. You never left me and stopped me every time I went too far. You forgave me for being a fool to think You were not all I needed, and I needed more. You are my Savior and my Rock and all I will forever need. Amen.

## CREDITS AND/OR INSPIRATION

John Bevere. *Good or God? Why Good Without God Isn't Enough.* Messenger International. Audio Book, Oasis Audio. August 11, 2015.

# The Devil Made Me Do It

## CONCEPTS

Use this Spur to relate the gospel to those who think themselves too far from God to receive His acceptance because of their temptations and inability to overcome them.

## PURPOSE

To lead people to Christ and allow Him to help them overcome their temptations and sin.

## SCRIPTURE BASE

1 Corinthians 10:13, Ecclesiastes 1:9, Hebrews 4:15, Matthew 26:41, Mark 14:38, Luke 22:40, James 1:12

## BACKGROUND

We are all tempted, sometimes we fall, and other times we overcome, but we are not immune or unique when it comes to being tempted. Jesus overcame temptation, and as our advocate, He understands and is there to lean on when our strength is not enough, His is. You can overcome temptation and sin, but not alone. And you are not alone. With God, you can overcome temptation and sin. For He alone is faithful and has the power to overcome what we cannot on our own.

## SPUR

The title is far from being original. A well-known comedian, Flip Wilson, made the phrase a tag title for jokes and commentaries, probably about a zillion sermons and devotions in the late '70s and early '80s. I thought it might still be an eye-catcher for interest's sake because young people may not have ever heard it, and older folks who know it might smile and remember the comedy of Flip Wilson. Unfortunately, Flip passed away at age 64 on November 26, 1998.

Do you know anyone who has not struggled in some way with temptations? Simple to complex, from the temptation of grabbing the last donut left in the box at work to the next-door neighbor who seems way too friendly. Our lives get confusing. We all have temptations that fit the time and social pressures at each age. Each age segment or season has its temptations from childhood through senior citizenship. Due to circumstances beyond our control, everyday temptations seem insurmountable, and we rationalize how others get away with sinning. We scheme how we might be able to as well. Our motives are so strong that we begin to believe we are unique and that a particular temptation is more than we can bear. Then we fall into the big trap—"I'll do it because I know God will forgive me." He will, but the consequences of your actions are bound to make you pay in some way. Those consequences may become your hell on earth. A big lie is the one that says, "I want this so much, I'll pay the price of the ultimate consequence." Not very smart.

We are unique. Everyone of us is different. We live with different needs, bodies, minds, ages, looks, resources, and jobs. Do I need to go on? We are unique, but not so much in terms of temptation and sin.

1 Corinthians 10:13

*There hath no temptation taken you but such as man can bear: but God is faithful, who will not suffer you to be*

295

*tempted above that ye are able; but will with the temptation make also the way of escape, that ye may be able to endure it.*

Ladies, that doesn't get you off the hook here. You are part of the "man" spoken of here.

Let's begin at the beginning of this verse. Please, repeat after me. NO temptation. Not one, not any, none are unique to just you. All temptations are common to every man and woman. As Solomon says in Ecclesiastes 1:9, *there is no new thing under the sun.*

In my ministry, I have encountered men and women who had an addiction they couldn't shake off or were addicts of some habitual drug of one kind or another. Most addictions come from the sins you feed.

Short story. A man called a rodent expert and asked him to come to his warehouse because he had a rat problem. The inspector looked around and said, "Where's the food?" The warehouse owner said, "This is a warehouse of auto parts. There's no food here." The rodent expert smiled at him and said, "If there ain't no food, there ain't no rats."

Temptation and sin are like that—no food, no temptation. If you feed your mind with the very sin you struggle with, the temptation for more sin will follow very quickly. Take the spouse cheater, adulterer, pedophile, or sex-monger. What sensual reading or viewing have they filled their eyes and minds with? Porn? Sensuous movies or salacious books and magazines? Feed the rats, and it is hard to get rid of them.

Some people succumb to peer pressure and take newer drugs that hook you on the first high. Others get you just when you think you can handle it. One addict told me (and you could tell he was well-versed in biblical theology) that "Jesus can't help addicts because He never had the temptation of addiction." He rationalized that because Jesus never sinned to begin with, He had never been down the road of addiction and the sensations and physical urges that drug addiction can bring. So, he was sure that he was lost and unrecoverable because God did not understand what he was going through.

He's right about Jesus never being addicted physically to addictive drugs or alcohol, but I know this. God created us, and He knows us much better than we do. Therefore, I never ever limit the power of our Holy God, creator of the universe! Never!

Hebrews 4:15

*For we have not a high priest that cannot be touched with the feeling of our infirmities; but one that hath been in all points tempted like as we are, yet without sin.*

He knows.

And that's what I told the addict. After that, I never saw him again. I pray I will see him in heaven someday.

Many of you have read and heard the temptations of Jesus. I couldn't relate to any of those. But, as the all-powerful Son of God, satan thought he knew what temptations Jesus might succumb to. And we know that Jesus responded to those temptations using Scripture verses that stopped satan in his tracks. Satan knows our buttons to push too. The temptations he draws us with are the ones we can have if we want them enough. Satan is the great liar. He prowls around, waiting to devour us—enticing us to sin and driving us away from God. Because we are tempted, satan also convinces us that we are already guilty of sin. You know that cannot be true. Satan tempted Jesus, and He did not sin. So, toss that guilt trip in the wastebasket. Everyone is tempted, and being tempted is not a sin; yielding to temptation is a sin.

We know our weaknesses, and quite honestly, sins can be addictive. We like it. Hate to say that, but for some of us, it is true. We must examine ourselves and seek God's intervention to pursue holiness. Ask the Spirit to convict us of what sin separates us from His love, blessings, and grace. How? Pray and read His word.

Here's an example. Jesus with His disciples in the garden of Gethsemane while on watch for the enemy that would soon come to take Jesus to the cross. Matthew 26:41 and Mark 14:38 write about what Jesus said: *"Watch and pray, that ye enter not into temptation: the spirit indeed is willing, but the flesh is weak."*

Luke 22:40 says,

*And when he was at the place, he said unto them, Pray that ye enter not into temptation.*

I don't know about you, but when I read the same thing in three places about what Jesus said, I think that might be something I should do too.

There are several other Scripture passages and verses about temptation. Almost too many to list. Read your Bible, because overcoming sin yields great rewards. But let me leave you with one more scriptural pearl I love most. I like the incentives. This one is written in James 1:12:

*Blessed is the man that endureth temptation; for when he hath been approved, he shall receive the crown of life, which the Lord promised to them that love him.*

Do you love Jesus? That's the question. Do you love Him more than your addiction? More than your sin? Do you want to overcome your temptations? You start here, and you start now. Come to the Lord Jesus, believe in Him, and let Him save you from sin, tribulation, and the consequences of sin in your life. Let Him throw you a lifeline to grab when temptation comes. Come to Him today, rededicate your life, and give up your sinful habit through Him. He's here, ready for you to draw near to Him, and He will draw near to you.

## PRAYER

God, I pray this Spur pricks the heart of those who read and hear it. May it inspire everyone to pray and meditate on the fact that we are all human. Temptation and sin are in each of our lives, but we who believe have You, Lord, to save us not only from our sin but You are also there to lean on when temptation knocks on our lustful minds and wicked hearts. Cleanse us today, make us pure and worthy of becoming a vessel of holiness to pour out our love, gratitude, and glory on You. Amen.

## CREDITS AND/OR INSPIRATION

Bruce Wilkinson. "Three Secrets About Temptations." YouVersion. Accessed May 13, 2025. https://www.bible.com/reading-plans/12956-three-secrets-about-temptations.

# GPS—God's Piloting Spirit

**CONCEPTS**

The verses listed below fit the analogy of driving with a GPS. Most people can identify using a Garmin or Google Maps on their phones or in their cars. The Spirit of God guides our life; all we need to do is tune in and listen to or read God's Word. Hundreds of other Scripture verses tell us how God leads and how we are to follow. You may know even better Scripture references than the ones I chose.

**PURPOSE**

Use these verses and others to remind people that the guidance and wisdom of God are flawless. If we will listen to His Spirit and voice within us and read His Word, the journey of our lives will be a mere walk in the park with Jesus.

**SCRIPTURE BASE**

Exodus 13:21–22, Luke 4:1, Proverbs 12:15, John 15:26, 1 John 1:7, Psalm 119:105

**BACKGROUND**

I use Google Maps whenever I go over twenty miles from home, not because I don't know how to get somewhere but because it tells me alternate routes when accidents, road work, and obstructions are noted. I'm not too fond of traffic and want to get where I'm going with ease. God's Spirit has led me through my entire life, sometimes forcing my turns or blocking my intended way. Thank God, He cares for me. He watches over me, and He makes my way. Never forget what God does for you; thank Him daily for it.

## SPUR

Most people make travel plans when going somewhere far off, even if they don't know how to get there beforehand. We used to unfold big paper maps or road atlases and plot our way with a colored marker. Today's latest technology is right in the dashboards of many cars with screen-driven guidance systems. Every smartphone has Google Maps or other apps that use the Global Positioning Satelite (GPS) system (Alpha International).

Once you begin your journey, your phone's or car's GPS starts with a man's or woman's voice telling you which way to go, starting right out of your driveway. It doesn't matter if it is the only way to go; it will still tell you to constantly go straight, right, left, or slightly one way or the other. These voice systems can get annoying. The directions are given with map information too. You will see a nice colored line of your path, and the screen may indicate if the road is stopped, slowed down, or has a hazard on it. In addition, reading the map might tell you how far to the next turn, the road names and labels, or the best lane to get in because you need to make an upcoming turn. I like to check my watch to see how accurate it is when the "time to destination is 1 hour and 40 minutes." I especially want to know that I am on the fastest route.

You can ignore GPS. Maybe you know a better or faster way; it might even recalculate and join your route. If you miss a turn, it will tell you it is recalculating, and then it will have you make a U-turn and go back to the turn you missed, or it will pick an alternate route and keep you going. Some GPS units will move you around traffic jams or let you know of an alternate course than the one you are on because of an accident or road work ahead. Some will tell you about speed traps or dangerous road conditions. It might even warn you when you are going too fast. I use mine all the time—big smile.

We can choose to ignore it and go our way based on what we remember or when we get close to home and know the rest of the way. We can turn it off when we are tired of the voice saying "Recalculating" all the time. I know that somewhere in that artificial intelligence guide's electrons, she's thinking I'm an idiot driver and can't follow simple instructions.

Sometimes I don't trust it. It must be wrong; as fallible technology goes, sometimes it is wrong. And that's where God's Piloting Spirit and a Garmin or Google Maps differ. You see, God has infinite and perfect wisdom—everyone else fails.

I don't like the bumper stickers that say, "God Is My Copilot." Folks, you'd better switch seats if He's your copilot. He needs to be in the pilot's seat every day.

We often pray, "Please, God, guide us," and His word says He will, but then we ignore Him, turn Him off, and go our own way. Sometimes, our GPS loses the satellite link, and we don't have a local map handy. Jesus used Scripture to navigate. He spoke God's words to guide Him through times of temptation. He often prayed to receive guidance from His Father. We have the same ability to plug into the throne of grace and ask for help when we are lost. His linkup is always open to us.

My destination is heaven, and I ask God to lead me to live righteously and holy each day. But instead, I get a lot of "Recalculating." I make a lot of U-turns and repent about the things He convicts me of doing wrong. I want Kingdom living right here, right now, and when I don't read His Word and when I don't listen to that inner voice, I disobey and make the wrong turns only to hear in my head, "Recalculating."

But that's the best part. No matter how bad I screw up navigating my way through life, just like the GPS on my dashboard, God is faithful and will never give up. Instead, He will correct, convict, and forgive you every time you make that wrong turn. If you listen, He will get you back on the road to glory, full of blessings, grace, and the love of Christ until you're home. I can't wait to hear my God say, *"You've reached your destination. Welcome home."*

People, this is no small matter. We are talking about your life's journey. God wants us to be blessed along the way, and the trip is essential, but the destination is our eternal reward. Memorize the following verse and live by it.

Psalm 119:105

*Thy word is a lamp unto my feet, And light unto my path.*

Your GPS will be with you all the days of your life.

## PRAYER

Lord, God our most gracious and heavenly Father, guide us with Your omnipotent Spirit. We believe that You love us and always want the best for us. Teach us to trust in You alone and listen to Your Word and inspiration as we pray. Thank You, Lord, for opening doors and closing others as we sometimes feel our way through life, blind in our thinking. Show us Your eternal light and guide us to walk with You. Amen.

## CREDITS AND/OR INSPIRATION

Alpha International. "Five Ways God Guides You." The Bible with Nicky and Pippa Gumbel, Day 110. Accessed April 30, 2025. https://bible.alpha.org/en/classic/110/index.html.

# Posers

**CONCEPTS**

Paul preaches the gospel. His example is our challenge to witness as he did for Christ. Know God's Word, speak God's Word, live God's Word.

**PURPOSE**

This Stem reminds everyone who hears it about their daily responsibilities as Christians.

**SCRIPTURE BASE**

Acts 13:14–41 (NIV)

**BACKGROUND**

This background may begin to read like a rabbit trail, but it has a point. During my years in Motorcycle Ministry, my wife and I took motorcycle trips across the east and southeast. We visited several dozen churches and Christian venues created by bikers to raise funds, perform services, and give praise and worship God. I've met thousands of bikers, both Christian and non-Christian. I've learned from meeting all those bikers and their families that people want to belong to something.

Christian bikers like to say they are do-gooders and enjoy telling people they are Christian bikers. They wear their cuts (vests) and ride their bikes, representing their loyalty to God and the organization. Most join Christian biker clubs because they are good people who want to identify with being a biker enthusiast, and being a

Christian biker keeps them from the rigid rules of actual biker clubs. Some will give twenty dollars as an entry fee to a charitable event to ride their bike in the event. Some are satisfied they did their part doing God's work or something good for the community. Those same ones don't belong to a church or attend any church regularly.

I call these people Posers. They are well-meaning seekers as lost as any other non-believer. Praise God! Some seekers eventually find Jesus through the excellent gospel to become doers of the Word and strong Christians.

The above was not written to educate you on Christian bikers. And though what I just wrote might insult many of the less faithful riders out there, I only wish to point out that Christian bikers are like every other group of Christians and churchgoers we know. Within every identifiable group of Christians, there are true believers and Posers. You might call them Groupies. Jesus called them tares sown among the seedlings. Some of Jesus' followers fell away once they heard Him speak the hard truth to follow Him. They were Posers too.

Today, churches and other religious groups have members who show up, give, remain active, lead, inspire, testify, evangelize, teach, and reach out to make disciples of Christ. The others only want to hang out and identify with other people.

I no longer give the benefit of the doubt to the entire group of members within organized groups of individuals, whether they are devout Christians or followers of a group that has accepted them as members. Likewise, I no longer give the benefit of the doubt to anyone I meet from another church or denomination because they occasionally gather in the name of the Lord.

Why? Because I've met too many Posers. People who want to say they belong are often not genuine workers spreading God's Word, sharing His Spirit, or making disciples. Some do not know God's Word. Some are so confused speaking about their beliefs, you know they don't know God's Word. Some are so far away from God in their sin and their old ways that it is shocking to see them play the part of a Christian. Not all of these organizational groups build disciples for Christ. They don't teach or share sound doctrine or theology. Some entire churches function like this.

Does this seem familiar? You get to know people from some group. Among a few Christians, you share your faith and listen to their testimonies and stories. Then you meet the Posers. You can see it before you even get a chance to talk to them. They say things like, "Sure, I'm saved! I believe in God. Me and Him are on a first-name basis. But I don't belong to any church. I don't care for church; I like riding (attending/participating) and being out in the wind." For some, this might look like unrighteous judgment. It's testing.

I don't know if you're saved. I don't know if anyone I've ever met is saved. God knows. We are to be fruit inspectors. The fruit of people's faith and the Spirit within them is what you can see as being evident in their lives, what they do, and how they serve Jesus. It is what Jesus has told us all to do—spread the gospel of His saving grace and make disciples. That's our job; few were better at it than Paul. His message was simple. His approach was BOLD. His works revealed his faith.

**SPUR**

This story begins with Acts 13:26–39. It is Paul's first missionary journey, and this Spur needs a little background and perspective before the climax of his sermon.

A Brief Outline of Acts 1–12:

Written by the physician Luke, it is a record or log of God's Spirit in action.

- Chapters 1 and 2 reveal how the first church was empowered through the Pentecost.
- Chapters 3–7 are the formations and recordings of the early church in Jerusalem.
- Chapter 8 is the Samaritans and Philip's witness.
- Chapter 9 is the conversion of Saul to Paul.
- Chapters 10–11 are about Judea and Peter in Caesarea, continuing through chapter 12 and beyond, spreading the gospel to the ends of the earth.

These chapters are rich in text and lesson. But we start in chapter 13 with Paul's first missionary journey.

The Stem focuses on what Paul does and how he brings the gospel to both the Jews and Gentiles.

Acts 13:14–15. Paul and others go to a synagogue where they are invited to speak and ultimately share some good word. It's unclear whether the hosts knew what they thought Saul would say. Saul had a reputation, and he was an educated Jewish scholar (Pharisee); he was also a Roman citizen. At that time, that was potentially a lot of weight to throw around to get you where you wanted to go or speak. Nevertheless, converted Saul, now Paul, is the one who is there, and he is called to speak and gives a message to a crowd of Jews and Gentiles who are there to hear about the latest movement coming out of Jerusalem.

So again, after the people had heard the standard message and reading of God's Word from the Torah or Pentateuch of the time, the synagogue rulers went unto them, saying in verse 15 *"Brethren if ye have any word of exhortation for the people, say on."*

Paul, still identified as Saul, begins by identifying with his audience—he's one of them. He says he has news of salvation—something everyone wanted to know about, but few knew how to obtain it.

I giggled to myself when I read this because I didn't think they had a clue about what they were going to hear. When the crowd listened to a religious bait and switch, I'm sure some were surprised, some were angry, and some were changed.

Verses 16–22. Paul stands up and gives a brief history lesson—a reminder of where they came from and what has happened in the path God had brought about to the children of Israel. Family, patriarch, royalty—Paul is just sucking in the crowd and the leaders with his knowledge. I'm thinking at this point, he has all the synagogue leaders shaking their heads and agreeing with every word, smiling, and endorsing this good message, when BANG!

Verse 23. Paul drops a bomb on them and says, speaking of David, *"Of this man's seed hath God according to His promise raised unto Israel a Saviour, Jesus."*

Now, I'm thinking here a few jaws drop, and a few others' ears pick up, and the curiosity of others won't let them leave because they want to hear the rest of this. Paul doesn't miss a beat.

Verses 24–25. He reintroduces a legend—John the Baptist and his role in the introduction of Jesus.

Then we get to our text in verse 26. Paul brings the crowd back into this revelation, speaking directly to them and how this revelation of salvation is the Word of God being given to them right now. That's big! It must have grabbed their attention.

Verses 27–32. He tells them of the more unrecognized prophecy of the Messiah and how one man had fulfilled the prophecy of old and that man was here, was slain, was raised from the dead, walked among us, and I (Paul) am here to tell you about it. This man Jesus is God, and He is alive and not buried in the grave even though those in Jerusalem all saw He had died on the tree—He is not rotting in the grave.

Verses 33–37. Paul continues speaking about how this was all ordained and written in the books they had just read.

Then he lays the kicker on them. Read aloud verses 38–39 (NIV):

> *Therefore, my friends, I want you to know that through Jesus the forgiveness of sins is proclaimed to you. Through him everyone who believes is set free from every sin, a justification you were not able to obtain under the law of Moses.*

He adds cement to his declarations later in verses 40–41 with even more prophecy fulfilled from the Old Testament. What a sermon! He blew them away, and instead of stoning him like others for teaching similar sermons, they invited him back so they could hear more.

This theme is nearly identical to virtually all of Billy Graham's sermons. He only preached the gospel. The core of this sermon is the same. Death, burial, and resurrection of Jesus, and He is God's saving grace, His One and only Son.

His sermons were the same message, repeatedly surrounded by a thousand stories and proofs, and they segued into the only message that Billy Graham ever preached. If that message was our only message, it would be enough for all time.

Test the fruits of the Spirit. Paul knew the talk, and he walked the walk. Challenge your group to do the same. They have to know God's Word and work His fields. Test them and find who your Posers are. Preach to them this gospel.

## PRAYER

Lord, God and heavenly Father, today, in hearing Your Word of truth, Your Good News, may we never discount that this story, this presentation, and this doctrine are the only testaments we need to tell others. Jesus is Lord. He is our banner. Lord, we ask that everyone who hears Your Word will speak it and live it like Paul. Help us, Lord, with Your power and might to be the example of You and Paul in his bold witness. Amen.

## CREDITS AND/OR INSPIRATION

I have always envied, worked, and studied to be able to teach and preach with Paul's wisdom and boldness. He inspires me through his letters in God's Word.

# Walk Like a Man

## CONCEPTS

The Old Testament (OT) and the New Testament (NT). have many things in common when telling people of God to go out and be courageous. The comparisons and contrasts are numerous. Comparing two or more Scripture lines between the OT and NT can become confusing as stories between the two can get lost in teaching. Be sure to note where you are in the comparisons.

## PURPOSE

Men and women seem to lack faith in stepping out to do as we were commanded in the Great Commission. Undershepherds must prepare and encourage their flocks to become uncomfortable if they sit back and watch the lost sheep perish. Our failing churches are not seeking, serving, or teaching our people to be soul-winning evangelists or disciple makers for the Kingdom of God.

## SCRIPTURE BASE

Romans 15:4; Joshua 1:1–18 (quoted below)

## BACKGROUND

I was honored to serve with several Christian organizations that worked tirelessly to seek and serve the lost. We worked closely with people, similar to what Jesus did, to witness to them about the grace and love of Jesus. The personal rewards and blessings of doing that ministry are hard to describe. Some churches are built entirely from those concerted efforts; others are dead because they did nothing.

# SPUR

In Joshua 1, God tells His people that the land He promised is in front of them, but they need the courage to take it. As New Testament Christians, our Great Commission is similar. The fields are ripe, but if you expect all those who need to be saved to walk through your front doorway and fill up your pews, that just is not going to happen by going out and doing a prayer walk around the neighborhood. We need to make and prepare our soldiers. Lead your people to go out and engage that neighborhood, and everywhere there are lost for Jesus to save.

The following Scripture is a comparison-contrast of how the OT is an example of NT commandments.

Joshua was one of the bravest and most successful commanders in military history. He had faith, and he had God to command him. As NT Christians, we have the Word that contains all we need to give us faith and courage to fulfill our commission. The Bible provides us with the weapons we need to defeat satan.

This is the commission God gave to Joshua in chapter 1, verses 2–3:

*Jehovah spake unto Joshua the son of Nun, Moses' minister, saying, Moses my servant is dead; now therefore arise, go over this Jordan, thou, and all this people, unto the land which I do give to them, even to the children of Israel. Every place that the sole of your foot shall tread upon, to you have I given it, as I spake unto Moses.*

This is our commission in the NT—Jesus' last words in Matthew 28:20 before ascending to heaven commanded us to:

*Go therefore and make disciples of all the nations, baptizing them in the name of the Father and the Son and the*

*Holy Spirit, teaching them to observe all that I commanded you; and lo, I am with you always, even to the end of the age.*

Through the following several verses of Joshua, God tells Joshua the depth, breadth, and width of what the people of Israel would receive and who they had to fight to get it. The passage from verse 4 through verse 18 is very specific. The words "Be strong and of good courage" were repeated by God to Joshua not once but three times. Please read it.

Verses 6–7, 9:

*Be strong and of good courage; for thou shalt cause this people to inherit the land which I sware unto their fathers to give them. Only be strong and very courageous, to observe to do according to all the law*

*Have not I commanded thee? Be strong and of good courage.*

This story should be as significant to us as any story in the Bible. It is filled with what it takes to succeed as Christian soldiers. The encouragement and promises fit for us as they did for them.

All of verse 7:

*Only be strong and very courageous, to observe to do according to all the law, which Moses my servant commanded thee: turn not from it to the right hand or to the left, that thou mayest have good success whithersoever thou goest.*

Could it be that simple? Or is it too difficult to trust and obey God's Word?

All of verse 8:

*This book of the law shall not depart out of thy mouth, but thou shalt meditate thereon day and night, that thou mayest observe to do according to all that is written therein: for then thou shalt make thy way prosperous, and then thou shalt have good success.*

Coincidentally, verse 8 exactly says what we need as Christians to be armed and ready to fight the wiles of satan, who wanders about like a lion attempting to devour those unaware. Knowledge and devotion to God's Word are the tools Jesus used to defeat satan, and we need to do the same. Therefore, we need to be prepared with the knowledge of His Word and meditate on it day and night.

Ask your people how many read their Bibles daily, twice daily, or more. A LifeWay Survey January 14–29, 2019 asked that question online. These were church members: Every day, 32 percent; a few times a week, 27 percent; once a week, 12 percent; a few times per month,11 percent; once a month, 5 percent; rarely/never, 12 percent (Briggs). I contend that the pandemic of 2019–22 may have changed those numbers for the worse.

Begin Bible reading and study. First, it may be the very thing to get people in the pews and, secondly, out into the world to share what they are confident knowing. At this point, our congregations should profess.

Verse 16:

*And they answered Joshua, saying, All that thou hast commanded us we will do, and whithersoever thou sendest us we will go.*

Would you love to hear that from your church?

315

God's people followed His commandments by faith and trust to do His will. Those attributes lead to working out faith and obeying God's Word.

Proverbs 3:5–6

> *Trust in Jehovah with all thy heart, And lean not upon thine own understanding: In all thy ways acknowledge him, And he will direct thy paths.*

Isaiah 41:10

> *Fear thou not, for I am with thee; be not dismayed, for I am thy God; I will strengthen thee; yea, I will help thee; yea, I will uphold thee with the right hand of my righteousness.*

Read and study God's Word.

Deuteronomy 6:5–7

> *And thou shalt love Jehovah thy God with all thy heart, and with all thy soul, and with all thy might. And these words, which I command thee this day, shall be upon thy heart; and thou shalt teach them diligently unto thy children, and shalt talk of them when thou sittest in thy house, and when thou walkest by the way, and when thou liest down, and when thou risest up.*

Encourage one another.

1 Corinthians 1:10

> *Now I beseech you, brethren, through the name of our Lord Jesus Christ, that ye all speak the same thing, and that*

*there be no divisions among you; but that ye be perfected together in the same mind and in the same judgment.*

Hebrews 10:24–25

*And let us consider one another to provoke unto love and good works; not forsaking our own assembling together, as the custom of some is, but exhorting one another; and so much the more, as ye see the day drawing nigh.*

Prepare for battle.

Ephesians 6:10–13

*Finally, be strong in the Lord, and in the strength of his might. Put on the whole armor of God, that ye may be able to stand against the wiles of the devil. For our wrestling is not against flesh and blood, but against the principalities, against the powers, against the world-rulers of this darkness, against the spiritual hosts of wickedness in the heavenly places. Wherefore take up the whole armor of God, that ye may be able to withstand in the evil day, and, having done all, to stand.*

Walk like a son of the King.

Colossians 2:6–7

*As therefore ye received Christ Jesus the Lord, so walk in him, rooted and builded up in him, and established in your faith, even as ye were taught, abounding in thanksgiving.*

Look down at your feet. Repeat this march of a Christian Soldier. Left foot, trust. Right **foot, obey**.

## PRAYER

Holy God and gracious Father, I pray this day these words strike deep in the hearts of those who read them. That they would be inspired by Your words and be encouraged to revive their people as You have provided. May their faithful action bring others closer to You and that Your Kingdom would grow throughout this land to glorify You. Amen.

## CREDIT AND/OR INSPIRATION

Years of experience in motorcycle ministry as home missionaries being God's faithful few.

Megan Briggs. "Do You Read Your Bible Every Day? Most Churchgoers Say No." ChurchLeaders. July 25, 2019. https://churchleaders.com/news/356089-do-you-read-your-bible-everyday-most-churchgoers-say-no.html.

# Special Service of Love

## CONCEPTS

The church administration appears to be reluctant to talk about giving. Sermons detailing giving and the reasons for doing so usually include the bills owed, the large mortgage, or the budget required. Paul's method of enticing the church to give is much better. He calls it a *special service of love*. The Scripture of 2 Corinthians 8 and 9 details the reason, the way, and the benefits of giving.

## PURPOSE

We have both a spiritual and business side in bona fide tax-exempt churches. Consequently, churches as a whole, often led by disillusioned pastors and deacons, committees, lawyers, accountants, and businesspeople, begin to change the reflection of our attitudes and beliefs toward the worldly path of loving money, and hence the root of evil. We hear the need for programs, and programs need money. Forget about all that. Give unto Caesar what is Caesar's and give unto God the worship He deserves. Glorify God with your giving as worship and works. The rest will care for itself if the Lord is in with you.

Proverbs 16:2–3

*All the ways of a man are clean in his own eyes; But Jehovah weigheth the spirits. Commit thy works unto Jehovah, And thy purposes shall be established.*

## SCRIPTURE BASE

2 Corinthians 8–9, Proverbs 16:2–3, Exodus 20:2–3, Matthew 22:37 (Jesus was quoting Deuteronomy 6:5), 2 Corinthians 9:6–14, Psalm 116:12–14

## BACKGROUND

Churches are closing their doors all over this nation. They are closing because they can no longer pay the mortgage or the heating and lighting bills. But that is only the result of something more profound. Too many have misplaced the mandated emphasis on preaching the gospel of Jesus, making disciples, and worshipping God. The blame, lost on many wrong things, replaces service that is not right. The right thing is to make the first things first. Preach the gospel of Jesus and worship God. Make giving what it is supposed to be—worship. Worship that is honorable, worthy, intense, respectful, and most of all, filled with thankful love and devotion to the One who has given us indescribable gifts.

## SPUR

What are the things we consider worship? What do we do to worship our Lord and Savior? Let's make a list. I don't think there is much argument that we worship God when reading and studying His Word. We pray and worship through thanksgiving. We glorify Him through our works and worship Him through song, praise, preaching, and teaching. We observe the sacrificial elements, baptism, and the recognition of Jesus' birth during Christmas and His death, burial, and the victory of resurrection during Easter. These are all times of worship. But what order of importance or value would you give them? What comes first? What comes in last or is no longer considered an act of worship? What service of worship comes in later on our list of importance? Tough questions. How about if we go to God's Word for the answer?

Let me begin with the Ten Commandments.

Exodus 20:2–3

> *I am Jehovah thy God, who brought thee out of the land of Egypt, out of the house of bondage. Thou shall have no other gods before me.*

Let's follow some Old Testament (OT) with some words from Jesus in the New Testament (NT) as Jesus quotes the OT. First, in Matthew 22:37:

> *And he said unto him, Thou shalt love the Lord thy God with all thy heart, and with all thy soul, and with all thy mind.*

You might ask, "What does this have to do with giving the church my hard-earned money?" It is that exact perspective that needs modification.

Let's inspect the elephant in the room. People often say to themselves, "You churches just want our money! Your pastors are seeking a higher salary. You deacons want to make a bigger building. You all want to spend it on extravagant stuff on a bloated budget. God doesn't need my money; He's God! You need my money, and you'll squeeze every dime out of me you can. Put me on a guilt trip by telling me I owe God what I have for saving me and giving me all I have. And that it's all His anyway." That list does not include all the complaints, but I believe I have addressed the major ones—wrong attitudes, wrong thought processes—not worship.

Here's another. We take our little envelope and insert a check based on what we might not miss too much. Chuck it in the basket or plate at Sunday school with our name on it so the recorder will ensure we get our tax credit or throw it in the offering plate as it's passed around, and the music is sweetly playing. Have you done any worship yet? Did you give from your heart in worship to your Lord? Even better, have you heard this one? "I have my tithe taken automatically from my bank each month, and I don't even miss it. I don't have to think about it, it's just gone."

Are you feeling the pain yet? Wow, some of that may look like the truth, and if you think about it, that perspective might be what people consider reality. Unfortunately, it is not what God's Word says.

I hate to use this passage as some pastors use the exact words to twist and swing the pendulum too far in the other direction, which leads to wealth and rewards ministry. However, God's Word is the truth written to cut through the flesh, bone, and marrow.

Paul writes in 2 Corinthians 9:6–8 how thankful he is to the church for their generosity to him and what that means to them:

> *But this I say, He that soweth sparingly shall reap also sparingly; and he that soweth bountifully shall reap also bountifully.*

Sounds great! Did he say anything about money here? There are many things we can give that don't include money. Think of the things we can sow. Goodwill and personal testimony, gifts of food, time, energy, professional talents, leadership, administration, and the list goes on with the things you can give to your church that do not include money. Can you do those and worship?

> *Let each man do according as he hath purposed in his heart: not grudgingly, or of necessity: for God loveth a cheerful giver.*

Have you heard anything about money yet? A few key points here. *As he hath purposed in his heart*—don't do it if your heart isn't in it. God knows your heart, and if you are giving *grudgingly, or of necessity,* it is probably better to not give at all, *for God loves a cheerful giver.*

Does that mean God will love you less if you don't give, or will He love you more if you do give? Neither one. God loves you, period. We should take Paul's expression as he meant it. It is better to be a cheerful giver than a regretful one; it's not about God; it's about you. It is about your attitude when you give anything. What does *blessed* mean? God can bless you, make you happy, and make you feel good when you give. That's a reasonable expectation and reward in itself:

> *And God is able to make all grace abound unto you; that ye, having always all sufficiency in everything, may abound unto every good work.*

Three big words here ... *all.* The last time I checked, all meant all—not some, not enough, but all. The other words are in two parts. What things? Everything. For every good work. Not some but *every* good work. That's what God can make—*all grace abound toward you.* He has already. If you are saved from the sin of your life, you have received an indescribable gift of grace. Free. Did you pay for it? Do you have to pay for it? Do you have to or want to for what He has done for you? After all, He sent His Son to die on the cross for you and all your sins. Jesus didn't go through a couple of hours of torture and didn't just die like every other human in history. He took on your sins, my sins, and all the sins of the rest of humanity. He bore them in His death as a sacrifice; He absorbed them like a sponge and wiped all sin from you and me to make us as clean as God requires of us to enter heaven. Justified—just as if I had never sinned.

I don't know about you, but I couldn't take the punishment I deserve for even my sin, let alone yours and everyone else's. He took it all. That's what hurt. That's what was so painful. He was without sin. That cleansing power, the gift of doing all that for me and you, is His holy sacrifice. His grace is He gave you His lifeblood to pay for your sins and my sins.

2 Corinthians 9:15

*Thanks be to God for his unspeakable gift.*

Now, here's the right attitude. Gratitude. Do you feel like you owe Him something? You don't need to feel guilty for what Jesus did on the cross for you. You should be grateful, though. You should be shouting, "Hallelujah!" Jesus did that for me, my wife, kids, parents, friends, and everyone else I know or meet. He did that for everyone. Everyone will receive that gift of grace if they only believe in faith that Jesus Christ is Lord and that He did it all for them.

Paul goes on in 2 Corinthians 9:9 to break it down when we all have the attitude of thanksgiving and gratitude:

*As it is written, He hath scattered abroad, he hath given to the poor; His righteousness abideth for ever.*

The passage is talking about God, not you. He doesn't need your money. He owns the cattle on a thousand hills—by the way, He owns the hills too. Verse 10:

*And he that supplieth seed to the sower and bread for food, shall supply and multiply your seed for sowing, and increase the fruits of your righteousness:*

Again, this is what God does for you. So basically, He does all this with or without you. Verse 11:

> *Ye being enriched in everything unto all liberality, which worketh through us thanksgiving to God.*

Be grateful for what you have received from God—beyond the grace He has already given. It is you who needs to give. It is you who will receive the blessing. God gives to those in need, and He outgives everyone. Verses 12–14:

> *For the ministration of this service not only filleth up the measure of the wants of the saints, but aboundeth also through many thanksgivings unto God; seeing that through the proving of you by this ministration they glorify God for the obedience of your confession unto the gospel of Christ, and for the liberality of your contribution unto them and unto all; while they themselves also, with supplication on your behalf, long after you by reason of the exceeding grace of God in you.*

This is worship. Thanksgiving of your abundance by giving whatever gifts you provide supplies the needs of the saints, which proves the ministry is vital and glorifies God that you are obedient to Him. And by sharing with all, they who receive return prayers of thanks for you because you have received God's abundant grace. WIN! WIN! WIN! Blessings to all who give and receive.

*Thanks be to God for his unspeakable gift.*

It's complex. But it is also simple. You can't outgive God. Your offering isn't for Him; it is for you. He doesn't need it; you do. Your need is to glorify God in whatever good works you do.

People have asked the question, "What do I owe God?" The same question is in Psalm 116:12–14:

> *What shall I render unto Jehovah For all his benefits toward me? I will take the cup of salvation, And call upon the name of Jehovah. I will pay my vows unto Jehovah, Yea, in the presence of all his people.*

Now, we need to go back to the beginning of this Spur. First things first. What are your vows? How about your vow of love? How do you show your love?

Paul began his sermon on giving in 2 Corinthians, chapter 8. In verse 7, he says:

> *You are so rich in all you have: in faith, speech, and knowledge, in your eagerness to help and in your love for us. And so we want you to be generous also in this service of love.*

That's the question for you to consider today. It's not about the money, folks. It's about your love for the One who cares for you and all your needs. Worship your Lord God with all your heart, with all your soul, with all your mind. Whenever you give, whatever you give, your gifts need to be accompanied by prayer each time. Your prayer of thanks, gratefulness, praise, and loving worship of the One Creator of heaven and earth will glorify our God.

## PRAYER

Lord, God and Father, I cannot even conceive of all You have done and do for me. Like what You have paid on the cross, what You have made for my life, health, wealth, and the blessings You provide me daily. I came into this world with nothing, and You gave me everything through Your love. I will leave with nothing but Your love, which is everything I will ever need. All You have given me in time, talents, gifts, protection, life, and salvation; I have everything because You provided for me. Please, Lord, show me what I can give You that glorifies Your name for all You are and what You have done for me. I give You my love and adoration. Amen.

## CREDITS AND/OR INSPIRATION

Too many sermons are begging for money to pay the bills. If it's God's will, it's His bill. And He will pay on time. Making priorities for eternity.

# I Miss Church

**CONCEPTS**

Here's a joke that doesn't seem funny anymore. You might hear an occasional testimony about the speaker's severe drug problem in his youth. The story goes that while they were very young, their mama drug them to church on Sunday and Wednesday, and every other day the church doors were open. An old joke, really, but there was much truth in it for many of us boomers. The church today is very optional, and it seems for some that it's the last resort because it is too easy to find an excuse not to go. A church service doesn't command the respect or reverence it once maintained in society. In my opinion, we need to reculture our community of Christians to think otherwise (Hebrews 10:24–25; see Introduction). Multifaceted aspects exist to this loss of desire to attend church and observe reverence for our Lord and designated sanctuary. We are the church; I get it. Where we worship our Lord as a congregation is more than just a building or address. Some readers here will not like this Spur, but everyone needs to hear it. If the shoe fits, test yourself.

**PURPOSE**

Have we lost our awe, honor, and respect for God? Is the church auditorium still considered the sanctuary? Do we follow the first commandment from God? I believe this is the downfall of our churches and extends to our society because we no longer put God first with respect and honor. A church sanctuary is a place of prayer and worship. Protecting the atmosphere that brings the Spirit of God into the midst of a congregation is paramount to moving people into God's presence.

**SCRIPTURE BASE**

Hebrews 10:24–25, Hebrews 12:28, Matthew 22:36–38, 1 Peter 3:15, Isaiah 40:8, Romans 1:21, Revelation 19:5, Ecclesiastes 7:10, Revelation 4:11

**BACKGROUND**

I miss the old church I grew up in. I often reminisce about the days when most of this country attended church. Sunday school, Sunday morning services, singing the doxology of praise, spirit-filled worship, partaking of the elements in the Lord's Supper, and Sunday night services. I miss Wednesday night prayer meetings, religious holiday programs, youth-night participation, revivals, and special music and speaker events. Full-page announcement bulletins and especially traditional gospel music from the hymnals. I miss full choirs and frequent special music from soloists, duets, trios, and men's barbershop quartets; those were great times. If you still have all that, you are blessed. If not, maybe you reminisce as I do. Cherish those things and try to keep them.

What happened to people's participation? Did we get too busy with the world and its programs? Or did we just get lazy? Chipped away bit by bit, we see Christianity being left behind in the lives of our members, schools, and society in general. The result is dwindling churches with too few people who sustain them with more than a checkbook. Satan seems to be winning, and time is on his side. We know the truth. Satan is a loser, and God controls time.

I miss preachers who were jealous to guard their pulpits. I miss the days when people went to church because their church family was there. There were no excuses to dismiss a night or Sunday because of a holiday. I must swallow hard when I read a phone-delivered text message from the church canceling service. I remember when a deacon would conduct service when the pastor was out due to illness or another event.

During a service filled with one announcement after another, we might hear there will be no service on the Wednesday night before Thanksgiving so everyone can spend time with their family. I think, "The church is their family!" Do you have church on Christmas Day, regardless of what day it falls? Or Christmas Eve? We used to. That is when we did our youth programs, and that is when we did our choir cantatas. That is when we greeted and gifted friends and family and gave little kids gift bags of food, oranges, apples, and even a tiny toy. I miss those memorable times and the blessings from the fellowship of believers.

It pains me to consider that church leaders must weigh between keeping the doors open for the faithful few because it costs too much for the heat and lights to stay on.

Hebrews 12:28

*Wherefore, receiving a kingdom that cannot be shaken, let us have grace, whereby we may offer service well-pleasing to God with reverence and awe.*

Excuses not to have service irritate me. The weather is another good one. The reason goes like this: "Well, the roads are bad, and we don't want anyone to have an accident on their way to church." In reality, that could be any day. Grown-ups know whether or not they can make it to church. "Well, we won't have enough people to make the choir." Alternatively, "Our Sunday school teachers can't make it," or "Our preacher can't get here." All excuses. Improvise, adapt, overcome, and God will be glorified with the worship you bring. If you believe in loving the Lord your God with all your heart and with all your strength, you will beat satan, who is happy to keep your doors shut. Have church, in season, and out of season. Depend on God. Have faith. Be obedient and meet. Allow a deacon or layman to step up and teach or preach. It is time to repent and put first things first. Let us begin with the first commandment in the OT and NT.

Matthew 22:36–38

*Teacher, which is the great commandment in the law? And he said unto him, Thou shalt love the Lord thy God with all thy heart, and with all thy soul, and with all thy mind. This is the great and first commandment.*

## SPUR

I know the arguments and understand the desire to attract those "in the world" to attend church with entertainment. But have we become so much like the world that it is hard to tell the difference? Have we lost our salt? Is our light like every other street light, shining without brightness?

1 Peter 3:15

*But sanctify in your hearts Christ as Lord: being ready always to give answer to every man that asketh you a reason concerning the hope that is in you, yet with meekness and fear.*

Popularity with specific groups determined by age, income, and education is more important than the purpose of teaching and preaching sound doctrine and the gospel of Jesus Christ. Size does not matter—well, maybe it does to the hireling who will justify a bigger paycheck. The size of the church and the variety of people in attendance are not up to the preacher or the deacons—it is up to God.

Think about this. Have you ever heard people say, "These are the things we must do to bring in those to grow our church?" That is nuts! How long has the Church survived? Who insured the survival? God's Word states it plainly:

Isaiah 40:8

*The grass withereth, the flower fadeth; but the word of our God shall stand forever.*

The church has seen every political system, social empire, flavor of the year or decade, progressive church, and anti-church, and still, God draws those He desires to serve and worship Him. He is still on the throne, and His will shall be done. He draws His own. Not the colored lights and smoke, drums, or steel guitars. The computer-driven 120-inch flat panel displays can't do it; God deserves all the praise, honor, and glory. Does having all that stuff make a difference? It might help if your priorities are straight. Jesus first! Let's get that right before we get a new sound system, okay?

Romans 1:21

*Because that, knowing God, they glorified him not as God, neither gave thanks; but became vain in their reasonings, and their senseless heart was darkened.*

If the church of today does not recapture the sacrificial spirit of the early church, it will lose its authentic ring. It will forfeit the loyalty of millions and be dismissed as an irrelevant social club with no meaning for the twentieth century (adapted from King).

I am not sure what you want to call this Spur. A call to repent or a call to revive. Maybe both are in order, but if this Spur calls you to action in your heart or church, my prayer is fulfilled by reading these words:

Revelation 19:5

*And a voice came forth from the throne, saying, Give praise to our God, all ye his servants, ye that fear him, the small and the great.*

I will leave you with two Charles Spurgeon quotes that came to me while writing this Spur:

> "The devil has seldom done a cleverer thing than hinting to the church that part of their mission is to provide entertainment for the people, with a view to winning them." (Spurgeon)

> "Other men may teach socialism, deliver lectures, or collect a band of fiddlers that they may gather a congregation, but I will preach the Gospel." (Biblehub.com)

Lastly, I understand and have been pricked to know I need correction and wisdom. The following verse tells us not to look back at the better days of our lives. It is not wise. So, here we are—take it or leave it:

Ecclesiastes 7:10

> *Say not thou, What is the cause that the former days were better than these? for thou dost not inquire wisely concerning this.*

## PRAYER

Lord, God and Father, today we ask You to forgive us for putting You second or third in our lives. We ask that You forgive us for not giving You all the honor and glory with awe and reverence in Your presence when we call upon Your name. Lord, revive us as the body of Christ to remember who we are and who You are. Powerful Creator of all things, Giver of all that is good, Master, Redeemer, Savior, and Lord above all. King of Kings, Almighty, and First and Last. God, may we never forget. Amen.

Revelation 4:11

*Worthy art thou, our Lord and our God, to receive the glory and the honor and the power: for thou didst create all things, and because of thy will they were, and were created.*

## CREDITS AND/OR INSPIRATION

The signs of the time. One morning during a Breakfast Club meeting our group shared a conversation about the above topic, and one man said, "Our church is full of old folks, and they are all going to die very soon. The church will disappear with them. Somehow, we have to attract some youth. That's the way to grow a church." We all knew what he meant, but what does it take to keep the church doors open? It seemed as though this man and those in his congregation felt it was up to them to create an environment that would attract younger people to join their church. I am sure they have already tried everything except doing church as they were raised. This dilemma is impacting churches across this nation. The answer is in this Spur. People need, want, and are looking for a Savior. Give them the only One to honor and respect.

Biblehub.com. "The Mustard Seed: A Sermon for the Sabbath-School Teacher." Accessed August 3, 2022. https://biblehub.com/sermons/auth/spurgeon/the_mustard_seed_a_sermon_for_the_sabbath-school_teacher.htm.

Martin Luther King, Jr. "Letter from Birmingham Jail." Csuchico.edu. Accessed April 30, 2025. https://www.csuchico.edu/iege/_assets/documents/susi-letter-from-birmingham-jail.pdf.

Charles Spurgeon. "Feeding Sheep or Amusing Goats?: Biblebb.com. Posted by Tony Capoccia, 1986. https://www.biblebb.com/files/spurgeon/amusement.htm.

# You Get What You Deserve

**CONCEPTS**

This is a call to sinners to be saved.

**PURPOSE**

There are thousands of sermons preachers have preached, and witnesses have confessed drawing sinners to Christ. This Stem is one of them, and I have always found it logical and spiritual. Christ saves; we testify of His grace and mercy. People need to know they are sinners, and without recognizing what Christ did on the cross to save us, sinners will pay in full for their sins. Hell is eternal death.

**SCRIPTURE BASE**

Romans 3:23, Romans 6:23, John 3:17

**BACKGROUND**

We are called to be disciples of Christ and spread the gospel to all who may believe and accept Jesus as Lord. He is the whole gospel. His sinless life, His death on the cross, and His resurrection from the grave are the story and what the gospel of Jesus is all about. People tend to forget that Jesus came to save us from our sins and from death. The point is that many in our present-day society feel that somebody owes them something.

**SPUR**

And what is that, exactly? What do we deserve? Does anyone owe us anything? This nation? This county? Does your mom or your dad owe you anything? Does your brother or your sister? How about your kids? Do they owe you anything? Do those rich folks who have everything owe you something? Does your local church owe you for giving all that money each Sunday? Does God owe us anything? If so, what did you do to deserve it?

I do not feel I deserve anything, even though I fought in a war and have become a disabled veteran. Occasionally, getting some respect and recognition is nice, but I do not insist on or pan for it. I enlisted and served my country to live well in a land of plenty. I pay my taxes, so I guess I deserve to have the roads paved, the sidewalks made, and traffic lights that work. I even pay taxes for law enforcement officers to give me a ticket when I drive through one of those lights. Is that what I deserve for paying my taxes?

My folks brought me into this world, and they should owe me a living, education, money—they owe me all they own. I am their kid. Not really. When you become a grown-up, you are responsible for yourself.

Why do all those rich folks have everything, and I don't? Good question! They have what God gave them, even if they think they earned it. He shines on those He chooses and rains on those He chooses. That is called God's sovereignty.

Now, we are at the root of it all. Why doesn't God give it to me? He brought me here. He made me who I am. He put me in this circumstance. He's keeping me here for some reason. Didn't you say He loves me? What is up with that?

You are right. You figured it out. God will give you all you deserve.

Romans 2 tells us that those who judge others and remain in their sin will also be judged and receive God's wrath.

Romans 3:23 says,

*For all have sinned, and fall short of the glory of God.*

Romans 6:23 says,

*For the wages of sin is death.*

You get what you deserve.

I know what you're thinking. You think I made up this Spur for sinners. Is that who you think you are? Do you think you are a sinner?

You would be right about that. You are a sinner, just like me— a sinner. Do you see? It doesn't matter if you work in a high-rise building and make six figures a year, are voted into office, or drive a fancy car. You could be in prison, working at McDonald's, or standing at the pulpit preaching. Everyone sins. Everyone does not sin the same way, but we all fall short of God's glory. Sinners cheat and swindle, lie and steal, beat their wives, abuse their kids, curse the older adult driving slow on the highway, pray to God, and maybe even go to church every Sunday. Every day, sinners hate and talk about their neighbor like a dog, thinking dirty wicked evil thoughts. I am a sinner, you are a sinner, and everyone else will get what we all deserve.

Just because some sinners didn't get caught, or I didn't get caught, or you didn't get caught does not mean God doesn't know what we've done. We cannot fix this. Call it karma if you want to, but you will get what you deserve. Some will get their punishment here on earth, but everyone will be judged before God in our after-life.

Do you deserve to be arrested for what you have done? Do you deserve to get slapped around, punched, and kicked? Do you deserve to get spit on and cussed at and accused of stuff you didn't do? Do you deserve to get whipped until your back and every inch of your body is bleeding? Do you deserve to be tied to a tree and nailed through your hands and feet? Do you deserve to hang on that tree for hours until you suffocate and die?

I know someone who didn't deserve any of that. That someone gave Himself up to take your place for all that punishment for you and all the junk you ever did. You! Your sins. My sins. Her sins. His sins. The sins of the entire world. He took everything we deserve for us.

Why? So, you wouldn't get what you deserve—death. See? Let me read you all of Romans 6:23:

> *For the wages of sin is death; but the free gift of God is eternal life in Christ Jesus our Lord.*

John 3:17 says,

> *For God sent not the Son into the world to judge the world; but that the world should be saved through him.*

God made a way for you to be forgiven of all your sins, so you could be acceptable to Him—for He is holy, and He gave His holy Son to pay the price of your sins and to make you holy. Then He raised Jesus from the dead and will do the same for me and everyone else saved from death through Christ Jesus. Jesus is alive today and listens to our prayers every minute of every day, sitting at the right hand of God. Jesus took the punishment for you, and all you must do is accept that He did it, not as a mere man, but as God. He did it to save you, redeem you from your sins and the ultimate penalty of death.

Do you deserve that? No. You and I can never do anything in this lifetime to deserve what God gives to us through Jesus. That is grace. Grace is what God gives freely to all who will receive it.

Now, this is the hard part. Call on His name, Jesus. Confess to Him that you know and that you know He knows you are a sinner—and sincerely mean it. Thank Him for suffering and dying on the cross for your sins. Ask Him to forgive you for all those sins you know you committed. Ask Him to come into your heart and show you His love. Tell Him you cannot do it alone and you need His help. You want His grace. Tell Him you give yourself to Him because He gave His life for you. Call on the name of Jesus Christ to save you, and He will because He promised He would—if you mean it sincerely and humbly. That is called faith. Believing God will do what He says He will do. His Spirit will enter you and keep you forever. Make that leap of faith. Move to the next level in your life. Accepting the grace of God is the most critical decision you have ever made. You will be deciding your eternal life. You are hearing Good News that the Spirit of God is asking you to respond to today. The cost to you is nothing (it's already been paid); the value to you is priceless. I'm going to pray you make the right choice and that you will accept this gift.

Pray your prayer as the Spirit leads.

## PRAYER

Lord, God and heavenly Father, my prayer is that this Spur is used to the glory of You and the fulfillment of Your Kingdom on earth and in heaven. I ask that those who read or teach from this be empowered with Your Holy Spirit to reach the lost and lead the confused and backslid souls into Your unlimited grace and mercy. Lord, pour Your Spirit on all who read and accept this gospel. Amen.

## CREDITS AND/OR INSPIRATION

Inspiration is from Jesus Christ, my Redeemer, my Savior, my Lord.

# Bibliography

Alpha International. "Five Ways God Guides You." The Bible with Nicky and Pippa Gumbel, Day 110. Accessed April 19, 2020. https://bible.alpha.org/en/classic/110/index.html.

*American Heritage Dictionary, The.* "Fantastic." HarperCollins Publishers, 2022.

"Answers in Genesis." YouTube Channel. Accessed March 31, 2023. https://www.youtube.com/@answersingenesis.

AZQuotes. "Charles Grandison Finney Quotes," Accessed March 10, 2022. https://www.azquotes.com/quote/1380354.

AZQuotes. "Charles Grandison Finney Quotes," Accessed March 10, 2022. https://www.azquotes.com/quote/1373424.

AZQuotes. "Charles Spurgeon Quotes." Accessed March 10, 2022. https://www.azquotes.com/quote/703855.

AZQuotes. "Friedrich Nietzche Quotes." Accessed March 10, 2022. https://www.azquotes.com/author/10823-Friedrich_Nietzsche.

AZQuotes. "Phillips Brooks Quotes." Accessed April 30, 2023. https://www.azquotes.com/author/1975-Phillips_Brooks.

Barker, Kenneth L., Donald W. Burdick, John H. Stek, et al. *NASB Study Bible.* Zondervan, 2000.

Bevere, John. *Good or God? Why Good Without God Isn't Enough.* Messenger International. Audio Book, Oasis Audio. August 11, 2015.

Biblehub.com. "The Mustard Seed: A Sermon for the Sabbath-School Teacher." Sermon preached by Charles Haddon Spurgeon, October 20, 1889. Accessed August 3, 2022. https://biblehub.com/sermons/auth/spurgeon/the_mustard_seed_a_sermon_for_the_sabbath-school_teacher.htm.

Bible Study Tools. "Baker's Evangelical Dictionary of Biblical Theology—Amen." Accessed April 30, 2025. https://www.biblestudytools.com/dictionary/amen/.

Bible Study Tools. *New International Version Bible.* Accessed April 30, 2025. https://www.biblestudytools.com/niv/.

Brest, Marvin, dir. *Meet Joe Black.* Universal Pictures. 1998.

Briggs, Megan. "Do You Read Your Bible Every Day? Most Churchgoers Say No." ChurchLeaders. July 25, 2019. https://churchleaders.com/news/356089-do-you-read-your-bible-everyday-most-churchgoers-say-no.html.

Cahn, Jonathan. "Appointing Our Days: Part 1." The Creator's Calendar. Accessed April 30, 2025. https://www.thecreatorscalendar.com/appointing-our-days-part-1/.

CBS News. "Comedian Flip Willson Dead at 64." November 26, 1998. https://www.cbsnews.com/news/comedian-flip-wilson-dead-at-64/.

daledawn. "Art Williams— AL Williams Founder—The Coach—Prime America—Must See Videos," Pure Motivation. April 18, 2020, https://puremotivation.com/artwilliams/.

Dylan, Bob. "Gotta Serve Somebody." Bobdylan. Accessed April 30, 2025. https://www.bobdylan.com/songs/gotta-serve-somebody/.

Elder, Richard Paul and Linda Elder. *Critical Thinking: Tools for Taking Charge of Your Learning and Your Life.* Fourth edition. The Foundation for Critical Thinking, 2022.

Facione, Peter. *THINK Critically.* Pearson, 2010.

FrontPageMag. "Prager U Video: A Short History of Slavery Video." August 27, 2021. https://www.frontpagemag.com/prager-u-video-short-history-slavery-prager-u/.

Furtick, Steven. *(Un)Qualified: How God Uses Broken People to Do Big Things.* Multnomah, 2016.

Goodreads. "Charles Haddon Spurgeon Quotes." Accessed April 30, 2025. https://www.goodreads.com/quotes/10747543-a-sermon-without-christ-in-it-is-like-a-loaf.

Goodreads. "John Wesley Quotes." Accessed April 30, 2025. https://www.goodreads.com/quotes/12757-do-all-the-good-you-can-by-all-the-means.

Goodreads. "Ravi Zaccharias Quotes." Accessed April 30, 2025. https://www.goodreads.com/quotes/746709-sin-will-take-you-farther-than-you-want-to-go.

Indian in the Machine. "If You Think You're Too Small to Make a Difference, Try Sleeping in a Closed Room with a Mosquito." Posted by Ricardo Peterson Kuthumi. January 14, 2010. https://indianinthemachine.wordpress.com/2010/01/14/if-you-think-youre-too-small-to-make-a-difference-try-sleeping-in-a-closed-room-with-a-mosquito-african-proverb./

King, Martin Luther, Jr. "Letter from Birmingham Jail." Csuchico.edu. Accessed April 30, 2025. https://www.csuchico.edu/iege/_assets/documents/susi-letter-from-birmingham-jail.pdf.

Lillegjord, Kacie. "10 Best Quotes from the Mummy." Screenrant. June 1, 2020, https://screenrant.com/the-mummy-best-quotes/.

Lindgren, Caleb. "Someday You Will Read or Hear That Billy Graham Didn't Really Say That." ChristianityToday. February 21, 2018. https://www.christianitytoday.com/ct/2018/february-web-only/billy-graham-viral-quote-on-death-not-his-d-l-moody.html.

LiveAbout. "The Whitney Houston Story." Dotdash Meredith. 2009. https://www.liveabout.com/whitney-houston-biography-3245298.

Mason, John. *Believe You Can: The Power of a Positive Attitude*. Baker Publishing Group, 2020.

Mayson, Barry and Tony Marco. *Fallen Angel: From Hell's Angel to Heaven's Saint.* Doubleday, 1982.

Mcjovial. "Are You Saved?" *Everyoflife*. September 15, 2017. https://everyoflife.wordpress.com/2017/09/15/are-you-saved/.

Merriam-Webster.com. "Bigotry." Accessed April 30, 2025. https://www.merriam-webster.com/dictionary/bigotry.

Merriam-Webster.com. "Covenant." Accessed April 30, 2025. https://www.merriam-webster.com/dictionary/covenant.

Merriam-Webster.com. "Integrity." Accessed April 30, 2025. https://www.merriam-webster.com/dictionary/integrity.

Millard, Bart. "I Can Only Imagine." The Worship Project (album) released 1999, Ivy Park, The Indigo Room, Paradise Sound, IBC Studios. Independent.

Phelps, Dennis. "9 Things We Can All Learn From Billy Graham's Preaching." Sermon Central. June 26, 2021. First published by NOBTS.Edu. https://www.sermoncentral.com/pastors-preaching-articles/dennis-phelps-9-things-we-can-all-learn-from-billy-graham-s-preaching-1678?ref=PreachingArticleDetails.

Poonen, Zac. "The Broken Pot." Word4life. Accessed March 11, 2023. http://word4life.com/brokenpot.html.

P.U.R.E. (Parents Universal Resource Experts). "Family Consultants: Sue Scheff." Accessed May 13, 2025. https://helpyourteens.com/family-consultants/.

QuotesGram. "Alice Cooper Christian Quotes." Accessed April 30, 2025. https://quotesgram.com/img/alice-cooper-christian-quotes/10003262/.

Raskin, Rabbi Aaron L. "Yud: The Tenth Letter of the Hebrew Alphabet." Chabad.org. Accessed April 30, 2025. https://www.chabad.org/library/article_cdo/aid/137082/jewish/Yod.htm.

Sager, Jessica. "Whitney Houston's Tragic Real-Life Story." NickiSwift.com. Updated February 3, 2023. https://www.nickiswift.com/82552/untold-truth-whitney-houston/.

Sammis, John Henry. "Trust and Obey." Hymnal.net. Accessed April 30, 2025, https://www.hymnal.net/en/hymn/h/582.

Scriven, Joseph M. "What a Friend We Have in Jesus." Hymnal.net. Accessed April 30, 2025. https://www.hymnal.net/en/hymn/h/789.

Spurgeon, Charles. "Feeding Sheep or Amusing Goats?: Biblebb.com. Posted by Tony Capoccia, 1986. https://www.biblebb.com/files/spurgeon/amusement.htm.

Spurgeon, Charles. "The Two Effects of the Gospel." Biblebb.com. Posted by Tony Capoccia, 1986. https://www.biblebb.com/files/spurgeon/0026.htm.

Stanley, Andy. *Better Decisions, Fewer Regrets: 5 Questions to Help You Determine Your Next Move.* Audible Audiobook. Zondervan Reflective. 2020.

Study.com. "FAQ: Generation Y: Definitions and Characteristics." Accessed April 30, 2025. https://study.com/learn/lesson/generation-y-characteristics-personality.html.

Vitagliano, Joe. "Behind the Song Lyrics: 'That Smell,' Lynyrd Skynyrd." American Songwriter. December 21, 2021. https://americansongwriter.com/that-smell-lynyrd-skynyrd-behind-song-lyrics-meaning/.

Wikipedia Foundation. "I Can Only Imagine (MercyMe Song)." Last Edited on April 20, 2025. https://en.wikipedia.org/wiki/I_Can_Only_Imagine_(MercyMe_song).

Wikipedia Foundation. "Tell Me the Old, Old Story." Last edited on January 29, 2024. https://en.wikipedia.org/w/index.php?title=Tell_Me_the_Old,_Old_Story&oldid=1200284523.

Wilkinson, Bruce. "Three Secrets About Temptations." YouVersion. Accessed May 13, 2025. https://www.bible.com/reading-plans/12956-three-secrets-about-temptations.

# About the Author

Since childhood, Dr. Fuchs has been a born-again Christian, and he began his outreach ministry in 2004. He was with Heaven's Saints Motorcycle Ministry for ten years. He became a Chapter President, Chaplain, and State Representative during that tenure. In 2009, Dr. Fuchs founded BikerDownLiftedUp.org and served as a hospital chaplain to serve motorcycle accident victims.

Dr. Fuchs had a career in the public school system in Buncombe County, North Carolina. He holds an A.A. in Audio-Visual Technology, a B.S. in Computer Management, an M.Ed. in Educational Technology, and an Ed.D. in Education Administration focusing on Educational Technology. Dr. Fuchs has a total of 45 years of experience in administering educational technology for both military and public education programs.

He has authored *Preacher Spurs*, which was self-published through Christian Faith Publishing in 2022. He writes Christian ministry articles as a contributing author for a weekly newspaper called "The Cherokee One Feather."

Dr. Fuchs lives in Clyde, North Carolina, where he resides with his wife and nearby children and grandchildren. Although originally from Billings, Montana, he has made North Carolina his home.

www.ingramcontent.com/pod-product-compliance
Lightning Source LLC
Chambersburg PA
CBHW070903120626
46546CB00001B/120